You'll see Amarillo
Gallup, New Mexico
Flagstaff, Arizona
Don't forget Winona
Kingman, Barstow, San Bernardino
Won't you get hip to this timely tip?
When you make that California trip
Get your kicks on Route 66

BOOKS IN THE WEIRD HIGHWAY SERIES BY TROY TAYLOR

ROUTE 66 HISTORY AND HAUNTINGS & LEGENDS AND LORE

1. WEIRD HIGHWAY ILLINOIS (2015)
2. WEIRD HIGHWAY MISSOURI (2016)
3. WEIRD HIGHWAY OKLAHOMA (2017)
4. WEIRD HIGHWAY SOUTHWEST (2025)
5. WEIRD HIGHWAY CALIFORNIA (2026)

WEiRD
HiGHWAY
SOUTHWEST

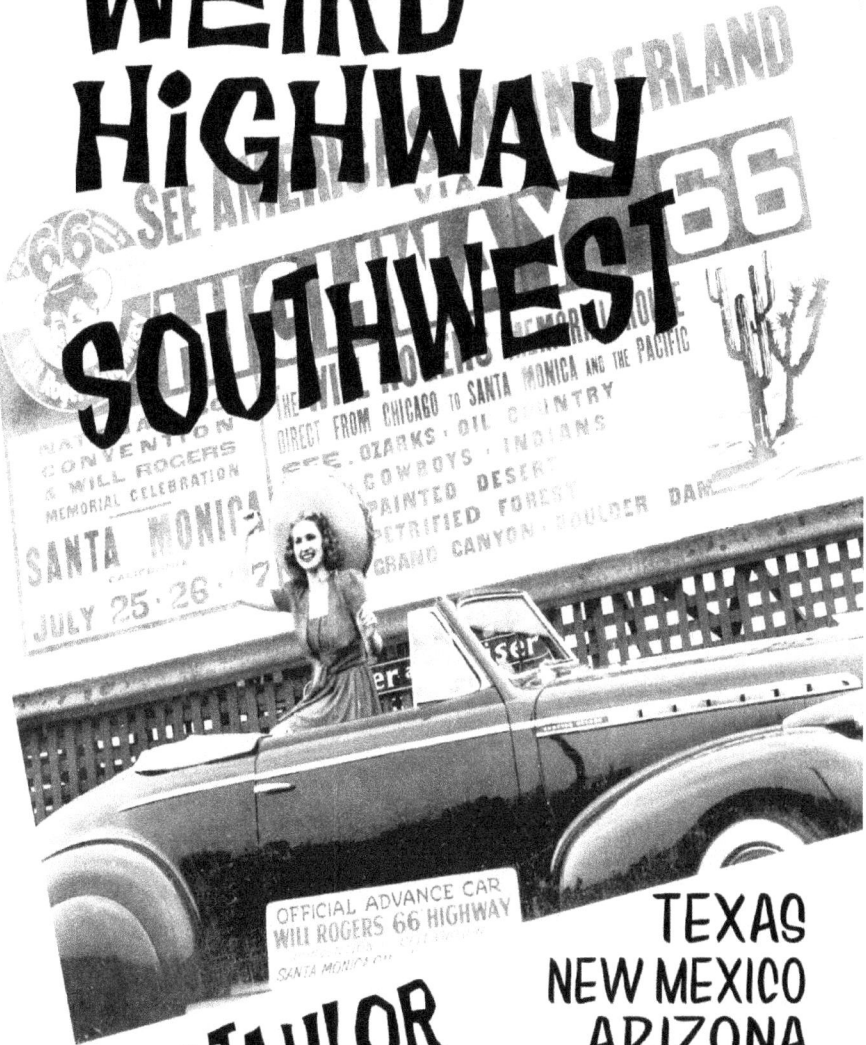

TEXAS
NEW MEXICO
ARIZONA

TROy TAyLOR

AN AMERICAN HAUNTINGS INK BOOK

WEiRD HiGHWAY SOUTHWEST
History and Hauntings & Legends and Lore

© COPYRIGHT 2025 BY TROY TAYLOR

Cover Design by April Slaughter
Interior Design by Troy Taylor

Printed in the United States of America

iNTRODUCTiON

THE GREATEST HIGHWAY IN AMERICAN HISTORY CAME to life a century ago. Route 66 began in downtown Chicago and stretched all the way to Los Angeles, coming to an end at the Pacific Ocean.

For millions of people who once "motored west" on Route 66, just hearing the name brings back a flood of memories about family vacations, road trips, and places that vanished decades ago. But as time marches on and Route 66 celebrates 100 years, there are fewer and fewer people left who traveled on the famous highway during its heyday.

And while many of us have been lucky enough to make the Route 66 journey since it was decommissioned in the 1980s, we know it's not the same as it was in its glory days – but we love it anyway.

We love its history and nostalgia, but we also love the roadside attractions, diners, and remaining relics that are making a comeback at a time when the world keeps moving faster and faster.

Just the name of "Route 66" offers a link to the past, the days of station wagons, two-lane highways, and lunches at roadside tables, greasy-spoon diners, and roadside stands. It conjures up images of souvenir shops, tourist traps, cozy motor courts, and cheesy roadside attractions that have since crumbled into dust. It revives thoughts of rusty steel bridges, flickering neon signs, classic cars, and drive-in theaters. It offers a few chills when it comes to stories of ghosts, haunted hotels, roadside spirits, mysterious vanishings, and bewildering anomalies, too.

It's America's most famous highway – even though it no longer exists.

Route 66 began simply to meet the needs of a growing nation. It gained notoriety during the Dust Bowl days of the Great Depression as an escape route for thousands of struggling families who were fleeing from the ruined farms of Oklahoma and Texas. They were migrants seeking salvation from drought, whose plight was immortalized in John Steinbeck's *The Grapes of Wrath*. In the book, he called Route 66 "the mother road, the road of flight." The nickname stuck, and for many years, Route 66 was seen as a passage to hope for struggling "Okies" and those who were down on their luck.

During World War II, Route 66 provided a fast-moving passage for soldiers, munitions, and equipment to move across the country. The military kept the highway busy – and the pockets of roadside merchants filled – but a road that had been built for civilian traffic paid the price in wear and tear. As it weakened and went into decline, officials took notice and began considering a wider, faster highway system that could handle the most challenging travel demands. By the time the war was over, the demise of Route 66 – although still years away – had become inevitable.

But not before the late 1940s and early 1950s brought new prosperity and a tourism boom to America. Spurred on by Bobby Troup's musical hit "Get Your Kicks on Route 66," families were anxious to travel the country, and the merchants of the highway cashed in. As traffic on the road increased, new businesses sprang up, and an explosion of tourist traps, curio shops, and neon signs began to appear in just about every town on Route 66's path. Motor courts became "motels," diners became "restaurants," and general stores changed into "trading posts." Hundreds of new billboards helped to spread the word about these booming businesses.

It was an era of good times that, sadly, would never last. By the middle 1950s, the new interstate highway system began making its way west, and in the decade-and-a-half that followed, Route 66 slowly began to disappear. It was ripped up, renamed, and re-aligned, with faster routes slowly strangling the hundreds of towns that had depended on Route 66 for their survival. Many of them became literal ghost towns, fading reminders of what they once were. By 1970, the damage was done, and the highway once called the "mother road" had ceased to be a direct route to California. It wasn't officially decommissioned, though, until the stubborn residents of Williams, Arizona – the last town to be bypassed – lost a legal battle to stop it in 1984.

Long stretches of Route 66 remain today. However, travelers often have to be creative navigators to make their way along from the original roadbeds to the access roads, abandoned fragments, and lost roadways. It's been reconfigured so many times in some places that even diehard road trippers can become lost while trying to follow the highway's often lonely miles.

Almost everyone who gets their kicks thinking about the old days on Route 66 has ventured out onto at least one section of the highway, looking for forgotten alignments and often finding broken pavement and dead ends.

But it's not for nothing – we often find true gems of the road, little-known places, and sites that can sometimes be found by tracing the rows of rickety telephone poles and abandoned railroad tracks that Route 66 usually shadowed. When we get lost and wonder if we're still on the right path, we watch for empty and crumbling stores, broken neon signs, and perhaps a rundown motor court that might still be eking out a living from travelers who are now few and far between.

The past often remains the present on Route 66.

And that's never been truer than it is today, as interest in Route 66 has revived with its centennial birthday in 2026. It's exciting that more and more people are discovering all the weird places, eccentric people, and fascinating sites that convinced me to begin this series of books a few years ago. When I started the series in my home state of Illinois, it was just going to be a collection of ghost stories along Route 66, but it quickly turned into more than that. I quickly realized that it was not just stories but a weird road trip that tackles all the oddness the highway had – and still manages – to offer.

It became a chronicle of the weird – ghost stories, haunted places, quirky hotels, abandoned places, favorite diners, forgotten spots, classic roadside attractions, and just about anything that entertained me, confused me, gave me a bit of a chill, or made me chuckle. My interests have always run the gamut from old drive-ins to oddball trading posts, UFO landing sites, spook lights, giant spacemen, natural wonders, and bizarre legends – all things that Route 66 had to offer. So, every bit of it went into this series of books.

The writing of this series will have covered about a decade of my life by the time it's finished, which makes me sad in a few different ways.

For one, that means I'm a decade older, but in truth, it means that I'll be coming to the end of a road that doesn't exist anymore. Or does it?

At one time, it was said that the whole world traveled on Route 66. For a long time, that was no longer true. Route 66 became a lost part of American history that, while gone, was not forgotten. But I'm not sure that we can even say Route 66 is gone anymore or that the "whole world" no longer travels on it. In recent years, Route 66 has seen a surge in interest not only among Americans but also among international travelers. In fact, some of the most diehard devotees of Route 66 come from overseas to drive those long and lonely miles.

Any other American highway would have faded into history a long time ago, but there is something about Route 66 that has remained within our collective imaginations.

So, join me for another volume of getting your kicks on Route 66 – you won't be sorry that you did.

Troy Taylor
Spring 2025

CYRUS AVERY AND THE HIGHWAY TO THE WEST

THE CROSS-COUNTRY HIGHWAY THAT EVENTUALLY became Route 66 didn't happen overnight. The demand for a highway that would stretch from one side of the country to the other began with the rise in the popularity of motor cars. As more cars were built and sold, drivers quickly tired of rutted, muddy trails and were desperate for good roads to drive on. It wasn't long before the demand began to be met, but a single highway was still years in the future. While it had to be built from a series of disconnected roads, the ultimate existence of Route 66 was thanks to the vision of a single man who saw the future, understood the needs of travelers, and put his ideas into action.

That man was Cyrus Avery, and he was the driving force behind the highway's creation. Long before he dreamed up the idea of Route 66, Avery had a passion for roads. He imagined a country with dependable, state-to-state motorways that travelers could use with ease and would not have to constantly worry about getting lost.

It's hard to say where his obsession with highways began. Avery was born in Stevensville, Pennsylvania, on August 31, 1871, and his family made their living from farming. When he was 10, his family moved west to what was then the Indian Territory of Oklahoma. After earning a degree from William Jewell College in Liberty, Missouri, he married Essie

Cyrus Avery

McClelland and returned to Oklahoma, where they raised three children together.

Avery initially tried his hand at several careers, including farming, selling insurance, and investing in real estate. This revived his interest in good roads and led to his membership in the Good Roads Movement of the early 1900s. This grassroots organization was started by bicyclists in the 1870s, but after the advent of motor cars, the organization changed and grew. With the ability to travel faster and at higher speeds, more people became interested in the fight for the improvement of existing roads and especially in the creation of new and safer ones.

In 1907, Avery moved his family to Tulsa and became involved in the oil industry, where he saw first-hand how roads affected his own and other businesses. Five years later, he entered politics and secured the post of county commissioner. He wanted the job for one reason – it gave him the opportunity to observe the need for an improved system of highways. It also gave him a platform from which to promote the idea of improving roads throughout the state of Oklahoma. His efforts helped to spur the development of numerous projects, and he furthered his mission in 1924 when the Oklahoma governor appointed him to the post of state highway commissioner. Then, just one year later, Avery was appointed to a federal board to develop a free, safe, and easily passable network of highways from one side of the country to the other. They wanted the roads to be easy to follow so people didn't get lost and there would be no dead ends along the way.

Working with a team of mapmakers, Avery designed a route that began in Illinois and Missouri and cut across his home state of Oklahoma on its way to Los Angeles. When first presented, this unconventional route wasn't well received. It took months for Avery to overcome the board's reluctance, and even when they finally accepted it, there was more disagreement over how it would be numbered.

Avery's first choice was U.S. Route 60, but he was immediately challenged by the governor of Kentucky, who wanted the more prestigious zero-ending number for a highway across his state. The governor then raised the stakes by demanding that the Kentucky highway be extended east to Virginia and then west to Springfield, Missouri, where it would connect to Avery's new route and create a true east-west highway. This would demote Avery's road through Illinois and Missouri to "branch" status, which Avery refused to consider. Finally, he let Kentucky have Route 60 and opted for number 66, which hadn't been assigned to anything. Avery liked the sound of the double sixes, and now, with everyone happy, Washington granted its approval, and Route 66 was designated on November 11, 1926.

The rest, as they say, is history.

In 1927, Avery helped found the U.S. Highway Association with the mission of getting the highway promoted and completely paved from end to end. Boosters began touting Route 66 in magazines, on maps, in travel brochures, and with staged events in various cities along the path. Through Avery's efforts, Route 66 was soon entrenched as America's premiere highway.

Cyrus Avery passed away in 1963 at the age of 90 and left behind a legacy as the "Father of Route 66."

THE ROAD OF MANY NAMES

CYRUS AVERY MAY HAVE SETTLED ON "ROUTE 66" as his second choice when the highway was created, but the road would turn out to be too prosperous, too historical, and too notorious to have just a single name. Over the years, it's had many monikers, each representing a different side of its character.

U.S. Route 66 was officially part of the United States Numbered Highway System, a set of routes for which the American Association of State Highway and Transportation officials were responsible for route numbers and locations. They followed a list of simple rules:

1. All routes that followed a north-south alignment were odd-numbered. If one of these federal routes was a major conduit, it was designated with a number ending in 1. The lowest numbers began in the east, and the highest numbers were in the west.

2. All routes that moved traffic east-west were even-numbered, with the major roadways ending with 0.

3. Last but not least, all highways with three digits were spur routes of parent highways, although they might not be connected.

But "Highway 66" didn't seem to have the gravitas that this road deserved. During its heyday – when traffic was heavy, and towns along its path prospered – promoters nicknamed it "America's Main Street." In the same way that the main street of a small town was the hub of the community, Route 66 tied together multiple states and gave them a sense of a connected community. Route 66 was a destination in its own right, and the towns and attractions that gave it life were the equivalent of the drugstores, movie theaters, hardware stores, five-and-dimes, and barber shops that once thrived on the main streets of towns across America.

Less than a half-decade after Route 66 was born, however, America was plunged into the Great Depression, a time when most people didn't have money for the necessities, much less extra cash for travel. Those were dark days when the highway was known by far too many as "the Road of Flight."

It was also around this time that John Steinbeck created the identity of Route 66 as a matriarchal pathway that pulled the migrants westward out of the Dust Bowl to what they believed was a land of dreams in California. He dubbed it, as mentioned earlier, the "Mother Road."

But the aura of the highway wouldn't always be grim. Humorist, writer, and actor Will Rogers was no stranger to Route 66 travel, and he knew how to bring laughter to those who even considered traveling the many miles to the West Coast. Although he grew up in a small town in Oklahoma when it was still Indian Territory, he became the most widely read newspaper columnist of the 1920s, penning entertaining articles for the common man, laden with a lot of good-natured humor and sage advice.

By 1933, he'd become a household name, a top movie box-office draw, wildly popular radio host, and a stage attraction who offered commentary on the news of the day. "All I know is what I read in the papers" became one of his most famous lines as she skewered current events and the state of the nation for comedic effect. He

Will Rogers

had a wry sense of humor and a knack for poking at politicians and all levels of society without offending anyone – even those who were the butt of his jokes.

Tragically, Rogers died in 1935 in an airplane crash in Alaska with famous aviator Wiley Post. However, in 1952, the U.S. 66 Highway Association bestowed an honor on the fellow who once said, "I never met a man I didn't like" – they unofficially started calling the road the Will Rogers Highway.

"GETTING YOUR KICKS" WITH A SONG

AFTER WORLD WAR II ENDED, AMERICA WENT A little crazy – although mostly in a good way. It was an era of prosperity for the country after the war with a housing boom, new cars on the market for the first time in years, and families that wanted vacations – which brought them to Route 66.

Among the tourists were Bobby Troup -- a Pennsylvania songwriter who was freshly discharged from the Marines -- and his wife, Cynthia. They left their hometown in Lancaster in February 1946 to seek their fortune in Los Angeles. Like everyone else at the time, they drove most of the way on Route 66. In their case, though, they wrote a jazz verse about their trip that became a post-war anthem that captured the imagination of the nation.

Bobby Troup was born to a musical family in Lancaster, Pennsylvania, in 1918. His father ran a successful music store, and when he passed away in 1937, Bobby enrolled at the University of Pennsylvania's Wharton School of Business to prepare himself to take over the family enterprise. But when he got to school, he found himself lured by the theater department, where he started penning production songs and musicals. Bobby joined the Embassy Club, a fertile ground for musical talent. It was with the Club that Troup met a young singer, Cynthia Harte, a society girl who had dreams of a theatrical career, who encouraged his writing.

In 1941, the Sammy Kaye Band recorded a song that Troup wrote for a production called "Daddy," and it spent nine weeks at #2 on the national Sunday Serenade radio hour. The record's success took Troup to New York to write for the Tommy Dorsey Band and Harry James. Royalties bought him a new car, a green convertible, which was mentioned in the song, and he bought a matching sedan for his mother.

Bobby and Cynthia Troup

But his show business plans were temporarily stalled by the attack on Pearl Harbor on December 7, 1941. Bobby joined the Marines in March 1942 and married Cynthia in May before he was sent to South Carolina for training. While he was there, Bobby composed a song called "Take Me Away from Jacksonville." His fellow recruits couldn't get enough of it, and it soon became the base's anthem.

A short time later, Bobby was shipped out to Saipan Island in the Pacific. While serving overseas, he met several service members with blues and jazz backgrounds that meshed with his own. They formed a jazz band, which included a soldier named Johnny Johnson from St. Louis, who would become a pianist for Chuck Berry a few years later. In 1945, Bobby was given shore leave in Long Beach, and he went to see the hot jazz clubs on the Sunset Strip in Hollywood. He began making plans to return to L.A. after the war was finally over.

Troup left the service in December 1945, and he returned to his mother's home in Lancaster, where Cynthia had been living, raising their two daughters, during the war. While waiting for his discharge papers to arrive, Bobby began talking about moving to California to try his skills as a songwriter in Hollywood. They would go to California, he decided, and try to make it there.

Bobby and Cynthia packed up their Buick on February 1 and left the girls with Bobby's mother. They set out on the new Pennsylvania Turnpike – the first modern expressway in the country – and headed west.

On the turnpike, Bobby and Cynthia enjoyed the peacetime joy of unrationed gasoline and the thrill of nearly unlimited speed. As they looked over the road map during a lunch stop at a Howard Johnson's, Cynthia suggested that they write a song about the Turnpike, but Bobby thought it was silly since they'd soon be on Route 66, the real road to the west. Still, the seed of a highway song had been planted in both their minds – and it would soon take root.

After leaving the Turnpike, they picked up U.S. Route 40, the old National Road, which took them across Indiana and Illinois to East St. Louis, where the highway joined Route 66 and took them across the Mississippi River.

Keeping herself occupied during the drive, Cynthia began rhyming new numbers into quick riffs, "Six, nix, picks, kicks," finally whispering to Bobby, "Get your kicks on Route 66." Bobby let out a laugh, knowing that the alliteration of suggestive sexuality was a surefire hit. He told Cynthia, "That's a darling title! God damn! That's a great title!"

With the rhyme in mind, they took U.S. 66 west out from St. Louis and then southwest across Missouri, stopping at Meramec Caverns near Stanton. When they made it to cowboy country in Oklahoma, they began collecting snapshots of cattle ranches and small-town cafes. They visited the recent memorial dedicated to Will Rogers in Claremore. By Monday, they had made it to Oklahoma City and began crossing the open vistas of the Great Plains, which had finally recovered from the Dust Bowl years. Driving west across the Texas Panhandle, they hit a midnight snowstorm near Amarillo and took refuge in a highway motel. Once it cleared, they kept motoring west on U.S. 66, now a narrow, two-lane road through the drylands of eastern New Mexico. In Albuquerque, they stopped for rest and haircuts. They followed the highway into the Indian lands at Gallup, then crossed the Painted Desert of Arizona. At Kingman, they detoured north to see Boulder Dam and the first casinos of Las Vegas.

For the couple, the trip over the California line and down into the Los Angeles valley was a welcome change. The fruit orchards and the warm weather were a reward for their long drive from wintry Pennsylvania. Route 66 ran along the foothills into Pasadena and down the new Arroyo Seco Freeway into downtown L.A. They took the last leg of U.S. 66 to Hollywood and a motel on Ventura Boulevard. It was now Friday, February 15, and they'd made remarkable time on what was then a narrow, two-lane road in the post-war winter of 1945.

Once settled, Bobby was eager to see the musical sights, especially the Hollywood nightclubs that he had visited while on wartime shore leave. More than anything, he wanted to see the Nat King Cole Trio at the Trocadero on Sunset Boulevard. Cole was well-known in the jazz circles of L.A. and was fresh from his wartime hit, "Straighten Up and Fly Right," which had been inspired by his minister father's sermons when he was growing up.

As a child, Nat's family had migrated north to Chicago, where the boy showed early talent on the piano. By high school, he had formed a

Nat King Cole

small band with his brother. In 1937, Nat joined a musical roadshow that folded, leaving the band broke and stranded in Los Angeles. Making the best of a bad situation, he decided to try and make his way in the local jazz scene, working with several small groups. He developed an elegant keyboard technique, traveled east to New York, and studied the be-bop style that was then emerging in Harlem. He returned to Los Angeles to form his own trio, which soon became the premiere jazz group in L.A., breaking the color barrier at the Trocadero.

Within days of arriving in the city, Booby arranged to meet Cole through the trio's new manager, whom Bobby knew through contacts with Tommy Dorsey. He was introduced as the composer of the pre-war hit "Daddy." When Nat asked about new songs, Troup played him a recently penned ballad, "Baby, Baby All the Time." Nat then asked if he had anything more appropriate for his upbeat piano style – and the rest was history.

Bobby told him that, while driving to L.A. with his wife, he had written half a song about Route 66, with lyrics set to a twelve-bar blues beat:

> If you ever plan to motor west, travel my way,
> Take the highway that's the best,
> Get your kicks on Route 66!
> It winds from Chicago to L.A.,
> More than two thousand miles all the way,
> Get your kicks on Route 66!

Nat was no stranger to highway travel, and perhaps that's what made him love the song so much. But whatever the reason, he urged Bobby to finish the song for a Capitol recording session in March, and the trio's manager arranged for Bobby to use a CBS studio on Sunset Boulevard. Amid the distraction of rehearsing bands, Troup unfolded his AAA highway map and began working on a second verse, trying to rhyme the names of towns between St. Louis and Los Angeles to give the song a sense of rapid motion.

Some of the city names – like Albuquerque – seemed impossible, but Bobby eventually worked out a lyric-bound itinerary with name drops happening about every 250 miles, including St. Louis, Joplin, Oklahoma City, Amarillo, Gallup, Flagstaff, Winona, Kingman, Barstow, and San Bernardino. Winona is the only town out of sequence -- it was a tiny community east of Flagstaff -- and might have been forgotten if not for the lyrics "Don't forget Winona," written to rhyme with "Flagstaff, Arizona."

I mean, it's the names of towns. You have to make them rhyme where you can.

The song was undoubtedly catchy, but there was one thing about it that bothered a lot of people – the pronunciation of "Route." Instinctively, Bobby used his eastern Pennsylvania accent in the song, saying "Root" instead of the Midwestern "Rowt," and never thought twice about it. Just as obvious at the time was that he dubbed the road "Route 66," instead of "Highway 66," which was its western name. Calling a highway a "route" was common in the East and, like the pronunciation, revealed the song as an outsider's description of 66 as a tourist road to California. The now iconic song changed the face of the highway from the Dust Bowl "road of flight" to a highway for dreamers in post-war America.

Nat King Cole loved the song and immediately decided to use it for his upcoming Capitol recording session. The Trio recorded three versions of the tune in March 1946. "Route 66" was released on April 22, and by mid-May, the national music weeklies were calling it a hit. Georgie Auld and his Orchestra immediately covered it on April 30, and Bing Crosby and the Andrews Sisters on May 10.

Within two weeks, the royalties from the Capitol release allowed Bobby and Cynthia to make a down payment on a house in North Hollywood. Their California dream had been realized beyond their wildest dreams. On May 2, their fourth wedding anniversary, they moved into a bungalow on Alcove Avenue. In celebration, Cynthia hung up their worn AAA highway map and pasted her U.S. 66 snapshots on it, together with sections of the song sheet, drawings, and colored lines to map the route and the towns where they had stayed overnight. Framed over the mantle, the Route 66 song map was a visual record of their journey and Hollywood success.

Once projected into the national culture, "(Get Your Kicks on) Route 66" became a musical map of the highway for post-war travelers. Years later, Bobby was told that his song had become wildly popular in the roadside diners along Route 66. He laughed about this in an interview:

"They'd drop a nickel into the jukebox and plan the next day's drive through 'Saint Loo-ey to Joplin, Missouri.'"

Since those days, the song has been subsequently covered by many artists, including Chuck Berry, who put his unique spin on the tune. He electrified it with guitar riffs, and whether intentional or not, he was the first performer to make the city of "Barstow" rhyme with "cow."

When Keith Richards from the Rolling Stones heard Berry's cover, he and Mick Jagger decided they needed to cover it, too. Their version started being played on the radio in 1964.

Since then, it's been covered by Depeche Mode, Brian Setzer, Tom Petty, and dozens of others. Depending on what version you hear, it's a great song, and it probably convinced more people to take a trip on Route 66 than anything else that has been written about it. It became the essential booster for getting people out onto the open road during the late 1940s and into the 1950s.

Route 66 wasn't just a highway anymore – it was a state of mind.

ROADSIDE NEON AND HIGHWAY GIANTS

DURING THE HEYDAY OF ROUTE 66, THERE WERE often long stretches of road that could be both ominous and perilous after dark. There were no overhead lights to illuminate the highway ahead – only the auto headlights that pointed the way in the darkness.

So, you can imagine the relief experienced by so many drivers when they spotted the glow of a town, diner, or service station lighting up the sky ahead of them – a warm glow provided by neon lights.

Neon changed everything. Because of it, towns along Route 66 became visual wonderlands. Back in 1898, British chemists discovered an element remaining in the air after the removal of oxygen, nitrogen, argon, and carbon dioxide. When electrically charged, it glowed bright red, and suddenly, the possibilities were endless.

Introduced in the U.S. in 1923, the first outdoor commercial neon sign was installed at Earle Anthony's San Francisco Packard car dealership, and soon, variations of that first sign began appearing everywhere.

Roadside culture would have evolved without the magic of neon signs, but it wouldn't have been nearly as much fun. Imagine rolling into a town along Route 66 after dark in the 1950s. Without neon, the motel signs would have been illuminated by tungsten bulbs, casting a weak yellow light and failing to illuminate the fact that a vacancy was available.

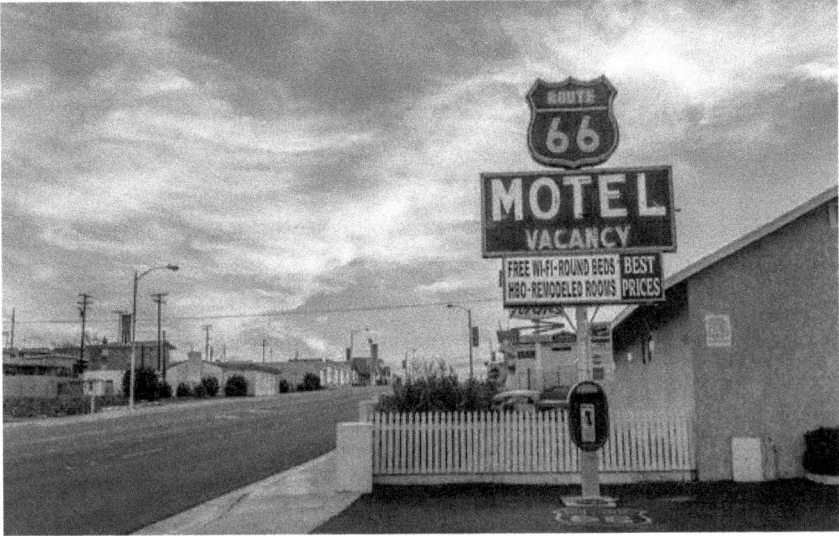

Otherwise, the town would be dark, encouraging motorists to keep driving instead of stopping for the night.

But thanks to neon, towns along the highway greeted travelers with a dazzling array of flashing lights in every color imaginable. Even the smallest towns and isolated roadside stops boasted neon signs that advertised motels, diners, souvenir stands, trading posts, and attractions using electrified gas to lure in customers and turning otherwise dark places into bright carnivals of color.

Today, most of the neon signs of Route 66 have blinked out. Those that remain – or have been rescued and restored – still draw travelers to bask in their glow. Everyone wants a little bit of the history, symbolism, beauty, and magic of the signs that illuminated Route 66 for a generation.

AND THOSE REMAINING NEON SIGNS OFTEN GO hand-in-hand with America's giants – the lumberjacks, cowboys, spacemen, and waitresses that served as advertising for decades along the highway. Unfortunately, while many of them have been toppled, discarded, removed, and sent to the local landfill with other unwanted advertising mascots of the past, a concerted effort has been made in recent years to save as many of them as possible.

The story of the fiberglass roadside giants began in 1961 when a man named Bob Prewitt started toying with the idea of building a

* GEMINI GIANT *

lightweight double-horse trailer out of fiberglass. He was a rodeo cowboy who was known for his roping skills, though not his trailer building. None of his friends believed the trailer he designed could hold a single horse, much less two. To prove the doubters wrong, he decided to craft two fiberglass horses to demonstrate his trailer's capabilities. It worked, the skeptics became believers, and Prewitt was in business.

Before long, word got out – not about the trailer but about his fiberglass horses. One day, he received a call from the PB Café in Flagstaff, Arizona, and they made an odd request – "We need a 20-foot-tall Paul Bunyan, ax and all."

Prewitt was happy to build it, creating the original mold that would one day be used to make scores of roadside giants that were eventually dubbed "Muffler Men."

He had no idea that he had created something that would one day become an icon of roadside America and Route 66. But he did know that he could earn a living making fiberglass animals like the horses he'd made. Bob quit his rodeo job and started a new company called Prewitt Fiberglass Animals.

He soon started crafting creatures in all shapes and sizes while his Paul Bunyan mold lay forgotten until 1963. That was when Steve Dashew of International Fiberglass came along and brought him back to life. He had an idea that the giant figure had enormous marketing potential, so he tracked down Bob and purchased the mold from him. At the time, Dashew specialized in building fiberglass boats, but he dropped that angle and switched over to larger-than-life roadside statues.

As it turned out, Paul Bunyan was very versatile. With a beard and an ax in his hands, he was a lumberjack. Leave off the beard and change the torso; he was an Indian. Bolt on a helmet, and he was a spaceman. All the giants had one thing in common, though: the position of their hands. The original configuration had the statue with the right palm facing up and the left palm facing down since the Paul Bunyan mold held his ax horizontally. This meant that the statue could hold anything – an ax, a rocket, a hot dog, or even a muffler.

Dashew began supplying the giants to small businesses everywhere, and they quickly became beloved by travelers. They were so popular that even big companies started using them too.

The trend began with Texaco's "Big Friends" ad campaign and an entirely new set of molds. The resulting giant featured a left arm raised in a "hello" wave with the right palm facing up. Soon, Dashew made mascots for oil companies like Texaco and Phillips, and he even made dinosaurs for Sinclair. Other muffler men – and women – followed, including a giant Uniroyal Gal, which came with a removable dress that had a painted bikini underneath.

The business thrived for a few years and then closed. Sadly, in 1976, the original giant forms were destroyed. The roadside giants that remain today are the last of the originals, kept alive by those who love them as they wave a friendly goodbye to Route 66 travelers who are lucky enough to discover them.

THE END OF THE ROAD

ROUTE 66 ENDURED THE GREAT DEPRESSION, THE DUST Bowl era, and World War, serving as an escape for poor Okies and helping the military to move troops and supplies from one side of the country to the other. The rationing of rubber tires and gasoline to help the war effort kept traffic sparse on Route 66 for years.

By The 1950s, though, the highway had become a genuine celebrity. It offered a way for families to leave their homes in the east and drive all the way to the Pacific Ocean on a highway that passed through towns where Abraham Lincoln once lived, where Jess James robbed banks, and Will Rogers learned to twirl his rope. They could visit the Grand Canyon or the Painted Desert, visit ranches where cowboys still punched cattle, buy chunks of petrified wood in Arizona, and souvenir spoons in the Ozarks. There were snake pits, prairie dog towns, wild critters, genuine Indians who sat like wooden statues and sold turquoise rings and bracelets, amusement parks, dance halls, and oddity museums. The lure of Route 66 became even greater in the late 1950s when the creator of Mickey Mouse built Disneyland among the orange groves of Southern California.

But it was also in the 1950s that the bright lights of Route 66 slowly started to dim. When President Dwight D. Eisenhower established a committee to explore the creation of a national interstate system, it marked the beginning of the end for the legendary highway.

The committee's findings were announced in 1956, and the plans for the new highway system were laid out, and the long and laborious task of building it began. Construction cost tens of billions of dollars, and over the next decade, pieces of Route 66 were replaced here and there, bypasses were built around towns and cities, and bit by bit, stretches of the old highway were turned into service roads, closed, or vanished altogether.

By the 1960s, travelers were no longer taking their time, motoring from one place to the next. They were now intent on getting to their destination as quickly as they could. As the interstates replaced the blue ribbons of highways, automobile vacations began to change. With their smooth surfaces, gradual curves, and occasional exits, the new expressways allowed a scenery-killing speed of 70 and 75 miles per hour.

Travelers embraced the new roads and, thanks to the continual flow of money from the government, they were constantly being updated and improved – leading to frustration over construction delays and confusing road signs that often carried several names for a single route.

It was impossible to ignore that change was coming, and towns and cities that earned their fame along America's most famous highway knew they had to embrace it or be left behind by progress.

The inevitable end was coming for Route 66.

Originally, the national interstate plan was supposed to take 12 years to complete. It ended up taking twice that long. Finally, the last stretch of U.S. Highway 66 was bypassed in 1984 near Williams, Arizona.

It had taken five different interstates to replace Route 66 -- Interstate 55 from Chicago to St. Louis; Interstate 44 from St. Louis to Oklahoma City; Interstate 40 from Oklahoma City to Barstow, California; Interstate 15 from Barstow to San Bernardino; and Interstate 10 from San Bernardino to Santa Monica. When the interstates were complete, someone commented, it became possible to drive all the way from Chicago to the Pacific Ocean without stopping.

The government called this progress, but thankfully, not everyone agreed.

Even as Route 66 road signs were being auctioned off and the road maps were being updated, history buffs and activists began trying to protect the legacy of the legendary road. Their numbers have grown over the years to become a veritable army of people from all walks of life. They are the people – like me and probably like you since you're reading this book – who want to see the highway's history survive. We're the people who get a thrill when we hear about someone reading *The Grapes of Wrath* for the first time, or watching the movie, or listening to the song, or actually getting off the mind-numbing miles of the interstate to "get their kicks" on a stretch of the surviving highway.

Route 66 lives on in the hearts and minds of thousands of people, and remnants of the road remain in every one of the eight states that it crossed. In many of those places, the old signs are returning, and the name never really surrendered. There are still motor courts, filling stations, curio shops, and tourist attractions that thrive on the nostalgia that is still felt by those of us who refuse to give up on America's past.

So, let's hop in the car, grab the wheel, and recapture some of the people, places, and ghosts that linger along Route 66 in the American Southwest.

TEXAS

The Lone Star State

GREETINGS FROM "So Big" TEXAS

DEPENDING ON WHO YOU TALK TO – AND WHICH alignment they used for their calculation – the length of Route 66 across the Texas Panhandle was somewhere between 178 and 189 miles. Except for Kansas, the border-to-border distance of Route 66 across Texas – where everything is bigger – was the shortest of any of the states the highway crossed.

This was the land of the Kiowa and the Comanche, who roamed the region just a century and a half ago. They were driven out by the white settlers, who built towns like Shamrock, Groom, and Amarillo – which owed their growth to the arrival of Route 66 in 1926.

Early on, the road across Texas was a rough, bumpy, and often hazardous ride. Because the Texas Highway Department gave priority to roads that served cities like Dallas, Houston, and Austin, maintenance on Route 66 was generally an afterthought, which meant the highway could be treacherous. One example of that was the dreaded "Jericho Gap" between McLean and Groom. When it rained, locals made extra money by pulling stranded motorists out of thick mud with teams of horses. In 1932, the section from McClean to Alanreed was bypassed and paved, leaving about 18 miles of dirt road from Alanreed to Groom. Construction started on that in 1933 but wore on for four years, which made the stretch that paralleled the Jericho Gap one of the last parts of Route 66 to be paved in 1937.

Military traffic further deteriorated the road across Texas in the early 1940s, but once the war ended, families braved the road in droves, finally leading to the improvements that had been needed for so long. By 1954, Route 66 was a modern four-lane highway from the Oklahoma border to just east of Groom and from Amarillo west to Bushland.

During the heyday of Route 66, a trip through Texas included dozens of "tourist traps," with live rattlesnake pits and cheap gas prices just a few of the marketing ploys to convince travelers to stop.

When a driver crossed the state line, they first passed the ghost town of Texola before arriving in **Shamrock**, the first Texas town on a westbound Route 66 journey.

The earliest settlers in this area were mainly buffalo hunters who were bent on eradicating the vast herds with the short-sighted blessing of the U.S. government. Because the hunters draped buffalo hides over their makeshift shelters, the area was initially known as "Hidetown."

The community gained a lasting name thanks to Irish immigrant George Nickel, who opened a post office at Shamrock in 1880. He was the first postmaster, so he was allowed to choose the name. When the railroads arrived in 1902, civilization came to Shamrock.

When Route 66 first came to Texas, the roads were so bad that the 90-mile trip from Shamrock to Amarillo was expected to take two days – and that was only in good weather.

That started to change in the 1930s, and Shamrock began to grow like wildfire. In the latter part of the decade, cafes, service stations, and motor courts sprang up all around the road through town. In 1937, thousands attended a parade to celebrate the paving of Route 66 through town. Far fewer people were on hand, however, when Shamrock was bypassed by Interstate 40 in 1972.

Neon lights from the dozens of diners, filling stations, and motels once lit up the evening skies of Shamrock and could be seen from as far as 20 miles away. Since then, however, most of the bright lights along this stretch of highway have quietly faded into the emptiness of the flat Texas landscape.

IN THE SUMMER OF 1931, JUST AS THE DEPRESSION was starting to decimate the nation's economy, Shamrock gained national attention for an incident that occurred just a few miles west of town. A westbound Greyhound bus was stopped on Route 66 by seven bandits who boarded the vehicle and robbed the passengers of cash and jewelry. Before they left, though, the robbers made sure that each of the passengers still had enough money to buy some breakfast.

On September 23, 1956, death occurred on Route 66 near Shamrock. Six people were killed, and four others were critically injured in a head-on collision four miles east of town. Highway patrolmen said that a car was attempting to pass a slow-moving truck when it collided with a vehicle that had Connecticut plates on the wrong side of the four-lane highway.

THE U DROP INN

The U-Drop Inn in Shamrock

THIS ART DECO-STYLE EATERY WAS BUILT AT THE intersection of Route 66 and U.S. Highway 83 in Shamrock in 1936. Legend had it that the plans for the building were drawn out in the dirt by John Nunn using an old nail.

The main building was brick with green and gold glazed tile accents, with two towers constructed from wood and covered with stucco. A contest to name the café was won by a local 10-year-old, who pocketed $5 for the winning idea. As the only café for about a 100-mile radius at the time, the U Drop Inn enjoyed great business.

In 1937, the space next to the café – which served initially as a store – was transformed into a ballroom with a large dining area.

The original proprietors, John and Bebe Nunn, sold the business a few years later but then repurchased it in 1950 and changed the name to Nunn's Café. After John died in 1957, Bebe sold it to Grace Brunner, who changed the name again to the Tower Café. The café now also served as Shamrock's Greyhound bus station and fed hundreds of travelers every day.

After a few more ownership changes, it was purchased in 1980 by the son of the original financier, James Tyndal, Jr., who repainted the place and restored its moniker to the U Drop Inn. It still stands today, not as an eatery, but as a Route 66 information center that continues to showcase this popular dining spot from the past.

THE UPLIFT CAPITAL OF AMERICA

WEST OF SHAMROCK IS THE SMALL COMMUNITY OF **McLean**, which got its start as a cattle-loading site for the Chicago-Rock Island Railroad in 1902. The land where the town started was donated by Alfred Rowe, a colorful rancher in the area who was known at one point as the largest landowner in the Panhandle.

At Jones Corner, one of the most popular service stations in McLean.

But Rowe's days were numbered.

In 1912, he was returning to Texas from England and was lucky enough to snag a first-class ticket on a new ocean liner called RMS Titanic. He was among the hundreds who were lost when it sank.

The town was named after Judge William Pinckley McLean, the secretary of the first Texas Railroad Commission, and after oil was discovered nearby in 1927, the sleepy little town grew rapidly. Dozens of new businesses opened – taking advantage of the arrival of Route 66 – like a brassiere factory that led to the town being unofficially called "the Uplift Capital of America."

During World War II, a German prisoner-of-war camp was opened east of town, which was designed to hold as many as 3,000 prisoners. Locals dubbed it "Camp Fritz." The camp incarcerated prisoners captured in North Africa and operated from September 1942 to July 1945.

During its heyday, McLean was home to as many as 16 service stations, six motels, and numerous cafes. One station, once operated by Phillips 66, remains in town as a preserved Route 66 photo opportunity.

McLean was one of the last towns to see an interstate bypass on Route 66. The townspeople fought the bypass for as long as they could. However, construction began in 1982 and was finished two years later, leaving McLean to deal with another economic blow soon after when the Rock Island Railroad declared bankruptcy.

McLean floundered but still manages to hang on today as interest in historic Route 66 continues to grow. These days, it plays host to the Devil's Rope Museum, the only museum in the world dedicated to the history of barbed wire.

And yes, it's a lot more interesting than you might think.

RATTLESNAKE HIGHWAY!

Alanreed service station

WEST OF MCLEAN, LOCATED ON A SMALL knoll, are the fading remains of **Alanreed**, a town that won't even count as a "wide spot in the road" anymore. While difficult to imagine today, the town's business district once included a hotel, bank, railroad depot, several saloons, several mercantile stores, a hardware company, and a blacksmith shop. But that was in 1904, when Alanreed was founded, and a lot of time has passed since then.

In July 1927, though, an incident in this small community made headlines around the country when neighbors of the Frank Weatherby family – after not seeing them for several days – discovered their badly decomposed bodies in their home. Frank, his wife, and their two small children had been shot to death. A mattress had been thrown over the bodies, and the room where they were discovered showed signs of being ransacked. The murder weapon was never found – and neither was the killer.

In the winter of 1949, after a snowstorm led to the closure of U.S. 66, Alanreed was again in the papers. For some unknown reason, some stranded travelers at the Standish Motor Court in town drank antifreeze, believing that the alcohol would be safe because they had strained it through bread. Three of them died because of it.

ONE OF THE ONLY ROADSIDE ATTRACTIONS that ever called Alanreed home was the **Regal Reptile Ranch**. The post-World War II tourist boom inspired a legion of tourist traps along Route 66 in the Southwest, many of which used reptiles to lure travelers off the highway. Rattlesnakes, Gila monsters, and pit vipers always made money, and no huckster on the road showed off things that slithered like siblings Mike and Addie Allred, who established their first reptile ranch in Elk City, Oklahoma.

When the highway bypassed Elk City in 1970, the pair moved their Regal Reptile Ranch to a new spot near Texola, which turned out to be a terrible decision for two reasons. One was that it was too close to Billie Henderson's Reptile Village, who didn't appreciate the intrusion and made their lives hell. Then, in 1975, they were bypassed again by a new highway.

They packed up and moved again, this time to Alanreed, where they opened what would become the last snake farm on Route 66.

That should have been the end of the story, but the brother and sister had a falling out. Mike rounded up his share of the snakes and leased a former gas station east of McLean, drawing tourists with a massive sign along the nearby interstate that read: RATTLESNAKES! EXIT NOW!

If Mike hadn't suffered a fatal heart attack in 1979, he might have outlived Addie to claim the title of "last snake farm." Instead, his snakes went back to Alanreed, where Addie continued to operate into the 1980s.

"JERICHO GAP"

THE PRESENT-DAY GHOST TOWN OF **JERICHO** got its start as a mail stop in the 1880s, and while it was never large, it had a couple of service stations and other provisions by the 1920s. Little remains of the

The Reed Grocery Store and Service Station in Jericho

town today, though, aside from the cemetery, an abandoned motel, and a weatherbeaten farmhouse, all in various states of permanent decay.

The demise of Jericho can be explained with a single word – "mud."

The drive from McLean to Groom was once infamously known as the "Jericho Gap." Route 66 originally followed this twisting dirt road through rugged and windblown stretches of ground, which, after heavy rain, became a thick, tire-sucking swamp. The mud was such a hindrance that when paving arrived in the 1930s, the highway was moved a mile to the north, which was the town's first step toward its doom.

To this day, the road through Jericho remains unpaved.

THE GOLDEN SPREAD MOTEL & GRILL

THE SMALL TOWN OF **GROOM** LIES BETWEEN Alanreed and Amarillo when traveling west on U.S. 66. It was named for the first general manager of the Francklyn Land and Cattle Co., B.B. Groom and was laid out on the Rock Island Railroad line in 1902. The oil boom of the 1920s brought prosperity to the area, which, when coupled with Route 66, tripled the town's population. As oil production faded, the tourist trade became the mainstay of the economy.

In 1953, Pete Ford, who had already made a fortune with oil and ranching, decided to get into the motel business. He bought an empty piece of property in Groom and hired an architect to design and build his 22-room motor lodge. Pete himself designed the unique, lighted arrow sign out front. A two-story building attached to the west end of the motel housed the office with an apartment for the manager upstairs.

Pete dubbed the place the Golden Spread Motel, a nod to the vast golden wheat fields across the Texas Panhandle.

The Golden Spread joined the Best Western chain of motels, and as competition in the area increased, so did the need for new amenities, like the heated swimming pool that was added.

The Golden Spread Motel in Groom

After the interstate bypassed Groom in June 1980, the pool was removed. The decline in business that followed the bypass could no longer justify its expense.

In 1992, the director of the Steve Martin comedy *Leap of Faith* wanted to shoot part of the film at the Golden Spread, but the owner at the time turned them down. The director liked the look of the motel so much, though, that he found another motel on the west end of town, built a second story and a sign to match the one at the Golden Spread, and filmed there instead. For years, travelers were puzzled by the fact that there were two Golden Spread Motels in town, but they could blame Hollywood for the confusion.

AFTER THE MOTEL WAS COMPLETED, PETE FORD decided to add a restaurant next door. The Golden Spread Grill opened in 1957, and while it was one of four restaurants, it was the most popular with travelers.

A few years after it opened, Ruby Denton took over the business, and its fame grew. The back of the postcards on sale at the diner read: "Always stop at the Golden Spread and be among the best fed." People did stop, were "the best fed," and the popularity of the place grew.

Business boomed until the interstate bypassed Groom in 1980 and crushed many of the town's small businesses. Today, the Golden Spread Grill still stands and continues to serve Route 66 travelers as simply The Grill.

ON THE WAY WEST TOWARD AMARILLO, THE highway passed through the town of **Conway**, one of the only communities of any size on this stretch of road.

Today, just off the interstate, is the Bugg Ranch, which was created in 2002 as an advertising gimmick for a corporate travel plaza that's meant to be a rival for the nearby Cadillac Ranch. The ranch consists of five Volkswagen Beetle wrecks that are planted headfirst into the ground.

It's not original to Route 66's heyday, but it's become a popular landmark in recent times.

AMARILLO

Cattleman's Club Cafe in Amarillo

THE TOWN OF AMARILLO WAS – AND IS – THE LARGEST community along Route 66 in the Texas Panhandle. In 1887, the Fort Worth and Denver City Railway was being built across the region, and as work progressed, a tent city was established along a local creek. Arguments began both for and against a permanent town, but the dispute was settled on August 30 when a site proposed by rancher Colonel James T. Berry was selected.

Originally called "Oneida," the name was soon changed to Amarillo – Spanish for "yellow" – which represented either the color of the soil along the creek banks or the many yellow wildflowers of the area. No one knows. Either way, by 1893, Amarillo's population consisted of "between 500 and 600 humans and 50,000 head of cattle."

One section of Route 66 that passed through Amarillo was dubbed "motel row," thanks to the dozens of motor lodges and tourist courts that lined 8th Street. It boomed until 1968 when the interstate bypassed the city. Even so, many of those lost motels have since become part of the U.S. 66 legend.

TRIANGLE MOTEL

BEFORE HE AND HIS WIFE, CORA, OPENED THE Triangle Motel in 1949, S.M. Clayton had been the mayor of Borger, Texas, dubbed by some "the wickedest town in the West." It's no surprise that he went looking for something quieter when he retired, so he and Cora moved to Amarillo and bought a wedge-shaped piece of property along Route 66.

Triangle Motel in Amarillo

The streamlined modern motel was designed as two parallel brick buildings that faced each other with a courtyard in the middle. Each building houses six rooms and a convenient two-car garage between every two rooms.

During its busiest time, the Triangle catered to the families of servicemen at the nearby Lackland Air Force Base. It would be the closure of the airbase that first slowed the motel's brisk business to a crawl. In 1968, the new interstate bypassed Amarillo, and its glory days came to a screeching halt. The motel closed a short time later.

BRONCHO LODGE

JUST DOWN "MOTEL ROW" FROM THE TRIANGLE was the Broncho Lodge, the first of many western-themed motels that will show up on these pages. When it was built in 1951, it was considered a superior motel, as evidenced by its high rating from AAA.

The western ranch-style motel was built in a U-shape with the office in the center. The original neon sign depicted a cowboy riding a bucking horse, but in the late 1950s, it was tragically replaced by a more contemporary design.

As auto vacations boomed during that decade, the motel satisfied tourists' demands for upgrades and amenities, like a café and steakhouse. The Broncho Lodge also added a heated swimming pool and a children's playground, as well as "free television," which was pretty upscale for the early 1960s.

The motel still operates today, is a popular destination for poker enthusiasts, and is known for its high-stakes games. It now features a card club that's co-owned by Doug Polk, a well-known poker player.

ARROW COURTS

The Arrow Courts later became the Arrow Motel and was also home to the popular Tam O'Shanter Cafe

By 1927, Amarillo was well on its way to becoming a popular tourist town. Motorists were already flocking to town on four major Texas highways, but the addition of U.S. 66 soon brought all the local traffic stops with all the business they could handle. In fact, the demand was so great in 1927 that there were as many as 29 auto courts and tourist camps competing for business in town.

The Arrow Courts – later the Arrow Motel – were located on the west side of Amarillo, almost outside the city limits. It was a good place to stop if you were motoring west and wanted to miss the city's morning traffic or the clamor of "motel row."

The Arrow's rooms were in two buildings, one with four units and the other with eight. The rooms provided guests with panel-ray heat, carpeted floors, and tile baths. A courtyard between the buildings was filled with plants and trees and the office at the front of the property doubled as a gas station. A café was conveniently located next to the office.

Advertised as "a clean, quiet place for a good night's rest," the motel survived until 1968 when the interstate bypassed Amarillo. There's nothing left of the Arrow today.

HOME OF THE "FREE" 72-OUNCE STEAK

DURING THE HEYDAY OF ROUTE 66, THERE WERE literally thousands of places to eat as you traveled from Chicago to the Pacific Ocean. Hundreds remain today, although I can promise you won't find a bigger meal than the one you can eat for free at the Big Texan in Amarillo.

The restaurant was built in 1960 by St. Louis transplant R.J. "Bob" Lee. He called it the Big Texan Steak Ranch because -- thanks to the stereotype of everything being bigger and better in Texas – he wanted it to be the biggest place on Route 66.

Bob made his dream a reality and created a restaurant like nothing else in the Panhandle region. He filled the interior with an eclectic mix of Western antiques and made sure that only the best steaks and the finest ingredients were used in the kitchen.

And he made sure the portions were huge.

Many of Bob's customers were true Texans – hungry cowboys who were always trying to outdo each other with their massive appetites. One Friday, Bob wanted to see how far some of his regulars would take things, so he pushed together some tables in the dining room and announced a challenge: Who could eat the most one-pound steaks in an hour? It only cost $5, and the top eater got to keep the cash.

To Bob's surprise, one of the contestants horsed down not one but two steaks – and it only took him 10 minutes to do it. Then, according to legend, he politely requested that a salad and a shrimp cocktail be served with his third steak. He ate it all, then asked for a fourth, along with a baked potato and bread. And he still had room to put away a fifth and final steak, too!

Bob was shocked but impressed by the cowboy's appetite. As the crowd went wild with delight, he stood upon a chair in the middle of the dining room and called out, "From this day forward, anyone who can eat an entire 72-ounce dinner in one hour gets it for free!"

And the "Texan King" was born.

This is not your typical steak dinner. It's a monster of a meal that is built around a 72-ounce slab of beef, grilled to your preference. It comes with one shrimp cocktail, baked potato, salad, and a roll with butter. Not all of Bob's customers were hungry cowboys with bottomless stomachs, so he figured that an occasional free meal would be worth the publicity.

He turned out to be right. Over the years, quite a few contenders have had their names written in the Big Texan record book, but for the most part, even the hungriest tourists end up having to pay for an unfinished meal.

If you love a good steak – or just want a good meal at a Route 66 icon – be sure to stop in at the Big Texan Steak Ranch when you're passing through Amarillo.

THE LEGEND OF "TEX" THORNTON

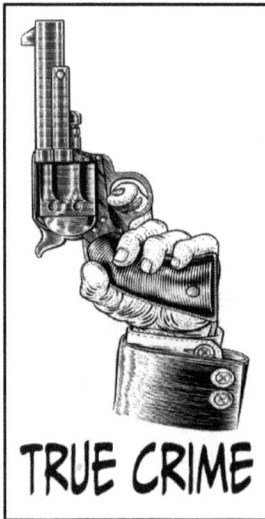

TRUE CRIME

ALTHOUGH WE'RE NOW LEAVING AMARILLO IN the rearview mirror, it will remain a part of our story for a little longer because in 1949, the city – as well as a string of communities along Route 66 in New Mexico – became part of a high-profile murder and its circus-like aftermath.

It's the story of the death of W.A. "Tex" Thornton, a larger-than-life character in the oil fields of the 1920s and 1930s. He became so legendary that it's almost impossible today to separate the fact from the fiction in the saga.

Tex was only six years old when his family moved from Mississippi to Goree, Texas, located about halfway between Wichita Falls and Abilene. A major oil discovery sparked a boom when he was 16, so Tex dropped out of school and went to work as a roughneck on the rigs. He was lured away, though, by a torpedo company. A torpedo was an explosive device used to fracture rock at the bottom of oil wells and to blow out well fires. Tex was such a good torpedo man that the company sent him to Ohio for more training – where he acquired the nickname "Tex," which he used for the rest of his life. In 1919, he put out his first well fire near Electra, Texas, and within a few years, he was the Panhandle branch manager of the U.S. Torpedo Company in Amarillo.

W.A. "Tex" Thornton

By this time, Tex's exploits were already becoming the stuff of tall tales. As one particularly difficult fire, he devised a valve system that became an industry standard. In 1924, in Hutchinson County, he snuffed out a fire that had been burning for a week. The following year, he managed to extinguish six blazes that had resisted every other team that tried to put them out. In 1926, an oil field was discovered in Borger, Texas, and the young man's career skyrocketed.

And his mythology grew. On April 11, 1927, a premature explosion occurred at a well, killing three men and injuring several others. Tex was there, and after racing into the inferno to pull the wounded to safety, he was hailed as a hero. These kinds of exploits led to his appearance on the front pages of papers all over the state, and the name Tex Thornton became even more widely known.

He never rested on his laurels, though. Just a month after that daring rescue, a major explosion and fire at Sanford, about 10 miles from Borger, killed eight workers. Tex was soon on the scene and, wearing an asbestos suit of his own design, knocked the fire out. Less than a day later, there was another explosion and another fire southeast of Borger. Tex climbed into his now-famous asbestos suit, ran into the fire, placed a charge, and put the fire out in front of an audience of several thousand people. On June 9, there was a well fire near Pampa. This time, Tex entered the fire zone, closed an open valve, and extinguished the blaze. Soon, he was being called to put down well fires throughout Texas, Oklahoma, and New Mexico.

Tex never slowed down, but he did revel in the publicity. At the Tri-State Fair in Amarillo, he not only gave a firefighting demonstration, but he also entered a race with a modified Cadillac.

Tex became famous throughout oil country for his innovative "well shooting" to put out rig fires.

His exploits continued in the 1930s. At a fire near San Antonio, he rescued a newspaper reporter who got too close to the flames. At Corpus Christi, he created an innovative process that used water from the Gulf of Mexico to put out a nasty fire. His wife, Sara, also stepped into the spotlight by driving 700 nerve-wracking miles to deliver a load of nitroglycerin that Tex needed. His wealth grew with his popularity, and by the 1940s, he was known in Amarillo for carrying large rolls of cash and wearing diamond rings on his fingers.

But then, on Sunday, June 19, 1949, the legend of Tex Thornton took a dramatic and fatal turn.

On that day, Tex headed west on Route 66 to work on a well in Farmington, New Mexico. Three days later, on his way home, he stopped at one of his favorite roadside bars in San Jon, New Mexico, east of Tucumcari. He wasn't alone when he arrived. Bartender Torrance Popejoy, a longtime friend, saw Tex come in and take a seat in a booth with a red-haired man and a young blond woman in a white blouse and dark skirt. He later recalled that Tex ordered three whiskey sours, but the couple seated with him asked for beer instead.

Tex gave the woman some nickels and asked her to play the jukebox. When the trio ordered a second round of drinks, the woman joined Tex and asked for whiskey. The man stuck with beer. Another round of drinks followed, and then the woman ordered a pint of Schenley's Black Label whiskey, six cans of beer, four bottles of Squirt soda, four packages of peanuts, and two packs of Camel cigarettes to go. She paid for all of it with some of the cash that Tex had tossed on the table when he ordered the first round of drinks.

Several witnesses – including Popejoy – noted that when they left, the red-haired man was driving Tex's black 1948 Chrysler sedan. The woman was in the middle, and Tex was next to the passenger door. They turned east on U.S. 66, headed toward Amarillo.

Shortly before 7:00 P.M., about two hours after leaving the bar, Tex's car pulled into Briggs Service Station on Route 66 in Adrian, Texas – only 50 miles from the bar. Why had it taken two hours to drive such a short distance? No one knows, and the police were never able to find anyone who remembered the trip stopping in any of the small towns along the way.

The gas station attendant later told investigators that Tex told him they couldn't turn off the car because they were having trouble with the ignition switch and were afraid it might not start again. The attendant also recalled a blond woman sipping whiskey from a pint bottle while he filled the tank and cleaned the windshield. Another reason he found the incident memorable is because he said Tex Thornton was so drunk he had to help him with his wallet to pay for the gas.

Around 8:30 P.M., the black Chrysler turned into the parking lot of the Park Plaza Motel in Amarillo. The woman entered the office and filled out the registration card for a room. She used the name E.O. Johnson from Detroit, Michigan, and paid $8.50 for a two-bedroom cabin. She didn't know the license plate number on the car, so the clerk looked out the window and wrote the number on the card himself. He noticed that Tex was sitting in the backseat. The motel's porter, Charlie Thompson, showed the trio to Cabin No. 18, unlocked the door, and turned on the lights. When he spoke with the police the next day, he noted that they had no luggage. He remembered Tex entering the cabin first and the young man asking for a restaurant recommendation.

Charlie left but was called back to the cabin a few minutes later because the radio wasn't working. He checked it and saw it hadn't been plugged in. He then went to the office to listen to a boxing match that was broadcast on the radio.

Around 10:00 P.M., Charlie saw the younger man and woman again. They asked once more for directions to a good restaurant before they left.

But they didn't get far. Unable to get the Chrysler started, a motorist passing by the motel stopped to help them push start it. Charlie Thompson saw the couple drive east on Route 66.

The next morning at 9:15, the motel's maid, Jessie Mae Walker, entered Cabin No. 18 and found Tex Thornton dead in the back bedroom. He was naked, and the covers had been pulled up to his chin. His shirt had been knotted around his neck so tightly that the funeral director who took charge of his body had to cut it off his neck. The mattress that Tex had been lying on was soaked with blood, and he'd been beaten so severely that his skull was caved in.

His clothing was on the floor next to the bed, along with a pair of bloody trousers that were too small for him. Those trousers offered the first clue in the murder case – someone had written the name "R.L. Leach" on the inside. The police believed they belonged to the killer. Tex's own pockets contained no money and no identification. At that point, no one knew who he was.

The police arrived at the scene just minutes after the call from the motel manager. One of the officers was a member of an organization called the Will Rogers Range Riders. Tex was also a member, and the officer identified his body. Other members of the group were called to the scene to confirm the officer's identification. They arrived just moments after Al Dewlen, the 27-year-old editor of the *Amarillo Times*. He couldn't believe what he was seeing. He later wrote: "Within 15 minutes of when I got there, there must have been 30 people in that room. Members of the Range Riders tramped around and tracked blood everywhere. They had their fingerprints all over everything."

Amarillo Police Chief Sid Harper was out of town that day, which left newly appointed Sheriff Paul Gaither to take charge of the case. Although the growing crowd in the cabin was contaminating the scene, evidence was gathered that included dirty glasses, empty beer cans, and a lipstick-smeared handkerchief. Blood was found in the bathroom sink, indicating that the killer – or killers – had washed their hands before leaving.

The murder became front-page news in Amarillo and across Texas and made it onto the national wire. One reporter, Norton Spayde, asked a question that everyone wanted answered: "How a young pair like described to officers take advantage of Mr. Thornton is a mystery. Both the young people are described as lightweights, and Tex had been schooled in the rough and ready oil fields."

After law enforcement agencies along Route 66 into New Mexico were contacted, Tex's steps were retraced, and a multi-state search for his car began. The Range Riders formed their own search teams to track the vehicle after it left Amarillo.

When the police interviewed Tex's wife, they learned he had been expected back in Amarillo on June 21. However, that afternoon, Tex had called Frank McCullough, sales manager of Meyers Motor Company in Amarillo, and said that he was east of Albuquerque and having trouble with his ignition. Detectives determined that Tex had spent the night in Albuquerque and theorized he had picked up the couple hitchhiking on his way home somewhere in New Mexico.

On Friday morning, a Potter County grand jury returned murder indictments against the pair, naming them as "John Doe" and "Mary Roe."

Meanwhile, the Range Riders were still following their own leads. They tracked the Chrysler east along U.S. 66 to Elk City, Oklahoma, where a service station attendant remembered seeing the car and the couple. They found more witnesses in El Reno and Oklahoma City and then found the car abandoned in Dodge City, Kansas. In a nearby field, they found the keys and a .45-caliber handgun that belonged to Tex Thornton.

The newspapers published updates on the case almost every day but despite the searches by the Range Riders and the tips and leads that poured into the Amarillo Police Department, the case quickly cooled.

By the end of 1949, it had turned ice cold.

ON FEBRUARY 7, 1950, AN 18-YEAR-OLD WOMAN named Diana Johnson turned herself in at a police station in Washington, D.C. – offering them a story so wild it was almost impossible to believe. In fact, after listening to her rambling story, officers considered admitting her to a mental hospital for evaluation.

Weirder still, this wasn't the first time the woman had surrendered herself to police. She had come into the station a month earlier, told the same story, and been shown the door. This time, though, Officer Porter M. Beale decided to send a telegram to the police in Amarillo, Texas, to see if her story was true. He was surprised to learn that Diana was the "Mary Roe" who had been indicted by a Texas grand jury.

Diana Johnson

In a colorful, long, and often-changing confession – made even more memorable by cigarettes that she chain-smoked and an impressive vocabulary of profanity -- she described how Tex had picked up her and her husband, Evald Johnson, west of Tucumcari. She claimed that Tex had already been drinking and asked her husband to drive. The trio continued drinking after they arrived at the motel, and when Diana stepped out to get some clothing from the car, she returned to find Evald beating Tex in

Diana's "drunk, abusive" husband, Evald Johnson

the back bedroom. According to her story, Evald told her to go out and get in the car, "or you'll get what he got."

Diana described her husband as an abusive drunk who had frequently beaten her. Overwhelmed with guilt, she decided to turn herself in to the police out of fear that her husband might kill her.

She told and re-told her story to the police and reporters, but it wasn't difficult to see that her version of events changed with each telling. At first, she said Tex was beaten with his own gun. Then, she changed the murder weapon to a hammer. During one confession, she said her husband acted in self-defense, but then she said Evald had started a fight. She told police that she'd spent time in a psychiatric hospital in Detroit but then later said that wasn't true. She said she was an orphan, but the police located her parents in California. She said that after abandoning Tex's car in Kansas, she'd fled to Florida alone – then police discovered the couple had traveled to Florida together.

Diana was, as one police officer noted, "completely nuts," but one thing she said proved to be true – where to find her husband.

On February 9, acting on Diana's information, police officers found Evald and his sister, Edith, at Tervo's Tavern in Munising, Michigan. They followed the pair to Edith's home and knocked on the door. Edith claimed her brother wasn't there, but when officers started to search the house, Evald came downstairs and quietly surrendered. He was arrested, even though he loudly proclaimed his innocence.

Al Dewlen, the Amarillo editor who'd been at the crime scene, sent the paper's police reporter, Bill Cox, to Michigan for what he hoped would be an exclusive story. Cox arrived ahead of other reporters and managed to get the first interview with Evald Johnson.

It turned out to be a bombshell.

The next day, headlines read:

JOHNSON TO PAY WITH HIS LIFE
BLAMES WIFE'S INFIDELITY FOR SHOCKING MURDER

SAYS HE WILL PLEAD GUILTY TO THORNTON SLAYING

The first line of the story under the byline spilled the best part: "Big-handed, square-jawed Evald Johnson blamed the nudity of his pretty young wife for the motel murder of Tex Thornton."

It included a colorful quote from Johnson:

I saw my old lady walking to the bathroom as naked as the day she was born. The next thing I knew, I was beating him with the butt of the gun. I don't remember nothing else. I remember holding the gun in the air and saw blood on my pants. I don't know whether I choked him with the shirt before or after I hit him. I had laid down on the bed in the front room to drink some beer. I must have passed out. But I woke up and saw her naked. I am ready to let them have what they want to make up for it – even my life.

Sex, violence, and murder – the story was a guaranteed page-turner – and it all started coming together after Johnson's arrest and confession. Evald claimed that Tex had started making improper advances toward his young wife almost immediately after they'd picked them up near Tucumcari. "He put his hands all over her," Evald snarled, choosing to forget the fact that his wife had voluntarily removed her clothes while he was unconscious.

But Evald did explain the bloody trousers left behind at the scene – he'd picked them up at a Salvation Army in Colorado Springs. The name "Leach" was already written inside.

The couple's story was further fleshed out by family members and by the testimony of Diana and Evald. Diana turned out to be a runaway who had left her home in California when she was only 15. She met Evald at a nearby army base where he was serving his second tour of duty. During World War II, he had been a gunner on a B-17 but had been dishonorably discharged after numerous AWOL violations. Evald claimed those had occurred because of his attempts to find Diana, who was running around with other men.

Evald and Diana were married in February 1947 in Ogden, Utah, where the legal age of marriage was 16. He later claimed that the local police chief had forced them to get married. Evald, who was a dozen years older than she was, said he was given a choice between marriage and being arrested for statutory rape. Even in California, he said, she was

Killer Pleads Written Unwritten Law

Amarillo, Tex., May 13.—Evald Johnson, veteran of 72 Air Force combat missions during World War II, testified today he bludgeoned W. A. (Tex) Thornton after finding his blonde wife and the famed oilfield troubleshooter in bed together.

The 30-year-old, self-styled wanderer, on trial fo r the murder of the 57-year-old Thornton in a tourist cabin a year ago, swore he walked into Thornton's room and found his wife, Diana Heaney Johnson, in the act of adultery with the oilman.

She Denies Story.

Diana, 18, whose father is an ordained deacon in the Baptist church, insists that she was out of when her husband at-

running around with soldiers who were older than she was. "Hell, I married her," he told a reporter. "And I did love the woman."

After his arrest, Evald found himself back in Amarillo. He hired attorney Ernest "Dusty" Miller, who was just as famous – maybe more so – than Tex Thornton. He specialized in defending clients facing the death penalty and he had yet to lose one. As soon as he hired him, Evald recanted his confession.

Diana had her own lawyer, Byron Singleton, while Tex's widow, Sara, hired another high-profile defense attorney, George McCarthy, to assist the district attorney's office. Judge Henry Bishop helped by appointing McCarthy as special prosecutor, setting the stage for a legal and media circus.

McCarthy immediately announced that the state would try Evald first and that he would seek the death penalty if he were found guilty. In a highly unusual move, the state asked for a change of venue, insisting that the local newspapers and radio stations had influenced locals about Tex and Diana's alleged "immoral relations." In the motion to move the trial, Diana now denied having sex with Tex and even claimed that he'd never made an advance toward her. But none of it mattered. The judge denied the change of venue, and jury selection was scheduled for May 8.

The newspapers, always eager for headlines, spent a lot of the space on their front pages focusing on the battle between the two attorneys, Miller and McCarthy. That fight began in earnest during jury selection, which took three days.

Once that was over, Miller immediately informed the jury that his defense would be justifiable homicide, which was legal under Texas law if a man found someone committing adultery with his wife – as long as he caught them in the act.

In response, McCarthy offered Evald's confession in Michigan into evidence, which clearly stated that he hadn't caught his wife and Tex together. He'd been asleep and woke up to find his wife walking out of the bathroom naked. Tex was asleep. There were also several instances described in the confession when Evald saw Tex with his arm around Diana or "feeling around on Diana," which McCarthy suggested meant that he hadn't beaten Tex to death in the heat of the moment.

McCarthy questioned dozens of witnesses who had seen the couple with Tex at various places on Route 66, including the motel owner and his employees, gas station attendants, patrons at the bar in San Jon, and the bartender, Torrance Popejoy. He also called the witnesses in Dodge City who found the abandoned car and gun and the police officers who worked on the case. By 1:00 P.M. on Friday, May 12, the state has rested its case.

Miller called Evald to the witness stand that same afternoon, and he answered questions about his childhood, his military service, and his life before and after the killing.

On Saturday, though, Miller promised the testimony the press and the public had been waiting for – what happened in that motor court cabin? The courtroom was packed as Evald once again took the stand, wearing a dark blue suit and looking nervous. He spoke directly to the jury, claiming that when he woke up in the front bedroom, he saw his naked wife walking toward the back of the cabin where the bathroom and Tex's bedroom were located. Evald stated:

I got up and went to the bathroom. I looked in and she wasn't there. The door to Thornton's room was halfway closed so that I couldn't see the bed. I pushed the door open, and the lights were on. When I opened the door, there was my wife on the bed and Mr. Thornton was with her. He didn't have any clothes on either.

He said that he remembered nothing about the struggle but vaguely remembered taking Tex's gun away from him and bashing him in the head with it.

Evald Johnson with attorney E.T. "Dusty" Miller

As he testified further, he tried to weave a thread through his story – that Tex had tried to get rid of him so he could be alone with Diana. He claimed that before they reached Amarillo, he'd tried to get Evald to pull off on a side road and take a walk. After he refused, Tex got into the back seat of the car and asked Diana to join him.

Miller made it a point to inform the jury that the trio had driven within blocks of Tex's home in Amarillo. He asked why Tex had paid for a motel room and stayed with the couple instead of going home to his wife.

McCarthy answered that question by calling Sara Thornton, Tex's widow, as a witness. She testified that her husband didn't like to come home after he'd been drinking because she "fussed at him." She also testified that when traveling with her husband, he often paid for rooms and meals for hitchhikers and people he could help because they were down on their luck.

Next, McCarthy called Diana's mother to the stand and attempted to portray Evald as an opportunist who had set up a tryst between his wife and Tex as a blackmail scheme. The jury was visibly moved when she wept while relating a past incident in which Evald had said that he saw no reason why Diana couldn't make money doing sex work.

As the trial neared its end, Miller and McCarthy became entangled in almost nonstop arguments and objections that finally forced Judge Henry Bishop to angrily step in. He also admonished the crowded courtroom for comments that were overheard during lulls in the heated exchanges between the two attorneys.

Finally, on Tuesday afternoon, the jury retired to decide their verdict. They returned three hours later – not guilty, Evald Johnson had been acquitted. The courtroom erupted in surprise.

But the story of the Johnsons wasn't quite over yet. They still faced charges of transporting a stolen car across state lines. A trial was scheduled for October 5, 1950, but on the advice of their attorneys, the pair entered a plea of "no contest." Diana received four years of probation. Evald ended up the same amount of time, but in federal prison.

Once he was released, he returned to his hometown of Munising, Michigan, and married Lillian Schultz on August 19, 1954. He started working as a house painter and later worked for the local telephone company.

Diana went back to California with her parents and found work as a housekeeper. A few years later, a reporter doing a follow-up story about the case learned that she was a nanny for a Hollywood movie producer. By the late 1950s, she had faded from history. Whatever became of her is unknown – like the story of Tex Thornton, she became a mostly forgotten footnote of Route 66.

"I'M GONNA MEET 'EM DOWN AT THE CADILLAC RANCH"

JUST OUTSIDE OF AMARILLO IS AN ART INSTALLATION that is worthy of the fame achieved by Route 66 – a tribute to Detroit steel, the cars that helped make America great, and the highway that changed history.

Created by the Ant Farm, a San Francisco art collective, the Cadillac Ranch began attracting interest back in 1974, the year that it sprang out of the Texas prairie. At the time, artists Chip Lord, Hudson Marquez, and Doug Michels concocted the crazy idea for an installation made from full-sized automobiles that were planted in the ground.

Like most artists, they couldn't fund the unorthodox artwork themselves. However, they had a willing patron in local millionaire Stanley Marsh 3 (yes, he was "the third," but he thought Roman numerals were pretentious). When he learned about the Ant Farm's idea of building a public monument to the Cadillac, he promised he'd come up with a funding plan for them by April 1 – April Fool's Day.

Marsh agreed to their plan – it wasn't a joke – but he had some ideas of his own. First, he asked the collective to come up with something that would inspire "delight and bewilderment" among the people of Amarillo. He was a well-known prankster known for his odd showcases, including a place in town he called the Dynamite Museum. At one point, his sense of humor had even landed him on President Richard Nixon's "enemies list" when he added one of Pat Nixon's hats to a display of decadent art.

With Marsh's money in hand, what would become an iconic Route 66 attraction was born right off the side of the highway in the middle of a wheat field. The installation showcased the birth and death of various Cadillac features, the most notable being the tailfin – used between 1949 and 1962. The 10 cars were planted in the ground nose first and set at an angle to copy the Great Pyramid of Giza in Egypt.

Unfortunately, the local community wasn't thrilled with the new art piece. At the time, Texans who had any appreciation for modern art installations were pretty hard to find. Some critics suggested it was that it wasn't an original piece but more like a derivative assemblage of spare parts. After all, famous auto designers like Harley Earl, who designed the Cadillac, deserved the credit for the sleek lines, angular forms, and sci-fi-inspired tailfins. The only "art" involved in the Amarillo installation was planting them in the ground.

But art critics aside, the Cadillac installation soon began a never-ending cycle of visual changes. The cars were their original factory colors when they were planted, but that didn't last long. Soon, the entire group was whitewashed for a television commercial. At one point, they were all painted pink in honor of the birthday of Marsh's wife. Then, when Ant Farm artist Doug Michel died, they were all painted flat black in mourning. In 2012, they were painted in the color of the rainbow for Gay Pride Day.

Since then, graffiti has become an integral part of the Cadillac Ranch – perhaps becoming even more important than the original installation itself. So, if you're traveling on Route 66, be sure to bring along whatever spray paint you might need so that you can contribute to a piece of art that has endured for more than 50 years.

HEADING INTO WILDORADO

LEAVING THE CADILLAC RANCH BEHIND, ROUTE 66 RUNS alongside Interstate 40 as it continues across the plains. The first community of note encountered has my personal favorite name of towns along this part of the road – **Wildorado**. It's a place so small that some people joke that First Street is the edge of town. Today, there's a feedlot, a few empty buildings, and the Windy Cow Café on the highway's shoulder.

There was a time, though, when this was a bustling little village – and was a hotbed for crime, which might explain its colorful name.

In 1928, a story ran in New York's *Syracuse Herald* that claimed the bank in Wildorado had been robbed eight times in the previous three years, and the general store next door had been raided by bandits so many times that the proprietors had lost count of the number of times "they have looked down revolver barrels." It added that the most recent robbery had occurred when two

The often-robbed Wildorado State Bank

armed teenagers entered the building, and locals, carrying guns of their own, managed to capture one of the bandits. They were forced to release him, however, when his partner threatened to kill the bank president.

The article ended on an ominous note: "Although discouraged by all these bandit raids, Wildorado is armed and ready."

In May 1933, another story appeared in the *San Antonio Light* about Wildorado and another audacious bank robbery. According to the Texas paper, "Burglars hauled off the one-ton safe containing more than $500 after breaking into the Wildorado State Bank sometime Friday night. Most of the bank fixtures were torn down by the burglars in getting the heavy safe out the front door."

By the early 1930s, bank robberies had become commonplace across Texas, Oklahoma, and Kansas. Wildorado may have made the papers because of the exceptional number of robberies that took place there, but no town was immune.

The First State Bank of Vega – the next town going west on Route 66 – was robbed at noon on November 15, 1932. Two employees were locked in the vault, and a young teller was tied up, blindfolded, and taken hostage. When the robbers stopped to switch cars outside of Amarillo, the fast-thinking teller stumbled from the highway to a fence line, used the barbed wire to cut himself free, hotwired the getaway car, and drove off to report the robbery.

"GRASSY MEADOW"

Along Route 66 in Vega

THE SMALL TOWN OF VEGA – SPANISH FOR "GRASSY Meadow" – hasn't changed much since that robbery took place back in the fall of 1932.

The town had its start back in 1897 when the state of Texas opened the land in the area for homesteading. Two years later, N.J. Whitfield purchased what would become the town for $1 an acre. In May 1903, A. Miller and Howard Trigg surveyed the area, and Miller opened the first general store in Vega later that same year. By 1904, it boasted a post office, a saloon, and a school, followed by a bank in 1908 and a depot for the Choctaw, Oklahoma, & Gulf Railroad in 1909. Once the tracks were laid for what would become the Rock Island Railroad, the community was complete.

Prior to 1926, the Old Ozark Trail carried the first automobile traffic through town, and when Route 66 was commissioned in 1926, it followed the original dirt road of the Ozark Trail through Vega. As automobile traffic increased, tourist courts, service stations, and cafes were built along the town's main street. Several storefronts on courthouse square were built after a devastating fire in May 1931 and another store fire later that summer. By 1937, the highway through town had been paved.

Vega was one of the last towns in Texas to be bypassed by the interstate, but the inevitable occurred in the late 1970s. Visiting the town today, travelers find that some of the old businesses that owed everything to Route 66 are still operating – or at least still standing, including the uniquely styled Magnolia service station, built in 1924 across from Roark Hardware, which later became a feed store.

MAGNOLIA STATION

THE MAGNOLIA STATION ACTUALLY PRE-DATES ROUTE 66, built by Colonel J.T. Owen, when the highway that ran in front of it was still the dirt highway known as the Ozark Trail.

It was the second service station built in Vega in the 1920s, and by the time U.S. 66 came through, Owens had leased the place to Edward and Cora Wilson, who lived in the apartment above the station. A few other operators followed, but in 1933, Colonel

Magnolia Station in Vega

Owens' son, Austin, took over the station's operations and entered into a lease with Phillips Petroleum Company, which cost him one cent of every gallon of gasoline sold.

In 1937, Route 66 was finally paved through town and was realigned through Vega so that it was just south of the station. It bypassed Vega's downtown completely.

The Magnolia Station continued to provide gasoline for passing motorists until 1953 when it was closed and turned into a barber shop. Abandoned in 1965, it sat empty for years until it was eventually restored and preserved as a Vegan icon on Route 66.

VEGA COURTS

ONE LOCATION IN VEGA THAT CONTINUED TO operate until 2022 was the Vega Motel. Constructed by Ervin Pancoast – and originally called Vega Courts – on Route 66 in 1947, the motor lodge had west and south wings, which contained 12 units. Cashing in on the importance of automobiles, Ervin had pairs of garages that alternated with pairs of motel units in each wing. At the same time, he also constructed a small house in the center courtyard that served as an office and personal living

The Vega Motel began during the heyday of Route 66 as the Vega Courts

quarters. Mr. Pancoast married the following year, and the couple lived on the property.

Business boomed for the young couple in the years that followed, and in 1953, they added an east wing that contained eight units with built-in garages. Many of the new rooms included kitchenettes.

Traffic remained heavy on Route 66 through Vega throughout the 1950s and 1960s, leading to a modernization of the motel – and the name change from "courts" to "motel" – in 1964.

Eventually, though, progress doomed the motel when the interstate bypassed the town. The Pancoasts sold the motel in 1976, and the new owners picked up right where they left off, making sure the motel remained in continuous operation since its construction.

The Vega Motel hung on for decades as a rare, surviving, and intact motel in the Texas Panhandle, but time caught up with the place again in 2022 when it finally closed for good.

MOTORING TO ADRIAN

WEST OF VEGA, THE INTERSTATE HIGHWAY TRANSFORMED Route 66 into a weed-strewn asphalt pathway that drops from the plains, through the broken rocks on both sides of the roads, and on toward the state line with New Mexico.

Before a traveler reaches the border, though, they pass through the small town of **Adrian**. The town's claim to fame is as the geographical "midpoint" of Route 66, with 1139 miles from Adrian east to Chicago and 1139 miles west to Los Angeles, which made the town's motto, "When you're here, you're halfway there."

Adrian got its start in 1900 when the Rock Island Railroad marked the site as a future station and shipping point, but it would take eight years for the line to arrive at the spot and for the settlement of the area to really begin. Like Vega, though, Adrian started to entice travelers with service stations and cafes when the highway that passed through town was still the Ozark Trail. It had an economic boom when the road was transformed into Route 66.

MIDPOINT CAFE

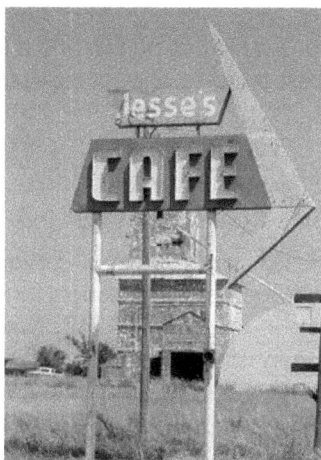

ONE OF THE MOST POPULAR – AND SURVIVING – EATERIES in Adrian was Jesse's Café, which was opened by Dub Edmonds and former Navy cook Jesse Fincher in 1956.

At that time, it was simply a cinder block building that sat next to a service station, but in 1965, a second-story A-frame was added above the café, and a new canopy was built over the pumps, which looked a bit more civilized. The apartment burned twice, though, and wasn't rebuilt the second time, so don't go looking for it today.

Jessie's Café became so popular that a second restaurant – called Jessie's #2 – was built in Wildorado, and the two men ran both locations until 1976 when they sold the Adrian café to Terry and Peggy Crietz. They changed the name to Peggy's – which was a terrible idea. When it failed, they sold it again, and the new owners called it Rachel's, but it also failed to take off.

Locals and travelers wanted to be reminded of when it was Jessie's because his pies had become famous in both Adrian and along Route 66. He baked pies in the morning, placed them on the counter, and they were almost always sold before

Midpoint Cafe

they had time to cool off. He continued to bake those acclaimed pies at the Wildorado location until he died in 1989. Dub Edmonds sold that last café in 1991 and retired from the business.

Meanwhile, Fran Hauser bought the restaurant in Adrian in 1990, and even though she first tried calling it the Adrian Café, she changed it in 1995 to the Midpoint Café to take advantage of the town's location on Route 66.

Today, travelers make it a point to stop in Adrian to take photos at the Midpoint sign, and they also make sure to stop at the Midpoint Café for a delicious burger and a slice of what's called "ugly crust pie," the next best thing to one that Jesse Fincher baked.

KOZY KOTTAGE KAMP

ANOTHER POPULAR SPOT IN ADRIAN WAS THE KOZY Kottage Kamp, which Manual Loveless built in the early 1940s. The café and attached service station thrived for a few years until it was destroyed by fire in December 1947. Unwilling to give up on Route 66 business, the family started renting cabins behind the ruins of the station, using the name Adrian Court.

Eventually, they sold the property where the station once stood to Bob Harris, who had worked at the Kozy Kottage Kamp before World War II. When he was discharged from the service, he came home with the idea of building something new on the spot – something that would convince motorists that they *had* to stop.

The nearby U.S. Army Air Force bases were selling surplus military items, and Bob decided to buy a decommissioned control tower and move it to the property. He then proceeded to build a café around it, which he named the Bent Door Café because of the angled door that needed to enter through the tower's slanted walls.

When Bob later moved away from Adrian, his mother operated the 24-hour-a-day café – now called Tommy's Café -- for a time, and then the

Loveless family decided to lease it. They kept it open until the late 1960s when the interstate bypassed Adrian and the steady traffic of the past slowed to a trickle. In 1970, the café closed its doors.

It sat empty for three decades until Bob Harris returned home for a visit. When he heard the café had been condemned, he repurchased the property with grand plans to open again in September 1995.

But it never happened. The plan to bring Tommy's Café back to life failed, and the café, which was built from a control tower, has been closed ever since.

BLOOD AND BULLETS AT THE STATE LINE

THE TOWN OF **GLENRIO** STRADDLES THE STATE LINE BETWEEN Texas and New Mexico. It's a ghost town today. It was one of the many towns that were snuffed out by the interstate, and today, only battered ruins – and tragic stories – remain.

But at one time, there were thriving businesses in town, including the Texas Longhorn Motel – Café – Service Station, although that one almost never happened.

Scared away from Glenrio in 1946 by talk of a new interstate that was going to bypass the town, local businessman Homer Ehresman packed up his family and moved to Plainview, Texas. However, by 1950, it became clear that the interstate was barely in the planning stages, so Homer, with his family in tow, returned to Glenrio and built the Texas Longhorn Motel on the Texas side of town. The motel – along with the filling station and café – ran smoothly, even after the Rock Island Railroad closed its depot in town in 1955. This dealt the town an economic blow, but Homer's business continued to thrive – the knockout blow was still years in the future at that point.

As tourist traffic grew in the 1950s, business flourished. The Longhorn's iconic "First/Last Stop in Texas" sign grew from a painted board to a giant, illuminated billboard that beckoned travelers to stop for supper and spend the night.

Then, the early 1970s arrived, and the interstate that had been stalled for decades finally arrived, spelling doom for Glenrio and its businesses.

Homer was down but not out, however. He built a new, modern motel and restaurant just five miles west of Glenrio at an interstate exit. It opened in 1975 but today, even the new motel lies in ruins.

As does the old Longhorn Motel. Like the rest of Glenrio, it's abandoned and slowly crumbling, still sitting at the edge of a highway that has gone from being hectic and alive to cracked and faded by the sun.

THE STATE LINE BAR

TRUE CRIME

ALONG THE FORLORN STRETCH OF ROAD THAT PASSES through Glenrio is a nondescript cinderblock building that has been ravaged by time. The windows are broken, and the front door vanished years ago.

It was in this building that a woman named Dessie Leach was senselessly murdered on July 10, 1973.

Dessie and her husband, Albert, had eked out a living on a failing ranch in Texas before moving to Glenrio and buying the State Line Bar in the late 1950s. Business was slow on that hot afternoon in July, a hint of what was to come once the interstate was completed outside of town. The bypass seemed to be all anyone in town wanted to talk about that summer.

When 58-year-old Dessie opened the tavern that day, it had been business as usual. She slowly cleaned up a few things that had been left unfinished the previous evening. She was a small woman who had painful arthritis, so her husband usually completed the harder tasks around the place.

According to the police investigation, Dessie was tending the bar alone, and her first customers of the day were a couple from Amarillo who were traveling west in a motorhome. Her second customer was John Wayne Lee, a friendly young man

The State Line Bar -- 1972 murder scene

who ordered a beer and asked the other customers if they wanted to shoot some pool. They declined. They were eager to get on their way. They mainly had stopped to use the restroom.

Not long after their motorhome rumbled out of the parking lot, Cornelia Tapia, who lived in an apartment behind the bar, saw Dessie stagger out of the tavern's back door. Her dress was soaked with blood. She stumbled a few steps and then fell to the ground. She had been stabbed four times and died before she could be transported to the hospital in Tucumcari, New Mexico.

John Wayne Lee was apprehended without a struggle a few hours later in Vega, Texas. He was covered in blood, and a bloody knife – and several guns – were found in his car. In a plea deal, he was charged with armed robbery and second-degree murder. On Halloween 1973, a jury found him guilty on both counts. Lee was given two consecutive sentences that should have kept him in prison for 50 years. But it didn't work out that way. He served just four years before the murder conviction was commuted in 1977. He served a little more time for the robbery, was released, and vanished into history.

But I'd say there's a very good chance that he didn't live a long and happy life.

The State Line Bar closed after the murder, and it never reopened. Albert Leach moved to San Jon, New Mexico, where he raised horses for the rest of his life.

Glenrio became a ghost town in the years that followed, and U.S. 66 became an empty stretch of asphalt to the state line. There, the last alignment faded into the desert, which is now recalled as only a memory.

NEW MEXICO
THE LAND OF ENCHANTMENT

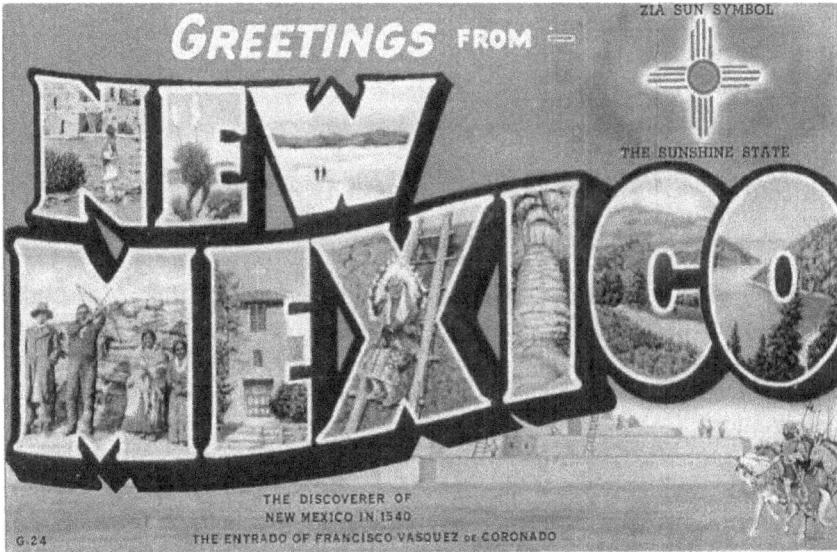

WHEN ROUTE 66 WAS CREATED IN 1926, THE STATE OF NEW Mexico had only recently celebrated its 14th birthday. Building a highway across 506 miles of rugged landscape was not an easy task. The planners faced many obstacles – deserts, twisting canyons, and treacherous hills.

Fortunately, they were not the first to traverse the land. Often, the route followed sections of the old Santa Fe Trail and the Camino Real, which, by then, was already more than 300 years old. The original alignment between Albuquerque and Santa Fe was considered the most treacherous stretch of road and included La Bajada Hill, which was Spanish for "The Descent."

From 1926 to 1932, the hill provided motorists with a slew of challenges, from sharp hills to more than 20 switchbacks. Before fuel pumps had been invented for cars, motorists often climbed the hill in reverse to keep fuel flowing to their carburetors. Descending La Bajada was an adventure of its own. Early brake pads were made from cloth and were not exactly durable. A motorist who rode their brakes going down the steep hill often set the pads on fire. So many accidents occurred that the state's highway department posted a warning sign at the top of the hill that read:

LA BAJADA HILL
WARNING
SAFE SPEED 10 MPH
WATCH SHARP CURVES
THIS ROAD IS NOT FOOL PROOF BUT SAFE FOR A SANE DRIVER
USE LOW GEAR

As automobiles became more popular, many of the older paths followed by Route 66 soon became obsolete. New Mexico saw its share of new alignments, just like other states, but none were as dramatic as that which took place just as the new highway was earning its official designation.

At the time, Governor Arthur T. Hannet was in the process of losing his bid for reelection in a closely fought race. Feeling that he'd been betrayed by his own political party and frustrated with state politics in general, he decided to avenge his loss by building a highway that bypassed the state capital.

Since the new governor, Richard Dillon, was going to take office in less than two months, Hannet had to act fast. He recruited state highway engineer E.B. Bail into his scheme and put him to work on a road-building project that would start six miles west of Santa Rosa and head straight into Albuquerque. At the time, Route 66 had been designated through New Mexico from Tucumcari to Santa Rosa, then to Romeroville, Glorieta, Santa Fe, and Albuquerque. Hannet's road would shorten the route to Albuquerque by about 90 miles and bypass Santa Fe's business community and political center. By the time the crews and equipment were secured, only 31 days were left to build 60 miles of road.

Angry residents on Route 66 to the north and Highway 60 to the south decided to try and ruin the governor's plans. Worried about the economic impact of the new route, they vandalized and sabotaged the equipment – but the crews kept working. Some of them even started sleeping close to the machinery at night to protect it from further damage. Cold weather slowed their progress, but they pushed on.

The men worked almost non-stop, but the new road wasn't quite finished when time ran out. On January 1, Richard Dillon took the oath of office and sent a representative to put a stop to the construction.

And then came the snowstorm.

Delayed by two days, the governor's man didn't arrive at the work site until January 3, but by that time, the work had been completed. The revenge road was finished. Although originally designated as New Mexico 6, it was paved by 1937 and redesignated as Route 66 that same year.

But of course, U.S. 66 through New Mexico only survived a little over four decades after that. The last segment of the highway was decommissioned in 1981, four years before the entire route (temporarily) faded into history.

"DEATH ALLEY"

BY 1969, THE INTERSTATE RAN STRAIGHT THROUGH FROM Oklahoma City to Barstow, with a few exceptions for small, unfinished sections that didn't pose much of a problem for travelers in a hurry. But one exception to the exception was a 20-mile or so stretch of road just across the border into New Mexico.

The state line town of Glenrio anchored the eastern end of the section while the town of San Jon was located at the western end. This piece of highway was so hazardous that it was commonly thought to be one of the deadliest stretches of roadway in all of New Mexico.

New Mexico residents, officials, and over-the-road truckers from all over the country called this part of the highway "Death Alley."

The original plan that had been drawn up to replace "Death Alley" with the interstate would have put the town of San Jon about five miles south of the new road – spelling certain doom for the small town. After a legal battle led by San Jon's former mayor, Earl Flint, the interstate was rerouted, and San Jon was saved. Six years later, when the new highway was built between Glenrio and Tucumcari, San Jon had its own off-ramp.

However, San Jon wasn't the only town located along "Death Alley;" the other – a present-day ghost town called **Endee** – didn't survive. There is very little left here today, aside from a long-abandoned motor court, the ruins of a service station and grocery store, and a handful of skeletons of houses. It was once a prosperous community, yet there's no hint that it played a role in New Mexico's history.

A newspaper clipping from the *Santa Fe New Mexican*, dated May 2, 1906, tells the story of two arrests that were made by Captain Fornoff of the mounted police that marked the beginning of the end of cattle rustling in the area. After a month-long chase "over dangerous mountain passes and lying for hours in wait for the desperados," the police arrested John Fife and Tom Darlington, the leaders of a gang of outlaws who had cost local ranchers thousands of dollars. The arrests had been made at Endee.

This was the last time that a horse-mounted posse was ever used in New Mexico.

ON THE WAY TO TUCUMCARI

IN THE 1940S, THE TOWN OF SAN JON HAD A BUSINESS district that boasted two auto courts, several cafes and stories, the San Jon Garage, the San Jon Implement Company, and a couple of service stations. There were also a few roadhouses, including the one that Tex Thornton stopped at with his killers while driving back to Amarillo.

Continuing west on Route 66, a motorist passes the ruins of Canyon Station and motors into **Tucumcari.**

Pronounced TOO-COME-CARRY, the town was originally called Six Gun Siding. In 1902, the citizens decided that it needed a more "respectable" name, so it began sharing the name of a nearby mountain – which, in turn, earned its name from an old indigenous legend.

The story goes that a tribal chieftain ordered two competing warriors to the top of the mountain to fight to the death for the honor of marrying his daughter, Kari. The man she favored most, Tocom, lost the fight, and in a violent rage, she killed the other man herself. Filled with despair, she then plunged Tocom's knife into her own heart. When he saw what had occurred, her father also took his own life. If you use your imagination and change the spelling a little, you've got a name.

During the heyday of Route 66, signs that read "TUCUMCARI TONIGHT! 2,000 MOTEL ROOMS!" lined the highway from Missouri to California, and the town became acclaimed for being "two blocks wide and two miles long." The highway through the booming community was lined with motels, filling stations, trading posts, and cafes.

When the interstate bypassed Tucumcari, the old town was hit hard, and even more so in the years as the population declined. Still, the resurgence in interest in the highway has made it a destination for 66 enthusiasts as well as business folks with vision.

The Motel Safari is a near-perfect time capsule from 1959, and the renovated Roadrunner Lodge offers travelers modern amenities with 1960s swankiness.

There are a few other motels and auto courts in town that have managed to reach legendary status over the years.

THE MOTEL GIVEN SPECIAL WRITE-UP IN THE SATURDAY EVENING POST.

CACTUS MOTOR LODGE

WHEN I.E. AND EDNA PERRY OPENED THE CACTUS MOTOR Lodge on the east side of town in 1941, they knew they would be the first motel that many travelers would see when they made it to Tucumcari, and for that reason, they wanted it to be special.

The motel was made up of four buildings that housed 25 guest rooms. Three of the buildings formed a U-shape, and the other building served as a dance hall that became a highlight for travelers and a hang-out for locals. Each of the guest rooms had its own private garage, as well as free radio and double insulated walls that blocked out the sound of vehicles on the highway – and whatever the neighbors were getting up to in the room next door.

After her husband passed away, Edna sold the Cactus to Norm and Irene Wegner in 1952. Hoping to modernize the look of the place, they had artificial stone applied to the exterior of all four buildings. They also converted the dance hall into an office and manager's residence. The Wegners operated the motel for the next 20 years until they retired in 1972.

They sold the place to Harry and Jean Schiermeyer, who sold it again to Frank and Elizabeth Kocab in 1976. It changed hands again in 1979.

When the interstate bypassed Tucumcari in the early 1980s, it killed most of the businesses in town, including the Cactus. By the 1990s, business was so bad that the motel units were closed, the swimming pool was removed, and the courtyard was converted to an RV park.

But all wasn't lost-- yet. In 2006, the Cactus Motor Lodge was listed on the National Register of Historic Places, and the motel's neon sign was restored two years later. It remained there, glowing the same way that it greeted travelers on Route 66 until 2018 when the sign was removed and relocated to a neon-sign park in Albuquerque.

What was left of the motor lodge was sold off at auction, and the property itself was purchased by O'Reilly Auto Parts. The company razed the remaining structures and built a store at the location, turning the Cactus Motor Lodge into nothing but a memory.

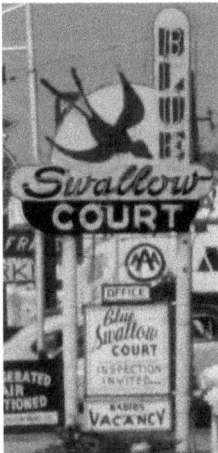

BLUE SWALLOW COURT

UNDOUBTEDLY, THE MOST FAMOUS OF THE MOTELS IN Tucumcari is one that still draws travelers today – Blue Swallow Court.

It's been a favorite with Route 66 motorists since 1941 when W.A. Huggins opened the classic motor court with 13 units laid out in an L-shape, each with its own garage. The office was located in the center of the lot.

It changed ownership a few times in the early years, and then in 1958, Floyd Redman purchased the property and gave it to his fiancé as an engagement gift. Lillian, soon-to-be-Redman, took over operations and then ran the place for the next 40 years until age and the high cost of upkeep took their toll.

BLUE SWALLOW MOTEL · 815 E. HI-WAY 66 · TUCUMCARI, NEW MEXICO

The motel crumbled, primarily due to lack of steady maintenance, and eventually, Lillian put the place up for sale – there were no takers.

Another Route 66 was doomed to fade away.

That's how it seemed until the place caught the eye of Dale and Linda Bakke, who saw the Blue Swallow listed for sale in a Denver newspaper. Looking for adventure and a change of scenery, they bought the place and started a substantial renovation of the place in March 1998. Room by room, fixture by fixture, they slowly brought the Blue Swallow back to life, and it's still in Tucumcari today, still greeting travelers who are reveling in the nostalgia of Route 66.

It's since become one of the most popular U.S. 66 photo ops in the Southwest, and spending a night here is on the bucket list of almost everyone who longs for the days when the highway was the only real way to drive across the country.

TUCUMCARI CRIME SPREE

BUT NOT EVERYTHING WAS "FUN AND GAMES" IN THIS ROUTE 66 town. On the evening of November 9, 1966, 20-year-old Bobby Gene Garcia began an unexplainable series of violent events that left several people wounded and two dead – including a police officer -- and the entire community in shock.

It began when Bobby went to the home of his mother-in-law, Annie Apalacio, looking for his wife. He stormed into the house and shot and killed his sister-in-law, Josie Baker. Moments later, he left the house, literally dragging his wife behind him. He shoved her into his car and drove

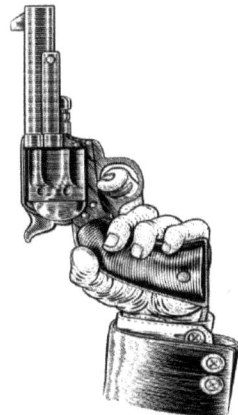

TRUE CRIME

five blocks to city hall. Leaving his wife in the alley outside, he pushed his way through the doors to the building and was confronted by two former classmates, Steve Grau and Ralph Murray. They were on the staircase that led to the second-floor police department and jail.

At gunpoint, he forced the two of them up the stairs to the police department, where he encountered dispatcher Mary Simpson and desk sergeant Jerry Wignall. He demanded that Wignall give him the key to the jail. Bobby's plan was apparently to free his brother, Albert, who had been arrested the previous day for disorderly conduct and assault with a deadly weapon.

To make sure that Simpson and Wignall knew he was serious, Bobby fired a shotgun into the wall. Covered by shards of plaster and dust, Wignall hurriedly pulled open his desk drawer and started fishing for the key. However, Bobby, manic with anger and anxiety, thought he was reaching for a gun and turned the shotgun on the police officer. He fired once, and Wignall was hit in the lower back. He later died from the wound.

Tragically, he'd died for nothing. Albert had already been transferred to the county jail earlier that day.

Taking Mary Simpson as his hostage, Bobby bolted down the back stairs of the building. On the way out, he ran into Officer Max Crespin and shot him in the leg.

In response to a call for help from the police department, a state trooper named Jack Kelly arrived in time to see Bobby and his hostage fleeing down the street. Kelly, joined by Quay County Sheriff Claude Moncus, followed Bobby to the Sands-Dorsey Drug Store, and after a tense but short standoff, Bobby Garcia surrendered.

The following morning, Bobby – who had been quiet throughout the night – went berserk in his cell at the police department. It took five officers to remove him from the cell and get him into the courtroom for

The Sands-Dorsey Drugstore

arraignment. His violent behavior continued to the point that the judge ordered the arraignment to be rescheduled.

Nearly a dozen charges against Bobby were already pending, including the murder of his sister-in-law. And when Sergeant Wignall died on

November 11, the murder of a law enforcement officer was added to the list.

When Bobby eventually went to trial, he was found guilty of all charges and received a life sentence. After two escape attempts, he was transferred from a New Mexico state prison to a federal prison in Terre Haute, Indiana. He committed suicide on December 13, 1980.

To this day, the cause of Bobby Garcia's crime spree remains a mystery. No one knows why he went looking for his wife, killing his sister-in-law in the process, only to leave her in the alley outside the courthouse. No one knows why he was so desperate to free his brother or why he was so quick to kill Jerry Wignall with that shotgun.

It will always remain a case of small-town murder that will never be truly explained.

CUERVO

WEST OF TUCUMCARI, WHAT REMAINS OF OLD ROUTE 66, is a stark contrast to the nearby interstate. At Cuervo, where the road has not been maintained for decades, all but the most daring travelers have no choice but to take Interstate 40 all the way into Santa Rosa.

But those who are brave enough – or who are driving a vehicle that can handle the broken-down road – may find themselves in a desolate ghost town whose name means "crow" in Spanish. Cuervo can be found along the old Ozark Trail, which passes over mesas and juniper-covered hills where, if you look closely, you might catch a glimpse of the

Guadalupe Church - one of the last remaining structures in Cuervo

shattered asphalt road and concrete culverts of a piece of Route 66 that once was.

Cuervo was originally a railroad water stop town whose main business was cattle ranching. When Route 66 passed through, the population of the town "exploded." A count of the residents in 1946 showed the number had climbed to 128 people.

But that was enough to run the two service stations and the motel in town and to fill the pews in the town's two churches. But when the highway was realigned in 1952, the town fell into an irreversible decline. Although a few people remain, most moved away in the years that followed, and even the post office closed in 2011.

Today, Cuervo is filled with ramshackle and crumbling wood and adobe homes, rusted cars, and sandy lots filled with weeds and brush. A small red sandstone Catholic church is one of the few surviving structures.

It's a place that now slumbers, never to awaken, under the wide blue New Mexico skies.

FRONTIER MUSEUM

Frontier Museum Santa Rosa, New Mexico

THE FINAL STRETCH OF ROAD WAS COMPLETED BETWEEN Cuervo and Santa Rosa in the early 1950s. The alignment today is, as mentioned, mostly buried beneath the interstate, but in 1954, the Frontier Museum was opened about nine miles east of town.

The building, with its multiple offerings, was built in the style of a western adobe by contractor Max Rivera for W.S. Wilson. It was a small version of what every Route 66 needed in the 1950s – a service station, tavern, café, souvenir shop, and a museum that offered hundreds of native and western relics from around the area. Wilson even kept a pair of buffaloes behind the museum. It soon became a favorite stop for highway travelers.

The Frontier Museum continued to draw people off Route 66 for the next 30 years, even after the interstate came through. The museum had its own exit, but the changing popularity of automobile travel – and the changing tastes of the public – eventually killed roadside attractions like this one.

The Frontier Museum closed in the early 1980s, and all the artifacts and most of the café kitchen equipment were auctioned off, including the magnificent, hand-carved wooden bar that had served cold beer to road-weary travelers for years.

But it wasn't completely lost. A few years later, Robert Rivera – son of the contractor who'd built the place – purchased the property. In 1985, though, he found the building was in terrible disrepair. He went to work remodeling the place as a bar and dance club and added a stage for bands. He called the place simply The Frontier and mainly catered to locals. There didn't seem to be much interest from travelers on the interstate, which was probably why its doors were closed again by 1993.

The building remained empty for the next decade and then was destroyed by fire in 2003. There's nothing left of it today, aside from some scorched bricks that are scattered in the grass at an interstate exit a few miles from Santa Rosa.

SANTA ROSA

LOCATED ON THE PECOS RIVER, THE TOWN OF **SANTA ROSA** started as a cattle ranch in 1865. Drawn by the abundance of local water, Don Celso Baca expanded his cattle empire and named the new settlement after his wife, Rosa, and Saint Rose of Liam, the first canonized saint of the New World.

The arrival of the railroad on Christmas Day, 1901, turned the sleepy community into an important transportation hub. Ironically, though, the abundant water that had appealed to Don Celso turned out to bring the end of the railroad in town. The water was so high in mineral content that it left gypsum deposits in the engines, ruining the locomotives. Soon, Santa Rosa became a sleepy little town again.

It would be Route 66 that brought the community back to life. It became an important stop on this stretch of the road and, at one time,

had as many as 60 service stations, 20 motels, and 15 eateries along the main street through town.

Despite the arid landscape, Santa Rosa maintains its long, watery reputation. There are many natural lakes near the town, including the famous **Blue Hole**, which is known for its crystal-clear water. The bell-shaped pool is over 80 feet deep and keeps a constant temperature of 64 degrees. Scuba divers from all over the country come to experience the Blue Hole, and many of them arrive via the small Santa Rose Route 66 Airport. During the Dust Bowl days, the Blue Hole and the surrounding area served as a campground for thousands of Okies on their way to California.

U.S. 66 arrived in Santa Rosa in 1926, but in late 1937, it was realigned to bypass the town, cutting out Santa Fe and heading straight to Albuquerque. For the most part, though, the town managed to hang on, and it still thrives on Route 66 nostalgia today.

It still boasts Bozo's Route 66 Auto Museum, along with a good selection of motels and lodgings like the restored Sun 'n Sand Motel, La Mesa Motel, and a couple of traditional campgrounds.

If you're hungry, the Route 66 Restaurant serves delicious Tex-Mex food and there's also Joseph's Café, which has a visible connection to the town's most famous defunct eatery.

CLUB CAFE

IF YOU TRAVELED ROUTE 66 THROUGH THE SOUTHWEST during its heyday, you were sure to spot one of the billboards for the Club Café in Santa Rosa. It was hard to miss them. Each was emblazoned with a cartoon of a jolly, smiling fat man who became one of the many icons of the Mother Road.

The Club Café was started in 1935 when Floyd Shaw and Phil Craig opened the doors of their small 24-seat restaurant. Floyd was working as a highway surveyor on Route 66 at the time, helping to plan the new alignment to

Albuquerque. Even though the café became immediately popular, its real success was still to come.

In 1937, the new route for U.S. 66 skipped Santa Rosa and Santa Fe and went straight on to Albuquerque. Even so, people kept stopping at the café in record numbers, which prompted the pair to sell the small building and move Club Café into a larger spot.

Knowing that business was only going to increase, Floyd and Phil invested in billboards all over the southwest that featured the café's jolly fat man mascot. Phil had crafted the character – leading friends to good-naturedly suggest that he'd based the mascot on himself.

Club Café's jolly fat man mascot, which became known up and down the highway

It wasn't long before the café became known nationwide, mostly thanks to the truck drivers and travelers who stopped in to enjoy the spot's excellent food and friendly service. The specialties of the house were their sourdough biscuits and pinto beans.

Club Café continued to enjoy success over the next three decades. It wasn't until the interstate came through, cut the town in half, and left the café far from the exit ramp that things started to slow down – a lot.

But in 1973, a former employee named Ron Chavez was passing through on his way home from California and saw for himself the terrible state of the town and the café. He decided to take a chance, and he bought the place, soon returning it to its former glory by doing the same things Floyd and Phil had done – putting up a slew of billboards and letting the Club Café fat man point the way to the restored diner.

Club Café hung on for almost another 20 years, but then, in 1992, it served its last meal.

In 1995, though, another man with a vision purchased the building. Jose Campos and his family owned and operated Joseph's Café in town since 1956, and he believed it was time to bring back the fat man mascot and Club Café. Unfortunately, it didn't work out as planned. The building was in bad shape, and it would cost a fortune to bring it up to code. The revival of Club Café was abandoned.

So, Jose did the next best thing. He purchased the rights to the cartoon mascot and brought him into the Joseph's Café family. He can still be seen grinning at hungry customers both inside and outside their place – looking happier than ever to have his old job back.

SANTA ROSA'S "DR. JEKYLL AND MR. HYDE"

IN 1939, IT WASN'T ROUTE 66, THE CLUB CAFÉ, OR THE BLUE Hole that caused Santa Rosa to become infamous across America. In January of that year, people were checking their newspapers for a verdict in the trial of Dr. John H. Sanford. They wanted to know the end of a story that had been making headlines since the previous summer.

The riveting story began about a month after Dr. Sanford – former mayor of Santa Rosa – rushed his wife to the hospital in Tucumcari. She died nine days later, on July 23, 1938. The official cause of death was heart failure, but it wasn't long before rumors began to spread around the community.

TRUE CRIME

An anonymous tip came into the police department that claimed Dr. Sanford wasn't what he appeared to be. He had been having a torrid affair with a red-haired waitress, Hallie Mae Wilson. She worked at a café on Route 66, and she and Dr. Sanford had been spotted meeting behind the building and disappearing to a local no-tell motel.

The tip led the police to exhume Mrs. Sanford's body in September, and the coroner came up with a very different cause of death than the one reported by the hospital – the doctor's wife had been poisoned.

Dr. Sanford was arrested, and he quickly hired an Albuquerque attorney who attempted to portray Mrs. Sanford as suicidal following discussions with her husband about a pending divorce. But the public wasn't buying it, and neither were reporters. One newspaper labeled Sandford as a "Jekyll and Hyde."

At trial, the waitress's husband, Walter Wilson, testified that Sanford had confessed his undying love for his wife and had even made the payments on the Wilsons' new car – an arrangement he didn't seem to mind.

On January 28, 1939, the jury deliberated for about five hours before returning with a guilty verdict. He was initially sentenced to death, but after a series of appeals, the sentence was commuted to life in prison.

"I STABBED THE SHERIFF"

SANTA ROSA WAS BACK IN THE NEWSPAPERS IN 1949 WHEN former Guadalupe Sheriff Jose Gonzales was murdered by a man to whom he had shown kindness just hours before.

On the evening of February 18, Gonzales and Abel Sanchez, who served as night marshals in town, were called to a public disturbance call involving a local man named Delfido Duran. This sympathetic character was known to both police officers and residents of Santa Rosa. It wasn't the first time that he'd encountered the two officers. Duran suffered from serious mental problems caused by his time as a prisoner of war during World War II. Rather than arrest the troubled veteran, the two marshals calmed him down and gave him a ride home.

TRUE CRIME

After their shift was over, the two men were unwinding at the Medley Lounge with friends. Seated at a table, Sheriff Gonzales unfortunately had his back to the door. That was why he didn't see Delfido Duran when he entered the bar, snuck up behind Gonzales, and plunged a large hunting knife into his neck, severing his windpipe and jugular. He fell forward onto the table and died in a pool of spreading blood.

Abel Sanchez and Officer Antonio Chavez quickly subdued Duran and dragged him outside to a car. He was taken to the jail at the courthouse, where Duran overpowered them and fled toward the train depot. The two officers, joined by law enforcement officers, went in pursuit. The

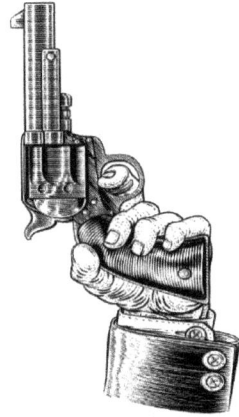

Sheriff Jose Gonzales

nighttime stillness of the town was shattered by cries, sirens, and even gunshots as officers fired at Duran as he ran. His break for freedom, though, was short-lived. They captured him – breathing and bullet-free – near the depot. With Duran's safety in mind, state officers transported him to the jail in Las Vegas, New Mexico. There were too many angry people in Santa Rosa that night.

Duran's trial was short. The jury quickly determined he was guilty of first-degree murder. Sentenced to 99 years in the state prison, he was transferred to a prison farm in Los Lunas two years later. After eight years there, however, Duran was given a fatal cancer diagnosis and was released early in consideration of his status as a former POW.

He died just one week after his release.

ROUTE 66 OLD AND NEW

WEST OF SANTA ROSA, ROUTE 66 TAKES ON TWO VERY different personalities. Before 1938, the highway looped north through Santa Fe and Albuquerque, but the later route went directly into the Rio Grande Valley. Only short pieces of the later alignment exist between Santa Rosa and Moriarty since most of it was buried under the interstate. The original Route 66, however, has mostly survived in the modern era as state highways and back roads.

Both alignments saw enough roadside attractions, memorable stops, murder, mayhem, and death to fill more than just one book. On the original portion, though, many of the stories predate Route 66 by centuries since the highway usually followed the old Santa Fe Trail.

So, I've done my best to pick and choose the best stories from the stretch of road between Santa Rosa and Albuquerque, and I hope that I haven't left out anything that you'd hoped to see in these pages.

IT WAS ALONG THE OLD ALIGNMENT WHERE YOU'D FIND AN old adobe that sat in the shadow of the Glorieta Pass, marking the last vestiges of the once-famous Pigeon Ranch. It was a hotel that had been established along the Santa Fe Trail in 1830.

Just west of the ranch, the Mexican army attacked a wagon train of traders from Texas in the pass in 1841. I mean, it was Mexican land at the time, so...

In 1848, on the east side of the ranch, General Manuel Armijo surrendered to U.S. General Stephen Kearney without a fight during the Mexican-American War. Finally, in March 1862, buildings on the ranch served as a field hospital during the battle of Glorieta Pass, an important western engagement during the Civil War.

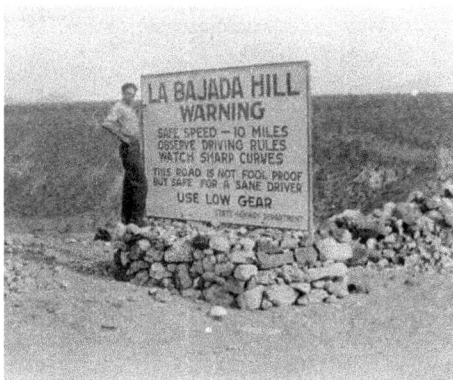

La Bajada Hill - one off the scariest spots on all of Route 66. It wasn't surprising that it was bypassed as early as 1931

Of course, these things have nothing to do with Route 66, but it's an interesting bit of history about the area.

This original alignment of Route 66 did include La Bajada Hill, which was mentioned at the start of the New Mexico chapter. In 1928, newspapers across the region were stoking fear in the public about the increasing amount of traffic on the highway and the danger represented by the steep, narrow roadway that was filled with sharp, treacherous curves. The story that kicked things off was about an accident that involved Paul Campbell of Fairfield, Missouri, who had overturned his Ford on the hill. He had fallen asleep at the wheel, drifted into oncoming traffic, overcorrected, and lost control.

The following summer, another accident on the hill made the news. An accident that occurred at the bottom resulted in the deaths of two men and tragic injuries of two women, one of whom later died. The accident and the legal proceedings that followed it fueled a crusade for

U.S. 66 improvements that didn't stop until a bypass of the hill was completed in 1931.

FOOD AND FUEL AT THE FLYING C RANCH

WEST OF SANTA ROSA, NEAR A TOWN SO SMALL IT'S HARD to find on a map, was the Flying C Ranch, built by Roy Cline in 1945. Roy is better known for establishing the very successful Cline's Corners (we'll get to that) in 1933, but he sold it before moving to Kingman, Arizona, in 1939. After a few other pit stops, he returned once again to the wide-open highway of New Mexico a few years later and built the Flying C Ranch.

The Flying C – so remote that its best advertising line was that it was 77 miles from Albuquerque, which was a long way in 1945 – was sorely needed along this stretch of desert road. It offered a Texaco gas station, a small café, and most importantly, a garage with a tow truck. Most of his business came from stranded motorists who knew nothing about traveling through the southwest in the summer.

A few years after the spot opened, Roy's son made some repairs to the stucco and decided to paint all the buildings gleaming white, which could easily be seen by highway travelers who were still miles away from the Flying C. It became so popular that it even became a regular stop for the Greyhound bus line.

And why not? There was nothing else for miles in either direction.

Roy owned and operated the Flying C until 1963, when he sold it to a corporate travel company that had been in business since the founder, Claude Bowlin, started his first New Mexico trading post in 1912. They still operate the Flying C today, offering souvenirs, food, drinks, and gasoline along what was once one of the most desolate parts of U.S. 66 in New Mexico.

THE VANISHING OF THE "EAST ST. LOUIS FOUR"

DURING ITS HEYDAY, ROUTE 66 WAS INVOLVED IN MORE than its share of crime, as we've detailed in this book and others in this series. One of the strangest disappearances in New Mexico's history took place along and around the famous highway, and it's still being talked about in the region nine decades later.

George Lorius was one of the lucky Americans who managed to weather the Depression. He was an executive for an ice and coal company in East St. Louis, Illinois – two items that consumers always seemed to need no matter how bad the economy seemed to get.

In fact, at a time when most people were trying to put food on the table, George was going on vacation with his wife, Laura, and another couple, Albert and Tillie Heberer. They had been close friends for years and often took weekend jaunts and overnight trips together. In late spring 1935, they set out on a great adventure together, motoring west on Route 66. They had a planned side trip to visit friends in Vaughn, New

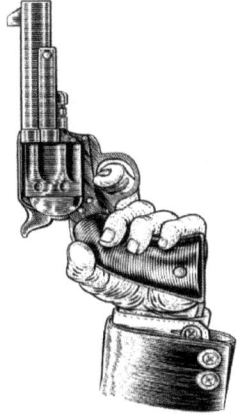

George and Laura Lorius and Albert and Tillie Heberer, the two Illinois couples that vanished during a Route 66 road trip in New Mexico in May 1935

The two couples spent the night at the Vaughn Hotel but after checking out the next morning, they were never seen again.

Mexico, and wanted to see Boulder (Hoover) Dam on their way to their destination of San Diego.

It was a destination they would never reach.

George, known for his attention to detail, carefully mapped out the trip. He purchased new tires for his 1929 Nash sedan and took the time to have it serviced before the trip. He didn't want there to be any chance for car trouble or a breakdown to ruin the trip.

As they followed Route 66 west, they mailed postcards home from Miami and Sayre, Oklahoma, entertaining their family and friends with tales from the road. There was every indication that they were having a great time.

On May 21, they left Route 66, dropped a little south to Vaughn, where their friends lived, and checked into the Vaughn Hotel. They spent the evening with their local acquaintances and returned to their rooms for the night. They had breakfast in the hotel's café the next morning, loaded up the car, and drove off into oblivion.

The two couples were never seen again.

By the time it was realized they were missing, the entire state police department got involved in the case. Even the FBI investigated their disappearance. New Mexico Governor Clyde Tingley worried about the stories that were appearing in newspapers about the two couples and how it might affect state tourism, and he posted a $1,000 reward for information that might lead to the resolution of the mystery. He also authorized the use of National Guard troops to assist law enforcement agencies with the search.

One of the few leads that turned up led to the discovery of some of the couples' luggage smoldering in a pile east of the Nob Hill area of Albuquerque. A call went out for assistance with a search, and more than 100 residents volunteered to scour the area as far east as Tijeras Canyon. A few days later, more of their luggage was found near El Paso, Texas, and another extensive search was launched in the surrounding desert.

Then, on May 29, George's badly damaged car was found abandoned near Dallas, Texas.

The Albuquerque FBI field office assigned Agent Albert Gere to the case, and he managed to find some vague clues that offered hints about where the couples had gone after leaving Vaughn. A postcard mailed to family back home indicated they had followed Route 66 north through Santa Rosa and Santa Fe to Albuquerque.

When Agent Gere was able to examine George's car, he found no signs of struggle or violence, but he did find receipts and a notebook with odometer readings in George's handwriting. The last entry was a receipt from a service station in Socorro, New Mexico – south of Albuquerque – dated May 23. Gere and other agents investigated every service station from Vaughn to Santa Rosa, along the highway into Albuquerque and south to Socorro. Only attendants at the last station in Socorro were able to offer a positive identification of the two couples.

Things soon took another turn when traveler's checks belonging to George, but with forged signatures, turned up first in Vaughn and then across New Mexico and Texas in the weeks that followed.

Acting on a hunch, Agent Gere expanded the search along a direct highway from Vaughn to Socorro and west along Route 66 to the Arizona state line. This turned up what came to be the last lead in the case. It came from a gas station owner in Quemado, a town on the west side of the state, who identified the missing travelers from a photograph.

After that, the trail went cold.

Both during the investigation and in the years that followed, thousands of possible leads were followed in the case. One came from a desk clerk named Josephine Ward at the Sturges Hotel in Albuquerque. She contacted the FBI and told them that the two couples had stopped at the hotel late in the afternoon on May 23. They inquired about rooms, rates, and availability and then, after a discussion, thanked her and said they'd decided to drive on to Gallup.

There were also claims of sightings in Madrid, Grants, Gallup, and Carrizozo, New Mexico, but by July 4, with nothing new to report, the disappearance faded from the newspapers. By the end of 1935, only Agent Gere and the families of the missing couples were still looking for answers.

When Gere retired in July 1947, he told a newspaper reporter that the greatest regret of his career was his inability to solve this case. He always believed they had been murdered and their bodies hidden somewhere around Quemado, New Mexico, but he could never prove it – nor could he find any trace of them.

Years later, however, one more tantalizing clue was uncovered. An Albuquerque real estate agent named Walter Duke, who was a distant relative of George Lorius and spent years of his own time investigating the case, announced he believed the couples had been killed in Vaughn. He said that in 1963, a woman had sent him an anonymous letter stating that she had been a waitress at the Vaughn Hotel café in 1935 and claimed the couples had been taken into the basement of the café and were murdered. She had only her story as proof, however. No evidence of this was ever found.

Today, despite the continued efforts of family and friends, the vanishing of those two couples from East St. Louis remains unsolved.

CLINE'S CORNERS AND THE GREEN BOOK

ROY CLINE, THE MARKETING WHIZ BEHIND THE FLYING C Ranch, which was covered earlier, didn't exactly get lucky with his first try out of the gate.

Clines Corners on Highway 66, New Mexico

After several failed businesses in New Mexico and Arizona, Roy and his son, Roy, Jr., leased 80 acres in New Mexico where Highway 6 and Highway 2 intersected. They built a small café and service station there and hoped this one wouldn't go bust.

In 1937, the two highways were paved and relocated, so Roy had his buildings jacked up and moved to a new intersection, where Highway 2 had become U.S. Highway 285 and Highway 6 became Route 66. He renamed the station **Cline's Corners,** and, by the way, that's how the intersection appears on maps, even today.

Despite the popularity of the new highway, Roy wasn't taking any chances. At night, he only turned on the lights at the station when he spotted a car approaching on the road. If they stopped, he left them on, but if they passed, he turned them off and waited for the next car that was coming from either direction.

Eventually, Cline's Corners became Roy's most lucrative business, but maybe he'd failed one too many times and decided that he needed to get out while the getting was still good. He sold the business in 1939 and moved to Arizona, but eventually came back to New Mexico and opened another Route 66 service station –the Flying C Ranch – which he owned and operated until 1963.

The biggest scandal that marred the history of Cline's Corners, however, had nothing to do with Roy Cline or his son.

On August 11, 1955, six travelers died in a fiery wreck at Cline's Corners – but this was no ordinary Route 66 auto wreck. Although the driver falling asleep at the wheel was blamed for the accident, it sparked an investigation by the National Association for the Advancement of Colored People (NAACP). Edward L. Boyd, the representative for the NAACP in Albuquerque, was quoted in an interview at the time, "It was not surprising that the men died in an accident. They could not have found a welcome at any of the courts on Route 66 from the Texas border to Albuquerque." He also noted that fewer than eight-present of the more than 100 motels along Route 66 would accept "Negro tourists."

The NAACP report about the accident sparked national outrage among African Americans but did nothing to change the sentiments of the time – mostly because black travelers were already well aware of the problems they faced on American highways, including Route 66.

In fact, things were so bad that African Americans had to have a separate travel guide that helped them navigate their way around the country safely. The *Negro Motorist Green Book* was a guidebook created by Victor Hugo Green, a black postal worker from New York City, and it was

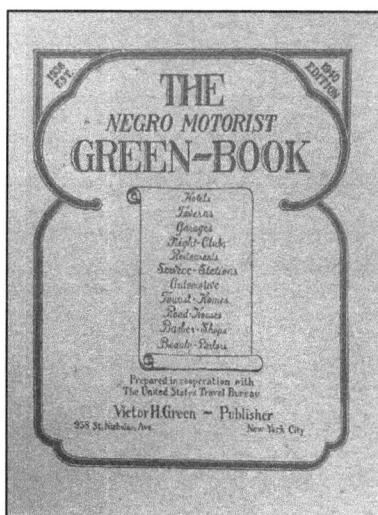

A copy of the Negro Motorist Green Book, created in 1920 to help African American travelers find food, and lodging ... and stay during the Jim Crow Law era in America.

updated and published annually from 1936 to 1966.

This was during the era of Jim Crow laws, when open and often legal discrimination against African Americans was widespread. While black automobile ownership lagged behind white Americans for years, an emerging black middle class began buying more cars in the mid-1930s, especially since it allowed them to avoid segregation on public transportation. Black motorists soon found a variety of dangers and inconveniences along the road, from refusal of food and lodging to arbitrary arrest.

On Route 66, African American travelers often encountered white-owned businesses that refused to serve them, wouldn't repair their vehicles, or provide food and lodging. Some threatened physical violence and forcible removal from whites-only "sundown towns." Green created and published the *Green Book* to help others avoid such problems, compiling resources "to give the Negro traveler information that will keep him from running into difficulties, embarrassments and to make his trip more enjoyable."

Starting with a New York-focused first edition published in 1936, Green expanded the book to cover most of the United States. The *Green Book* became "the bible of black travel during Jim Crow," helping black travelers find lodgings, businesses, and gas stations that would serve them along the road. It was little known outside the African American community.

The Civil Rights Act of 1964 outlawed the types of racial discrimination that had made the *Green Book* necessary, and publication ended two years later.

Sadly, the men who died at Cline's Corners knew they had nowhere to stay along the stretch of road between Texas and Albuquerque. It's very possible they even had a copy of the *Green Book* that alerted them to the fact. They had no choice but to keep driving – with fatal results.

LONGHORN RANCH

HEADING WEST FROM CLINE'S CORNERS – AND BEFORE reaching Moriarty – weary travelers arrived at the Longhorn Ranch and its adjacent motel. It was always a welcoming place because the big sign out front assured you that it was "Where the West Stops to Rest."

Bill Ehret, a former State Police captain from Lincoln County, New Mexico, opened the Longhorn with only a counter and a handful of stools.

The barren desert that surrounded the tiny café gave him a lot of room to grow, and it was eventually expanded – a lot. Bill turned the café into a full-scale restaurant and added a coffee shop, cocktail lounge, souvenir shop, and a full-service garage. The storefronts were designed to look like a western town out of a movie, and a pair of totem poles were stationed on either side of the door to the souvenir shop.

The wide-open desert between Santa Rosa and Alburquerque was barren and often harsh, with not many tourist facilities along the way. This was the perfect place for places like Cline's Corners, Flying C Ranch, and Longhorn Ranch.

The Longhorn was the first taste of the "Old West" for many travelers on Route 66, and the Ehret family took advantage of this by adding themed attractions like a cowboy town, Native American dancers, and rides in a bright red stagecoach pulled by four painted ponies with Hondo the Cowboy at the reins. After a ride, kids could have their photos taken with Hondo and the stagecoach.

The Longhorn also kept "exotic" animals on display for tourists to see and photograph, including oxen, a large Brahma bull, buffalo, and a longhorn steer named "Babe." The Ranch became an institution along Route 66, playing host to thousands of tourists every day, a number that climbed when the motel was added that kept those same travelers on the premises at night.

The motel was built on the north side of Route 66, directly across from the main complex. It offered 15 units and an office built to resemble a Western ranch house. The ranch-style setting was the perfect addition to the Old West theme of the complex across the road.

Bill Ehret sold the Longhorn Ranch and officially retired in 1955, but the place continued to thrive under new management, as popular as it had always been for the next two decades.

By the late 1970s, with the glory days of Route 66 fading away and tourist interest in cowboy towns starting to wane, the death knell for the Longhorn rang when the new interstate bypassed the old highway.

Today, little remains of the Longhorn Ranch. Most of it has been so thoroughly removed that it's hard to tell that the landmark attraction ever existed at all. For a few years, a single building with the two totem poles was still standing on the property. The motel struggled along for years, becoming more rundown as time went by until it finally closed for good.

HOME OF THE PINTO BEAN FIESTA

HELD EVERY FALL IN **MORIARTY**, THE PINTO BEAN FESTIVAL brings thousands of people to town to eat, celebrate, and stay the night, just as Route 66 did for decades.

Moriarty started as the heart of a ranching community, named after local landowner Michael Moriarty, who settled in the area with his family in 1887. The town grew when the railroad arrived and, like so many other places, saw a new wave of prosperity when Route 66 passed through in 1926. The highway wouldn't be paved until 1937, when the road was realigned in the "Santa Fe Cut-Off" project.

By then, Moriarty had troubles of its own. Located in the Estancia Valley, where the Sandia Mountain Range meets the high desert, and next to a salt flat that used to be a lake, the area around the community was severely affected by the Dust Bowl. The drought of the mid-1930s ruined farms and ranches, killed off cattle, and put scores of people out of work. Many in the area packed up and went west, hoping for a better life in California.

It took a few years, but the area was revived when irrigation was used to solve New Mexico's drought problem, and tourism along Route 66 saw a resurgence after World War II. Several new places opened in the

1950s, including the **Lariat Motel**, which was opened by Paul and May Danneville and boasted 13 steam-heated rooms with televisions, as well as a restaurant and service station.

The 12-room **Cactus Motel** was opened by Charles and Maria McPherson in 1952, and the **Sands Motel** opened in 1954 with six rooms and an enclosed garage next to each unit. As with many Route 66 motor courts, the garages were eventually converted into four additional rooms. Moriarty's **Sunset Motel**, which opened around this same time, remains in business today. It's been completely refurbished but still contains most of its original furniture.

BLACKIE'S PLACE

WHILE DOING A STINT AS A GREYHOUND BUS OPERATOR, Hubert Odell Ingram had a regular stop in the little town of Buford, New Mexico, at the Thunderbird Café. With a two-hour layover on his hands, he had a lot of time to chat and become pals with the owner, and he often pitched in to help the staff with dishwashing and other chores. The little eatery was one of the only establishments in town.

The owner of the Thunderbird was Hal Crossley, a local legend who'd been instrumental in getting Route 66 through Buford in the first place. He believed passionately in the little town's potential as a western highway hub, and between dirty dishes, Hubert – better known as "Blackie," thanks to his dark hair – came to agree with him. When a turn of events caused Crossley to look for someone to take over the café, Blackie let go of his bus run and took over the place.

The rest, as they say, is history.

HUBERT "BLACKIE" INGRAM WAS A TEXAS NATIVE, THE SON of a farmer from the small town of Abernathy. Although he worked in the fields with his father as a boy, he started wandering when he got older and ended up in New Mexico. He found work with the Greyhound bus lines and was assigned to the route between Santa Fe and Buford. He

Blackie's Place... one of New Mexico's favorite stops on Route 66

enjoyed the scenery, the people he met along the way, and the friends he made during his layover at the Thunderbird Café, which was where he ended up after ditching his bus driver job.

As the newest eatery operator in the tiny town, he had a tough time finding new waitstaff. He ended up going out to area towns to look for them. One day, he was in the nearby community of Estancia and heard about a young woman looking for work. He knocked on the door of Norma Danielson, and he hired her – and then he married her in January 1945.

Within a year of leasing the Thunderbird café, Blackie's business had outgrown its tiny location, and he decided to buy an enormous adobe building that stood in the center of Moriarty. It had been constructed in 1937 as a mercantile store, café, and filling station. Although it was a nice, western-style building with thick walls and artful wood beams that crossed the ceiling, it was filled with empty oil cans and debris left behind by the previous owners. Blackie bought the place for $1,250.

He refurbished the place and opened it for business, even though it didn't yet have a name. He didn't want to call it the Thunderbird and have it confused with the old place, so Blackie and Norma put out a suggestion box for customers. He asked the locals for a name for the new establishment, and when the votes were counted, the most popular suggestion was Blackie's Place.

The restaurant and Sinclair service station saw an immediate surge in business, and it was a good thing it did. Most people didn't know it, but Blackie had exhausted every dollar buying the building and getting it ready to open. He was so broke that on opening day, he'd had to borrow money for cash register change.

He didn't stay broke for long, and once the operation was in full swing, he did all he could to help his staff – and strangers, too. There was a little building to the west of the restaurant that they ran like a little motel, offering free rooms to the staff because there were no apartments to rent in town. They often hired people from other states who were passing through and looking for work. Norma and Blackie took a chance on them and were rarely disappointed.

Like many other busy spots on Route 66, Blackie's Place was open 24 hours a day. The Greyhound bus stop had moved from the Thunderbird to the new place, a mail drop was added, and postcards were sold to those who wanted to write home.

Blackie painted scenes of southwestern landscapes in his spare time – although I'm not sure how he had any spare time – hung them on the walls and sold them to travelers. He also turned himself into an attraction of sorts – dressing in Western clothing, boots, and a signature Stetson so he could treat all his guests to his version of the wild and wonderful West. Blackie became a legend on Route 66, just as his restaurant did.

Blackie's daughter, Sonja, later recalled: "Dad had a wooden box with a tail – it looked like the tail of an animal – sticking out of it. He would walk around the restaurant petting this tail, and he'd tell people there was a mongoose in the box. Customers would want to pet it, too, so he'd let them pet it. Then he'd pull a string on the side of the box. The top would fly off, and this tail – it was on a spring – would come bouncing out right into the person's face. He did that to tourists. He did that to friends. He just got a big kick out of it. Dad was always pulling something on someone."

Stories about Blackie's Place and the character that ran it spread up and down Route 66. Motorists who came looking for it found it easily, thanks to the signs that stretched from Oklahoma City to Moriarty and 500 miles beyond it. The black and yellow billboards were purposefully vague – most just offered the word "Blackie's" and a simple mile count – but anyone who stopped there was always glad they did.

Blackie was skilled at playing the accordion, banjo, guitar, and piano and would always sing on request. On some days, he performed behind the cash register, slapping palmfuls of nickels into his hand and counting the change by weight. On other days, he offered a full-fledged rodeo behind the café.

He started the rodeo to snag the attention of vacationers after realizing there was a large supply of untapped cowboy talent in the area.

It soon became a regular event and featured calf roping, bronco busting, and bull riding. Blackie built bleachers for those who stopped but, more often than not, motorists just pulled their vehicles up around the edge of the arena and watched the show through open windows. Blackie himself announced the shows, and between events, he'd show off his "trick shooting" for the tourists. He'd throw metal washers into the air, fire at them, and if they came down and weren't dented, he'd claim the bullet passed right through the hole.

In 1949, Blackie built an addition to the east end of the building and filled it with curios. The enormous souvenir store was the largest in the area and secured Blackie's Place as a highway landmark.

After that, he was happy to let his high profile take him where it would, even when it steered him into politics. He lent his popularity to several governors' campaigns and served on the Moriarty village council. When the interstate arrived and threatened to bypass the stretch of Route 66 that ran through town, Blackie loudly opposed it. So, when the U.S. Bureau of Public Roads ultimately adopted Moriarty's plan for access to the interstate, Blackie welcomed 550 state officials and legislators to a celebratory fried chicken dinner at his famous eatery.

Blackie passed away in May 1966, but after his death, the highway spot that carried his name continued to thrive. Buoyed by staff and customer loyalty, Norma operated Blackie's Place until 1975, when she sold it to John Kean, who made Blackie's Place a tavern before it was sold to a trading post owner, then a pharmacist.

Even through all those changes, though, Blackie's name never left the building. It remains today on a bar and grill as a reminder of a man who was a true character of Route 66.

GUN BATTLE AT SEDILLO

WHEN WE THINK ABOUT THE VIOLENCE OF THE PROHIBITION era in America, we tend to think of killings and massacres in Chicago and New York, not in the Southwest states. However, the regional newspapers of the era offer many stories about

TRUE CRIME

smuggling along the Mexican border and the violence that occurred along Route 66.

On January 29, 1930, C.U. Finley and two other federal Prohibition agents, accompanied by four deputies from the Bernalillo County sheriff's office, went east from Albuquerque to serve a search warrant on the ranch of Procopio Espinosa near the village of Sedillo. The three agents entered the house to investigate and left the four deputies – Emilio Candelaria, Pablo Lujan, Abe Sour, and Ablencio Romero – outside to stand guard. While Agent Finley was reading the warrant to Procopio Espinosa, his brother, Gregorio, and several other men confronted the deputies, and an argument began.

An investigation later determined that Gregorio fired a shotgun, and a blast of birdshot hit Candelaria in the face. Guns cleared leather, and a shootout began. Augustine Jaramillo – nephew of Procopio and Gregoria – was wounded in the leg and both arms. The agents inside the house took up positions around the house. As the gunfight intensified, Finley left the other two agents at the ranch to back up the deputies, drove to the village of Barton, west of Sedillo, and called Bernalillo County Sheriff Phillip Hubell for reinforcements. Sheriff Hubell, along with Charles Stern, the head of the Prohibition department for the state, soon arrived at the ranch with a dozen heavily armed deputies and federal agents.

They surrounded the house, which the residents had transformed into a small fortress, and demanded that those inside surrender their guns. After a brief stand-off, they gave up. No more shots were fired. Only one man died – Deputy Candelaria, who succumbed to his wounds while on the way to the hospital in Albuquerque.

As it turned out, no illegal liquor was found at the ranch. The bloodshed had occurred for no reason at all.

MOTORING TO ALBUQUERQUE

IT WOULD BE A MISTAKE TO SAY THAT ROUTE 66 WAS responsible for the growth of Albuquerque since the town predated the highway by well over two centuries.

The Spanish village of Albuquerque was founded in 1706 on the banks of the Rio Grande by Don Francisco y Valdes, the governor of New Mexico. It was named for the Duke of Albuqurerque, viceroy of New

Route 66 passed through on Fourth Street in Albuquerque

Spain, although the first "r" in the name was eventually dropped – which barely makes it easier to spell, trust me.

The settlement became an important stop on the El Camino Real, or "King's Highway," that connected Mexico City and Santa Fe, and it grew quickly, especially after it became American territory after the Mexican War. In 1879, the Atchison, Topeka & Santa Fe Railroad steamed into the area and established New Albuquerque about a mile-and-a-half east of what is now called Old Town. The first rail passengers arrived on April 22, 1880.

When Route 66 was designated in 1926, the highway passed through town via Fourth Street, crossed Barelas Bridge, and continued down Isleta Boulevard. In 1937, when the Santa Fe Loop was bypassed – making what some call "Retribution Road" – Route 66 traveled into town by way of Central Avenue. Before that, there were only three tourist camps on Central Avenue, while there were 16 operating on Fourth Avenue. That quickly changed, though, and soon Central became the focus of the city's tourist traffic. Within a few short years, motor courts had multiplied to 37.

After World War II and the end of gasoline rationing, the country once again gravitated to automobiles for their vacation travel. By 1955, there were 98 motels on U.S. 66 within the city limits of Albuquerque – ranging in style from western to Pueblo Revival to Streamline Moderne. Dozens of them still exist today, even though Albuquerque was bypassed by the interstate in 1970.

MANY OF THE MOTOR COURTS EARNED LEGENDARY STATUS in town, including the famous **Luna Lodge**. Built in 1949, it was one of the first motels that travelers encountered when arriving in the city from the east. It originally consisted of three one-story, white stucco, southwestern-style buildings that were arranged in a broken U shape. The office and manager's residence were located in front of the buildings on the west end, where the deluxe rooms with carports could be found.

The Luna Lodge had 18 rooms, but that number grew to 32 rooms by the late 1950s, when the carports were converted into rooms and a second story was added to the west end. A café called La Nortenita was also added around this time. But its popularity didn't last. The motel eventually closed and fell into disrepair but was restored and converted to low-income housing in 2013.

Tower Court was built by Ben Shear in 1939, just two years after Route 66 was relocated through Albuquerque along Central Avenue. The mostly single-story motel was constructed in the classic U-shape layout and was in the Streamline Modern style. Typical of other auto courts in the

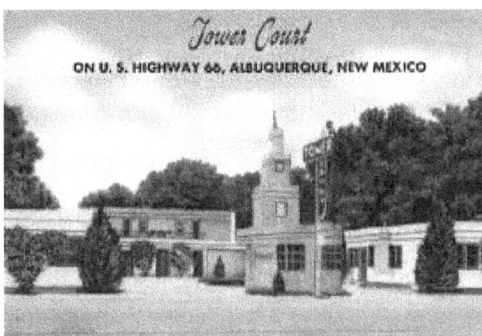

Tower Court
ON U. S. HIGHWAY 66, ALBUQUERQUE, NEW MEXICO

1930s, garages were located alongside each unit.

Originally, a 30-foot tower that contained the motel office was located at the front of the property (hence the name). It accentuated the unique design of the motel, and it pulled a lot of travelers in off the road. Eventually, it was removed.

Later, to keep up with the times, the "Court" was dropped from the name, and it started to be called the Tower Motel. It no longer serves nightly guests – it's an apartment building today -- but it still stands as one of the oldest tourist courts in Albuquerque and a classic example of how motor courts were built before World War II.

DE ANZA MOTOR LODGE

ANOTHER ALBUQUERQUE MOTOR LODGE DIDN'T FARE AS well as some of the other legendary spots along Route 66 in the city – at first, anyway. But against all odds, it's still thriving today. It would have been

torn down years ago if it wasn't for the secret that was hidden in the motel's basement.

Though the De Anza was named for a Spanish conquistador, it was started as an Indian-themed trading post. It became famous for its diner, the "Turquoise Room," which had thousands of shards of turquoise embedded in its floor.

The De Anza was built by Charles Wallace in 1939. He had first been successful operating a trading post in a Zuni pueblo in the 1920s but moved to Albuquerque to cash in on the automobile vacation boom. He was eager to offer Zuni jewelry to tourists on Route 66, which turned into a trading post, a popular restaurant, and one of the largest motor lodges in the city, eventually spreading out into eight stucco buildings.

In the decade that followed the war, Wallace expanded the motel into 67 units, then added a coffee shop and a swimming pool. The De Anza was such a popular stopover during its heyday that Wallace would regularly pick up and drop off VIP guests at the airport in his shiny pink Cadillac.

Wallace operated the hotel until he died in 1993. The place was subsequently sold and re-sold, eventually falling into disrepair. Its doors were finally closed in 2003.

The basement murals depicting the Shalako Ceremony of the Zuni Nation, which saved the old hotel from destruction.

The dilapidated old building was nearly razed to make way for a grocery store, and if it weren't for what was discovered in a basement conference room, it would already be a memory. Instead, it began to be protected by 24-hour security.

It turned out that the conference room

contained seven priceless 20-foot by 4-foot murals that depicted the sacred Shalako Ceremony of the Zuni nation. The Shalako ceremony is a series of rituals and dances unique to the Zuni people. It is performed each year at the Winter Solstice and is the most important ceremonial event of the year.

The murals were painted for Wallace by well-known Zuni artist Tony Edaakie, a significant figure in the First Nation art world of the twentieth century. This made the murals in the basement of the De Anza not just priceless but one-of-a-kind treasures like nothing else in the world.

This saved the rundown motel from destruction.

In June 2020, the property was rescued again when it was redeveloped and transformed into a luxury apartment complex. The murals have remained intact and are available for viewing twice each year during special ceremonies or when members of the Zuni nation are in attendance to accompany non-tribal members into the former conference room.

As a side note, the De Anza has also become known as the site of a scene from the television show *Breaking Bad*, which takes place in Albuquerque. While Skylar is in the hospital giving birth, Walt pulls into an abandoned motel after a major cash transaction and throws out his spare tire to hide the money. The De Anza is that motel prior to the 2020 renovations.

AZTEC AUTO COURT

THE AZTEC AUTO COURT WAS THE FIRST MOTEL constructed on Central Avenue in 1931, a full six years before Route 66 was realigned to bring more customers to Guy and May Fargo than they likely ever imagined. Until 2011, when it was torn down, it was the oldest motel in continuous use in the city.

The motel – which bragged about "innerspring mattresses, furnace heat, and moderate rates" – initially consisted of two buildings that ran parallel to each other with a

AZTEC COURT — ALBUQUERQUE, NEW MEXICO

ON U. S. HIGHWAY 66   3921 EAST CENTRAL AVENUE

courtyard in the middle. There were three carports adjacent to the rooms, but during a remodeling in the 1950s, they were walled in to create more guest rooms, increasing the total from 13 to 17. The office, also the manager's residence, was located at the front of the property, shielding most of the courtyard from the street.

The motel changed hands several times over the years. Guy passed away in 1942 but May continued to operate the Aztec until she sold it in 1944. Two years later, the property was sold again to a pair of couples – William and Emma Geck and Wesley and Bertha Meyer – who owned and operated it until the early 1950s.

Wildly, throughout the 1950s, the ownership and the name of the motel changed a staggering eight times until Floyd and Evelyn Lewis purchased it in 1958 and changed the name back to the Aztec, switching to "Motel" instead of "Auto Court." It was at this time that the place underwent its first renovations in years.

When the interstate bypassed Central Avenue, the booming business at the motel predictably collapsed, and it fell into both disrepair

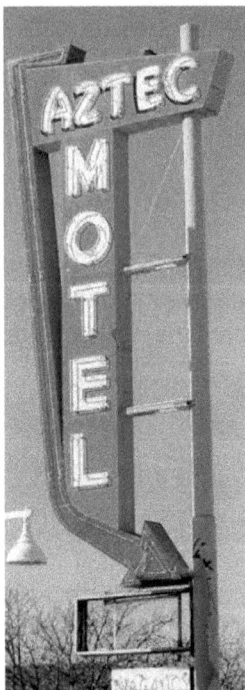

and disrepute. It soon became a haven for prostitutes and drug dealers and earned frequent visits from the local police. This lasted until it was purchased again by a new owner in 1991.

With a lot of patience and hard work, Mohamed and Shokey Natha remodeled and turned the motel into a short and long-term stay motel. The exterior was updated dramatically by a retired professor who lived there part-time, adding unusual decorative elements like velvet paintings, plastic flowers, and other ornaments to the outside walls, turning it into an "architectural art" stop for Route 66 nostalgia buffs.

In 1993, the Aztec was listed on the National Register of Historic Places as one of the best examples of a relatively unaltered tourist court on Route 66 in New Mexico. In 2003, it received cost-share grant funds from the National Park Service Route 66 Corridor Preservation Program to restore the original neon sign. This was part of a project to restore nine neon signs on Route 66 across the state.

The Aztec continued to serve a new generation of Route 66 travelers for several more years and then was sold to a development company in 2006. They had every intention of renovating the building – they had already purchased two other historic Route 66 motels and developed them – but after bringing in architects and engineers to study the Aztec, they decided it couldn't be renovated in a way that would be profitable. Despite its listing on national and state historic registers, the old auto court was razed in 2011.

For several years, the motel's neon sign was left standing, hoping it would be used as part of future development at the site, but then it was removed by the city with plans for it to be added to the neon sign museum located in Albuquerque.

All that remains where the Aztec Motel once stood is an empty lot.

EL VADO MOTOR COURT

THE EL VADO MOTOR COURT, WHICH HAS BEEN REOPENED to serve travelers once again, was constructed in 1937, barely predating Route 66's realignment on Central Avenue.

The motel was built by Daniel Murphy, an Irish immigrant who worked as a bellboy at the Waldorf-Astoria in New York City and who moved west to New Mexico. He had worked his way up to a management position at the Franciscan Hotel in downtown Albuquerque when word came that Route 66 was to be realigned through Albuquerque. He left his job and opened the El Vado just in time. He chose the motel's name, Vado, which means "ford" in Spanish, because of its location near the old ford that crossed the Rio Grande where Bridge Street is today.

The new motel had 32 units, some with covered carports, and was arranged in two parallel, one-story buildings facing a parking courtyard – so, pretty much the standard for auto courts of the era. When the place opened, it also offered a service station, and two gas pumps were located along Central Avenue in front of the office.

Murphy had the motel designed in the Spanish Pueblo Revival style, which featured irregularities that were purposely added to the buildings to give them the look of nearly pueblos. This included uneven parapets, curving roof lines, and exposed roof beams. When it opened, the local business journal described the units as "swanky tile cabin suites ready for the summer tourist trade."

To draw in the crowds from the highway, Murphy installed a flashy neon sign that was topped by a Native American wearing a colorful headdress.

Tourists who stayed at the El Vado were treated to soundproof and fireproof rooms and a nearby "bathing beach" on the Rio Grande and an adjoining public golf course. A swimming pool was also added later, around the time that "court" was dropped from the name and replaced with "motel."

For the most part, the El Vado remained unaltered over the years, with the exception of the removal of the gas pumps and the pool and the replacement of the original windows. Even most of the carports remained untouched, which is what made it such a significant spot for preservationists and Route 66 enthusiasts – who saved the place when a

local developer wanted to tear it down and replace it with luxury townhouses.

The motel has changed hands a few times, and by 2005, with business dropping, the developer announced plans to clear the site for his new buildings. However, the preservationists and historians lobbied to save the old auto court. The city of Albuquerque entered the fray, rescued the El Vado, and helped make plans to have the motel refurbished into a mixed-use development with a food court, amphitheater, boutique motel, and small events center.

And then nothing happened for 13 years. The old El Vado Motel sat behind a chain-link fence, with paint peeling off and weeds choking a courtyard that had once been filled with cars from all over the country.

Finally, the historic El Vado opened again to travelers. The 22-room motel – fitted with retro-style furniture and original art – is part of a complex that includes an event center, shops, restaurants, and a brewpub that features local beers.

THE HOTEL ANDALUZ

WHILE NOT A RETRO MOTOR COURT ENTICING GUESTS off the highway with a flashing neon sign, there is a hotel in Albuquerque that not only boasts a storied history but is also home to more than its share of ghostly encounters.

The La Posada de Albuquerque was built by Conrad Hilton, who honeymooned in Albuquerque with bride Zsa Zsa Gabor in 1939. As a New Mexico native, he wanted to build a grand hotel in the bustling Route 66 city, and while this was the third property he'd purchased, it was the first in his home state. He named it "La Posada," which means "resting place."

And the hotel was certainly grand. Handcrafted wooden railings surrounded the balcony that overlooked the two-story lobby. An elaborate Moorish brass and mosaic fountain stood in the center of the tiled lobby, gurgling beneath the tin chandeliers above. High archways surrounded the entry, creating the feel of an old Spanish hacienda. The Lobby Bar, with its hand-painted murals, carved beams, and balconies, became one of the city's most popular meeting spots.

Today, a 70-year-old key box is still in use behind the front desk, just like it was when Thomas O. Jones -- a security chief for the Manhattan Project, who was in charge of evacuating the area if the nearby project went off the rails – watched from his fourth-floor room as the flash of the first atomic bomb exploded on July 16, 1945. Just a month earlier, a hotel

HAUNTED

registration card had been signed by a spy named Harry Gold, and it became a key piece of evidence in the trial of Julius and Ethel Rosenberg. The ballroom of the hotel hosted both Senator John F. Kennedy in 1957 and Vice President Al Gore in 1998 and the hotel itself can boast stays by dozens of other historic figures over the years.

But things didn't always go smoothly at La Posada.

In 1969, the hotel was sold, and after a few renovations, it became the Hotel Plaza. For the next 12 years, it was a dominant business on Route 66, even after the interstate bypassed the city, but it closed in 1981. The building was purchased again, becoming the Hotel Bradford, but it sat vacant for three years, waiting for renovations to be completed. When it opened in 1984, it was again La Posada de Albuquerque.

It was at this time when the ghost stories first began to spread.

As most who are interested in hauntings know, violent history often leads to ghostly tales, and this hotel is no exception to that rule. During its history, it was the scene of several murders and brutal deaths. One of them involved a waiter at one of the hotel's restaurants who was killed on the seventh floor. When a maid came to clean the room he was in the next morning, she found him lying facedown on the floor in a pool of blood. He had been stabbed more than 35 times, his spinal cord was severed,

The Hotel Andaluz lobby

his throat was cut, and he'd been scalped. Not surprisingly, the hotel's seventh floor became a rumored hotbed of strange activity that included slamming doors, mysterious footsteps, and late-night knocks on hotel room doors that revealed no one in the corridor when the knock was answered.

In 2005, the hotel was sold and renovated again, eventually opening under its current name, Hotel Andaluz, in 2009. It's important to note that the building was closed for renovations over long periods of time during its history, which plays a part in the ghost stories that have emerged over time.

Many who have stayed at the hotel claim to have encountered unseen visitors and resident spirits within its walls. According to one guest who stayed there with her husband, she was relaxing in her room one afternoon and saw a woman in a stylish 1940s-era dress walk out of the bathroom. She was surprised because she'd thought the room was empty when she came in and knew she hadn't opened the door for anyone. At first, she thought it might be someone from housekeeping but couldn't understand why the woman was wearing a costume.

She stated that she wasn't afraid but was startled enough to be unable to speak for a moment, and when the 1940s-attired woman turned a corner, she never saw her again. She simply disappeared.

Another uncanny sighting occurred in 1980 when a maid saw a beautiful young woman walking near the hotel ballroom on a rainy morning. The girl was wet and appeared as if she had been crying, so the maid asked her if she was all right. The young woman paused, looked at her, and then turned and went into the ballroom. The maid quickly followed her and was shocked when she entered the ballroom and found it empty. She was even more shocked when she looked down and saw there were no wet footprints on the dance floor.

A separate witness to what may be the same ballroom ghost seemed to shed light on the origin of her presence at the hotel. The story was told to author Cody Polston by an older man who experienced it firsthand.

He explained that he had owned a small DJ service in Albuquerque in the mid-1970s and had a job at the Hotel Plaza ballroom. He arrived a couple of hours early to set up his gear and found the place busy and bustling as the staff prepared for the evening event. He had just finished setting up when one of the staff asked if they could unplug his equipment for a few minutes because they needed the power outlet he was using. He agreed and asked them not to change anything he'd already arranged. He was just getting his business up and running, and this was one of the biggest jobs he'd booked so far, and he wanted it to go smoothly.

He left the room and stepped outside for a cigarette with a friend, Eddie, who he'd hired to help him that night. After a chat and a double-

Ballroom at the Hotel Andaluz

check of the night's playlist, they went back into the hotel. While the DJ waited for the elevator, Eddie went to the restroom, assuring his friend he'd be in the ballroom in a few minutes.

The elevator door opened, and he stepped inside, punched the button, and rode in silence to the ballroom floor. As soon as the door opened, he heard music coming from the ballroom. He assumed that someone had a portable radio and was listening to music while they worked because it was country music, a genre he hadn't brought to the hotel that night. He recalled that it was a clear woman's voice singing about sunshine and birds. It was not a record from his collection.

However, when he walked into the ballroom and saw a redheaded woman on the stage playing a guitar, he realized the music was coming through his sound system. I was immediately angry. He'd spent a lot of money on his system, and the woman had managed to tap into it without his permission. He feared she had likely changed his settings, which meant he'd have to do another soundcheck to correct whatever she had done.

He stormed across the ballroom and started yelling at her to stop, but there was no response. She either didn't hear him, he later said, or she didn't care. So, instead of continuing to tell her to stop, he walked over to the electrical outlet to unplug the system.

When he reached the power outlet, though, he got another shock – the system wasn't plugged in. Startled and upset, his hands shaking, he gaped at the power cord lying there on the floor. He recalled that he was more scared than he'd ever been in his life – he didn't believe in that kind of thing, and yet, he couldn't explain what was happening. He said that initially, he was afraid to turn around and look at the woman again, but then, suddenly, the music turned to static. When he finally summoned the courage to turn around, the redheaded woman was gone.

The static noise suddenly stopped just as his pal Eddie walked into the ballroom. He immediately asked him if he'd seen a redhead with a guitar in the hallway, but he didn't. However, he did hear the music and was wondering what kind of show his friend had committed to that night.

He asked what was wrong, and the DJ told him what happened. His eyes got bigger and bigger as the story went on. When he was finished, Eddie told him about an old ghost story about this singer who died. Her last performance had been in that very ballroom.

As the man finished his story, he told Cody that just recalling the story again gave him chills. He added, "That was a long time ago, but I still think of it sometimes. For a long time, I wouldn't tell anyone, my friends or the people I work with, because they'd laugh in my face and never let me hear the end of it."

THE ENCOUNTER IN THE BALLROOM IN THE MID-1970S MADE it easier to track down the source of the ghost story that had been haunting the hotel for so long --- and likely provided the identity of the resident spirit.

Her name was Sandee Saunders, and she was born in March 1940 in the small town of Hatch, New Mexico. Growing up, she turned out to be a talented singer and musician and dreamed of a life on the stage. Her first album, *Reflections*, was released in June 1972 and featured a single called

Sandee Saunders on the cover of her only album, which was recorded in 1972

"Mornin' Kind of Feelin'," which climbed both the country and the pop charts.

The album came after years of hard work for Sandee. She had been performing at small venues all over New Mexico for years, and as her fame grew, the venues got larger. Soon, she and her supporting band began playing at upscale spots like La Fonda in Santa Fe and Hotel Plaza in Albuquerque.

But then tragedy struck during the early morning hours of August 1, 1972, when Sandee was driving home to Hatch after a show in Santa Fe when her car veered off a bridge south of Caballo Lake State Park. It

plunged into the Rio Grande and was ripped apart on its way down. Sandee was decapitated by metal and glass, and while her body was later found on the opposite riverbank – her head was never found. The cause of the crash was never determined, but investigators theorized that she possibly fell asleep at the wheel.

Peter Pickford, Sandee's manager, was the first to see her ghost. One early morning, he claimed he saw Sandee standing by the side of the road, waving at him to slow down. Pete slammed on the brakes and looked into the rearview mirror, but she was gone. Then, a short time later, he swore that Sandee's song, "Mornin' Kind of Feelin'," came on the radio just as he drove onto the bridge where she died.

In the years that followed, Sandee's ghost remained active. Many motorists driving on the same highway where she was killed claimed to see the face of a red-haired woman appear in their rearview mirrors, although, of course, they were traveling alone.

As the story of her ghost spread, many began to believe that she was a sort of benevolent force on the nearby highways, frightening sleepy drivers so they wouldn't end up the same way she did.

Her ghost was also reportedly encountered at many of the places where she performed during her too brief career, including the Hotel Plaza. She usually appeared in the ballroom – or just outside the door, where the main encountered her – wearing a pink western shirt with white fringe on the sleeves.

And she wasn't just seen – she also sang or played her guitar, just as she did on the night when that DJ encountered her in the ballroom.

Stories about Sandee's roaming spirit became a staple around the region, stretching from Albuquerque to Santa Fe. While many told of their strange encounters with her, the person who seemed to be most affected by her continued existence was her former manager, Pete Pickford.

He purchased her father's old service station in Hatch and established a small museum dedicated to Sandee. He displayed her favorite stage outfits, her guitar, and even pieces of the car that she died in. During this time, he claimed to have many other encounters with her ghost – and perhaps he did, so unable to let her go that he kept her tied to the places and people she loved in life.

Peter remained in Hatch until his death in 1997, sharing stories of Sandee – and her lingering spirit – with anyone who stopped at the museum. After he died, though, the museum closed and perhaps the two of them ended up together once again. With no one to keep the stories of her alive, the stories of Sandee Saunders faded away and were mostly forgotten.

Although the Hotel Andaluz continues its tradition of being haunted, especially on the seventh floor, it seems as if Sandee has finally found the peace she deserves.

COVERED WAGON SOUVENIRS

THERE ARE A HANDFUL OF OTHER LEGENDARY SPOTS IN Albuquerque that I don't want to forget as we pass through town. Although they're just memories now, I can't help but remind today's motorists about the unique and amazing locations that we've missed out on in the modern day.

COVERED WAGON SOUVENIRS WAS A HARD PLACE TO MISS if you were arriving in town from the east. It was right at the start of Central Avenue and featured an enormous covered wagon pulled by life-sized figures of oxen.

The souvenir store was the baby of Manny Goodman, a native of Pueblo, Colorado, who came to Albuquerque in 1935 to work for Maisel's Trading Post – hitting the highway to sell Native American jewelry for months at a time. When Manny built the Covered Wagon in 1945, he hoped that his traveling days were over, but city buses didn't run all the way to where his store was located at the time, so he felt obligated to pick up his staff every

SEE THE LARGEST COVERED WAGON IN THE WORLD
ALBUQUERQUE, NEW MEXICO

morning and shuttle them home at night.

In addition to what became his famous wagon, the shop also thrilled tourists with photo ops like a stagecoach, an antique fire engine, a buckboard pulled by a life-sized horse, and a large black jackrabbit crouched on the store's roof. After Walt Disney gave motorists a new reason to travel west in 1955, Manny started calling Covered Wagon Souvenirs the "poor man's Disneyland."

After being bypassed by the interstate, Manny moved his Covered Wagon to Old Town Plaza for a few years but retired long before he died in 1999.

LITTLE BEAVER TOWN

LITTLE BEAVER TOWN IN ALBUQUERQUE WAS COOKED UP by two Standard Oil executives – Howard Hull and Ernest Sudron – in the early 1960s who believed a new amusement park would provide a much-needed shot in the arm for local tourism.

Little Beaver from the Red Ryder comics

The park was planned as a place that would be half Native American village and half old Western movie town. Navajos and Apache were hired to construct houses and teepees, and a working replica of an 1865 train was custom-built for it. Howard then went looking for a personality to promote the authenticity of the park and he found his man with popular comic strip artist Fred Harman, Jr.

Fred was born in St. Joseph, Missouri, in 1902, but to the readers of his comics from the 1940s to the 1960s, he was the Wild West incarnate. He had only been two months old when his parents first took him to visit Colorado, but he grew up obsessed with the West. As a boy, he started drawing pictures of cowboys and horses and eventually moved to Kansas City to start a career as a commercial artist. He created his first western comic strip, *Bronc Peeler*, in 1934. When the Scripps Howard

Family fun times at Little Beaver Town

publishing syndicate showed interest in one of his characters – an American Indian boy named Little Beaver – Fred revamped the strip and changed the name to *Red Ryder*. The first installment of *Red Ryder* appeared in the comics section of Marshall Field's *Chicago Sun* on November 6, 1938.

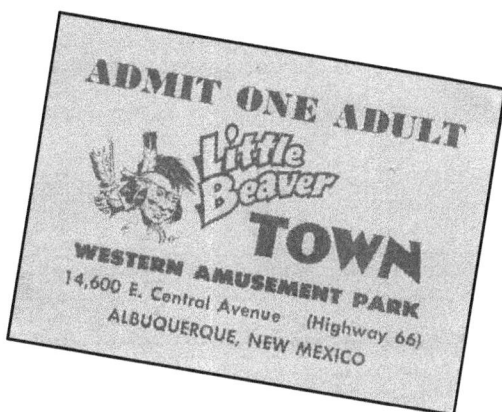

And yes, that's the same *Red Ryder* brand of BB gun that will "shoot your eye out" in the classic holiday film *A Christmas Story*.

When Little Beaver Town opened, *Red Ryder* boasted an estimated 40 million readers around the world. When the gates opened for the park's first weekend, 15,000 of those fans stormed the gates. They were greeted by Western film star Montie Montana, Jr. performing rope tricks for the crowds. At the same time, can-can dancers kicked up their legs in the Red Bull Saloon, and Troy Vincente – a 12-year-old Jicarilla Apache from Dulce, New Mexico – officially greeted the guests as Little Beaver. An area ranch hand named Dave Saunders took on the role of Red Ryder.

Although everyone predicted great success for Little Beaver Town – one newspaper predicted it would equal Disneyland, and the Daisy Air

Rifle Co. featured it in advertisements – the park closed within two years of its opening.

Fred Harman, Jr. retired in 1964, and he took *Red Ryder* with him. There was just no way for Little Beaver Town to survive without the characters that had been used to promote it.

EL SOMBRERO

WHAT SHOULD HAVE BEEN AN AVERAGE TEX-MEX restaurant on Route 66 in Albuquerque became anything but average in the hands of Sherman C. Anderson, who created something that was literally larger than life.

Located on Central Avenue, El Sombrero pulled in passing tourists as a south-of-the-border eatery that was topped by what appeared to be a gigantic Mexican hat. It certainly got attention, and according to those who were lucky enough to eat there, the food lived up to the hype at a time when most Americans – especially those from back east – were not all that familiar with Mexican dishes.

But that wasn't the most unusual thing about El Sombrero – it came to symbolize the confusion that many tourists experienced when they arrived in New Mexico. In April 1965, the restaurant was featured in a cartoon that accompanied a newspaper article titled "Is New Mexico in the U.S.A.?"

The article was written by Albuquerque newspaperman Arch Napier, who gently poked fun at easterners who believed that New Mexico was a foreign country. Even though it had officially been a state since 1912, there were still many people who confused it with our neighbor south of the border – and not all of them were tourists.

New Mexico residents often received letters that had been marked "Passed by Customs" stamped on them by the post office. Out-of-state companies frequently refused to send catalogs to them because they didn't do business "outside of the continental limits of the United States." Some companies rejected checks drawn from New Mexico banks. In 1963, when Sandra Fullingim of Albuquerque arrived in Miami to participate in the Miss Universe pageant, she was handed a Spanish-English dictionary by a hostess.

But that was nothing, he wrote, compared to what local merchants had been dealing with for years, nothing the most frequent questions from travelers who stopped in at their service station, museum, trading post, or curio were:

"Are we still in the United States?"
"Do you accept American money?"
And my favorite – "If it's Tuesday in the United States, what day is it in New Mexico?"

This was funny in 1965, but it still happens today.

ICEBERG CAFE

NESTLED ALONG EAST CENTRAL AVENUE AND LOOKING AS though it was waiting for an ocean liner to sink, the Iceberg Café was the perfect optical illusion for a hot and tired traveler on Route 66. The 75-foot architectural mirage was built in the shape of a giant glacier and promised something cool and delicious to motorists cruising into town from the desert.

It opened in May 1931, with one side serving as a filling station and the other half as a frozen custard shop. Located near the University of New Mexico, the Iceberg became a popular hangout for students since it blew cold air across a dance floor that was hopping almost every night.

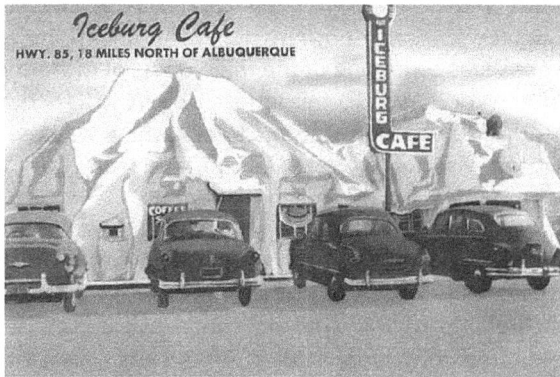

Iceburg Cafe
HWY. 85, 18 MILES NORTH OF ALBUQUERQUE

In the later 1930s, when a new development was planned for the Iceberg's property, the mammoth glacier was moved down the street. In the 1940s, a second frozen peak was added when the large dining room was opened. This was also when the large statue of the polar bear was added on the roof, drawing even more attention and selling a lot more custard.

Sadly, in 1953, the Iceberg was moved again. The Star Oil Company leased the property, so the Iceberg's owners hired a moving company to shuttle the place to U.S. Highway 85 in Bernalillo. The announcement caused a stir in Albuquerque and customers in mourning lined the streets to watch as their favorite ice cream shop slowly drifted out of town.

Out on U.S. Highway 85, the Iceberg continued to whip up cold treats for locals for another decade until finally closing for good in the 1960s. The owners later demolished the building, although – somewhere – the polar bear that once traipsed over the Iceberg's roofline still survives.

TOMAHAWK TRADING POST

WHEN JOHN KEAN DECIDED TO SELL THE TAVERN THAT HE'D opened after buying Blackie's Place in Moriarty, he sold it to a man named J.T. Turner, the famed owner of one of the most popular trading posts in New Mexico – a state that was filled with them, especially along the tourist highway of Route 66.

In April 1965, a newspaper writer named Robert Buber reported that tourists interested in Native American cultures had done what many in the tourism business had long predicted it would do – it had eclipsed interest in everything else that New Mexico had to offer.

This boom in interest had been building for almost 40 years by that time. From the day when tourists first started passing through New Mexico on Route 66, finding an American Indian with whom one could speak was often one of the main goals of motoring easterners. In the years after World War II, this quest began to reach ridiculous levels. Drivers stopped at service stations to ask which way the Apache went. Motorists visited Manuelito, New Mexico, expecting to find the famous chief after whom the town had been named.

Bob Claar, whose family operated the Hitching Post near Moriarty, recalled the tourists' itch to see Native Americans hitting a high mark in the early 1950s. Both Frank Chaves and Caytano Chavez – two gas station attendants of Hispanic descent – were harassed daily by tourists who assumed they were Native Americans. They even asked Bob, who had blond hair and blue eyes, if he was an Indian. It got so bad that he eventually just gave up and told them that he was. "Sure," he said. "No one challenged it, and no one ever asked me to speak Navajo."

Tomahawk Trading Post

Just west of Albuquerque – shortly before Nine-Mile Hill – J.T. Turner built the Tomahawk Trading Post for easterners who had Native Americans on the brain. One of Route 66's most enterprising business people, Turner knew what people wanted, and during his highway career, he operated more than 10 roadside souvenir shops. None of them served the tourists better than his first store, the Tomahawk Trading Post.

Turner had been born into a Texas farm family in 1926 and spent his early years working in the fields. What he called the "happy accident" of his life was when he married Ida "Reese" Abshire, who had an aunt who lived out west and was married to Route 66 business owner George Hill, Jr., who owned and operated Rio Puerco Trading Post. About 19 miles west of Albuquerque. The Hills had been open for eight years when they invited Reese and J.T. for a visit.

J.T. was thrilled by the trading post. "It looked like the World's Fair with the traffic out there," J.T. later recalled. "The Hills had a polar bear in a glass case. They were selling Indian curios to tourists. I thought, if they can do this, I can, too."

As luck would have it, George owned a second building on Route 66, an abandoned store just outside of Albuquerque. In 1953, J.T. made a deal with the Hills to renovate – donkeys and chickens were living in it – and reopen the store.

J.T. and Reese embarked on a two-year remodeling of the building, adding large windows, additions on both ends of the structure, jewelry showcases, new counters, and more. They also made sure the apartment area was livable again.

Just before they opened, J.T. purchased a burro at a bargain livestock sale, fitted the small animal with a saddle, and hitched it to a buckboard wagon out front. He hoped that tourists would stop for pictures.

And if the burro wouldn't convince them to pull off for a photo opportunity, then the arrows would. They were massive arrows that J.T. had fashioned from telephone poles. They were stuck into the ground, painted brightly, and fitted with feathers made from sheets of plywood. Eventually, there were 10 of those arrows announcing the Tomahawk – pointed promises that motorists had reached the land of the American Indian at last.

Other elements of the Tomahawk underscored this fast. A pueblo pottery oven was built on the premises, life-sized teepees flanked the gas pumps, and painter Everett Sloan painted southwestern scenes on the various buildings, reserving his liveliest work for the building that hosted Indigenous dancers from the Jemez Reservation.

J.T. had a friend from the Jemez Pueblo named Cristino Pianani, who often came to the store in traditional dress and greeted tourists. Bringing dancers from the reservation to entertain the tourists was the next step.

Long before Route 66, Native American pueblos welcomed white spectators to their religious and harvest ceremonies. In the late nineteenth and early twentieth centuries, southwestern tribes grew accustomed to outsiders watching their dances.

No event drew more interest than the Hopi Snake Dance, which was just a small part of a 16-day ceremony that was held in August, but it was so famous because the performers were known to dance with poisonous snakes clenched between their teeth. In 1912, the Hopi Snake Dance was photographed for the first time and, soon after, was attended by Theodore Roosevelt. In 1924, author D.H. Lawrence also witnessed it and preserved the power of the event on paper.

Credit for introducing highway motorists to traditional Native American dances goes to a businessman from Gallup named Mike E. Kirk. In 1922, Mike and several others established Gallup's Inter-Tribal Indian Ceremonial – an annual celebration of American Indian arts and customs. As the celebration continued in the years that followed, many of the participants discovered they could make money year-round by dancing at local roadside trading posts. Business arrangements varied, but all proved profitable for both store owners and dancers.

During the 1950s, Jemez performers at the Tomahawk were among the most popular on Route 66. They traveled from the reservation each day and performed tirelessly in traditional garb -- usually every half hour – throughout the day. J.T. charged admission to the performances and split the money with the performers.

The performances themselves consisted of tribal dances with spectators lining benches around a large concrete floor. A microphone wired to a loudspeaker – manned by Jemez women – allowed for narration, descriptions of the dances, and explanations of the costumes that were worn. Drums beat, bells jangled, all meeting in what was, perhaps, the highlight of the show – the Jemez Eagle Dance. For this, the performers put on masks, fitted their arms with feather wings, and portrayed the life cycle of the eagle, from its first flight to its slow, spiraling death.

The dances at the Tomahawk became so popular that J.T. started offering evening shows to satisfy demand. This meant that business in the store boomed, but despite this success, J.T. was not entirely pleased. The Hills still owned the property where the Tomahawk was located, so wanting control of his own fortune, he bought another roadside trading post on top of Nine-Mile Hill that he called Teepee Village. He dotted the new property with painted plaster teepees.

His subsequent dealings turned him into one of the most successful entrepreneurs on Route 66, and while he wasn't the first trading post owner on the highway, he certainly made a mark on its history.

MORE BLOOD ON THE HIGHWAY

AS WE'VE ALREADY NOTED, ROUTE 66 TOOK TWO DIFFERENT routes in Albuquerque, and the later alignment followed Central Avenue west, up Nine Mile Hill, and then along the present-day course of the interstate. The original alignment followed the Rio Grande south to Valencia before turning west. In April 1930, this portion of Route 66 became part of a headline-grabbing tragedy.

The horrific accident – resulting in 19 deaths and overwhelming the morgue in Albuquerque – happened because a bus driver, F.D. Williams, failed to see the Santa Fe Main Train No. 7 as he entered a railroad

crossing. The bus, traveling east from Los Angeles, was running behind schedule, and the driver apparently never saw the train coming. The locomotive slammed into the vehicle.

At the time, it was the worst accident to occur on Route 66 and the worst disaster to occur in the history of the Pickwick-Greyhound bus company.

An article in the *Albuquerque Journal* about the incident reported:

In a twinkling, the luxurious coach was a mass of wreckage twisted about the front of the railroad engine. Simultaneously with the collision came a terrific blast as gasoline tanks exploded, adding fire to the horror. Bodies of the bus passengers were hurled through the air, clothes ablaze, or dragged along in the wreckage and distributed along the right of way with debris of the coach. One or two were pinned in the chassis, which were carried along under the cowcatcher of the engine until the screeching brakes brought it to a halt. The bodies were extricated with difficulty.

The coroner's report added more horror to the story of the accident by noting that numerous bodies -- including those of women and children – would likely never be identified because of damage and burns. The manifest indicated there were 29 passengers on the bus, and none of them survived unscathed.

The impact carried the debris from the bus nearly 500 yards down the tracks, with pieces of wreckage found almost a mile away. The collision partially derailed the locomotive. The crew and passengers from the train did their best to render aid for those from the bus but were overwhelmed by the condition of the dead and the hideous condition of the wounded.

According to the *Albuquerque Journal:*

Scattered about were numerous bodies, mangled or with clothing still ablaze from the burning gasoline which had enveloped everything. One body, severed at the trunk, lay across the rails and the figure of a man with his forehead off was a short distance down the tracks. Moans of the dying and injured were heart-rending to eyewitnesses. Baggage strewn about was also burning.

News of the tragedy spread across the country because the passengers who were identified seemed to come from every corner of America.

Driver F.D. Williams was identified by the remains of his uniform. R.C. Stevens of Kankakee, Illinois, was identified by a business card case in his pocket. Potaclo Torteleto of the Santo Domingo Pueblo was identified later by six members of his tribe. Three passengers – eight-year-old Kenneth Huff, his mother, and a man named William Mickle – came from Santa Monica, California. Roland Anderson, a U.S. Army soldier, was on his way home to Merrill, Iowa, for his father's funeral.

And the list went on – a litany of death and tragedy.

THE BUDVILLE TRADING COMPANY

IF YOU'D BLINKED WHILE DRIVING THIS STRETCH OF ROUTE 66, you might have missed Budville. It never really amounted to more than a garage, service station, and store with a roadhouse, the Dixie Tavern and Café, across the highway.

But this little spot on the route could boast more violence, murder, and bloodshed than much larger towns along the highway.

In 1928, H.N. "Bud" Rice established a service station and trading post at this bend in the road, and in the years that followed, he and his wife, Flossie, carved out a solid business that was built on the needs of sometimes desperate travelers.

TRUE CRIME

In 1947, he dubbed the area "Budville" after he became the local justice of the peace, beginning a legacy of corruption and scandal that left a lasting stain on the area. Even as recently as 1995, a local man told a reporter: "If you want to live here, you mind your own business."

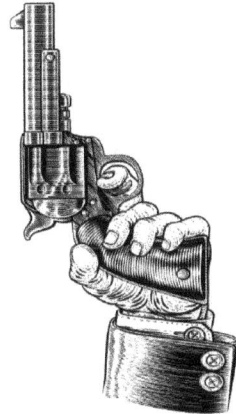

The Budville Trading Company, long after it closed

You see, Bud made most of his money not from running his gas station and trading post – it came from ticketing travelers and charging them with fees for speeding and reckless driving that even his contemporaries called excessive. Bud justified the fees by citing the ever-rising number of accidents. He was accused more than once of operating a speed trap but without consequence.

Bud also sold bus tickets and operated the local State Motor Vehicle Department concession. By 1950, he was the only available towing service for miles in every direction, which further assured the prosperity of the couple. Bud often joked about being "the only law west of Rio Puerco" and that just about anything was available for a price.

But it all ended on the frosty night of November 18, 1967, when Bud was closing the trading post for the day. With him were Flossie and Blanche Brown, an 82-year-old retired schoolteacher who worked part-time at the Budville store. Just before the door was locked, a young man came in, but he was not a customer – he was brandishing a gun and demanding the cash in the register. Details are sketchy, but when the man fled, he left Bud and Blanche shot and bleeding to death on the floor. Flossie had run screaming toward the bathroom when she saw the gun, and inexplicably, he spared her life.

Just as the robber was escaping, a Continental Trailways bus turned into the parking lot, and the driver spotted a small pickup truck roaring away from the trading post at high speed and heading east toward Albuquerque. He later reported that the truck was a 1946 or 1947 Ford, dark blue or black, except for the right door and right front fender, which were light colored. He didn't see the license plate but did notice that the truck had only one taillight.

Since there weren't any passengers waiting near the bus depot sign, he continued down the road instead of stopping. He didn't think anything out of the ordinary was going on. However, he did recall that the trading post and station were dark inside and outside – except for the globes on the two gas pumps – which was odd because he knew Bud usually stayed open until at least 8:00 P.M.

The man Flossie identified as the killer of Bud and Blanche turned out to be a discharged sailor, Larry Bunten, who was hitchhiking west – but it wasn't him. He was positively identified by at least a dozen witnesses that placed him miles from the crime scene.

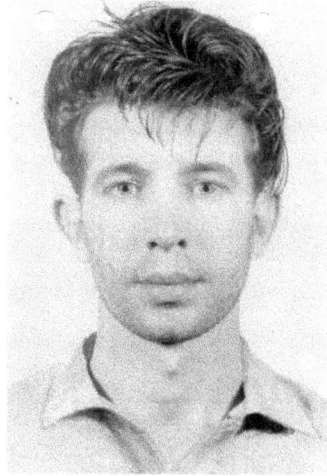

The main suspect in the murders was a drifter named Billy Ray White. Despite strong evidence against him, he was acquitted at trial, leavin the murders officially unsolved.

Several years later, three men arrested in Albuquerque offered details about the Budville robbery in hopes of getting a deal. They fingered Billy Ray White, a drifter with a lengthy record of petty crimes, as the killer. After his arrest, White stood trial for the murders, but the jury acquitted him despite overwhelming evidence against him.

Officially, the Budville murders are unsolved, but most believe that White was the killer, no matter what the jury decided. Soon after his release, he was arrested and convicted of a robbery and murder that was almost identical to what happened in Budville. While behind bars, White allegedly confessed to the earlier crime – just before he committed suicide.

But that's not the end of the Budville Trading Company story.

Bud's widow, Flossie, married a troublemaker named Max Atkinson in 1971. Soon after their nuptials, Max shot and killed his brother, Phillip, in an ambush following a brawl at the Dixie Tavern across the road from the trading post. Then, two years later, Max was shot to death by an area rancher named Gus Raney during an argument.

Flossie, who married a third time, died peacefully in 1994, outliving three husbands, including Bud, who remains one of the most controversial characters of Route 66.

KILLER ON THE ROAD

ON JANUARY 10, 1956, A SANTA MONICA, CALIFORNIA MAN named Ralph Rainey, was found shot to death on the side of Route 66 just west of Budville. He had two bullets in his head.

Weeks later, an incident in Las Vegas led to the arrest of Rainey's killer and revealed a string of murders along Route 66 and in Nevada.

Just before dawn on January 23, Police Sergeant Dick Barber was on duty in North Las Vegas – near Nellis Air Force base – and made a traffic stop on a Buick with California plates. The driver, a man of about 35 with wavy brown hair, responded politely when asked for his license. It identified him as Kenneth Short of Burbank, California.

But what the cop didn't know was that Kenneth Short was listed as a missing person who was last seen in Tucumcari, New Mexico. Without warning, the driver of the Buick hit the gas and fled the scene with Sergeant Barber in a high-speed pursuit.

On East College Street, the driver of the Buick lost control, rolled the sedan, crawled out of the wreckage, and disappeared into the surrounding neighborhood. A manhunt was soon underway, but the driver had taken refuge – and a hostage – in the home of Loren E. Tracy.

He managed to elude police until the following day when the man who claimed to be Kenneth Short was apprehended in nearby Caliente. By this time, though, the police had learned that the real Kenneth Short was an electrical engineer who had vanished. He had purchased a new Buick in Michigan in early January and had driven west to meet his wife, Mira, in San Francisco. He was supposed to have arrived by January 21.

So, who was the man arrested in Caliente? He now claimed his name was Samuel Stuart and told police that he suffered from amnesia. He said that he'd found the car abandoned on the side of the road in Santa Rosa, New Mexico.

Skeptical, police officers contacted the FBI, who soon revealed that the man was actually David Cooper Nelson, whose lengthy criminal record included six years served at the Montana State Prison for armed robbery. Additionally, his fingerprints matched those found in the recovered car of Ralph Rainey, the dead man found outside Budville. They also found that Nelson had cashed traveler's checks belonging to Kenneth Short in Lowe, Utah, and Santa Rose, New Mexico.

This guy was a one-man crime wave.

But, at first, he continued to insist that he had amnesia and had no idea who David Nelson was – although he eventually confessed to a string of murders through several states. Although he later recanted the confession, he told police that Rainey had picked him up hitchhiking near Flagstaff, Arizona, on January 9. They later argued, Nelson said, and Rainey ordered him out of his car near Grants, New Mexico.

At that point, Nelson said he removed a gun from his suitcase in the back seat and ordered Rainey to switch places with him. When he was behind the wheel, he said that Rainey repeatedly tried to take the gun from him. After striking him several times, Nelson finally lost patience and shot the other man in the head.

"I guess I had driven about 15 miles when Rainey moaned, 'Why did you do it?'" Nelson told the cops and then added, "It was then I fired the second shot."

While admitting to the murder, Nelson was unaware that the police had recovered the .38-caliber revolver he'd used to kill Rainey. It had his fingerprints all over it. When he learned this, Nelson again claimed to have amnesia.

Back in the interrogation room later that day, Nelson spilled his guts again, offering a rambling confession about killing Kenneth Short while west of Tucumcari and dumping his body in an arroyo along Route 66. Short had picked up Nelson hitchhiking near Sapulpa, Oklahoma, and when the men stopped to take a short nap on a farm road, Nelson overpowered Short while he slept. He tied him up, and even though he promised Short nothing would happen to him if he cooperated, Nelson killed him anyway.

During his confession, he dropped a bombshell: "And I also killed a fellow named John Valente on January 4." Nelson didn't know it, but Valente's body had already been found in the bathroom of his home in Pioche, Nevada. Until then, investigators didn't know if his death had been a murder or suicide.

Nelson was arraigned and went on trial for the murder of Ralph Rainey. Before the trial, he recanted his confession and, in front of the judge and jury, offered an insanity defense, which no one believed. The jury found him guilty – twice. He was charged and tried for Kenneth

Short's murder, too. After this second conviction, Nelson tried to escape from jail but was quickly recaptured.

He was executed in the gas chamber on August 11, 1960.

VILLA DE CUBERO TRADING POST

THE DRIVE WEST FROM BUDVILLE TO GRANTS IS THE KIND of Route 66 experience that the modern-day enthusiast imagines when planning their first trip on the legendary highway. There are faded villages that have been baked by the sun, western landscapes with mountains that rise in the distance, and stretches of desert unbroken only by buttes, mesas, and rock outcroppings that reach toward desert sunsets.

Villa de Cubero - Cubero, N.M. - Modern Auto Court, Cafe, Curios and Gen'l. Mdse. on Highway 66, 55 miles from Albuquerque - 83 miles from Gallup

The next stop on the road after the remains of Budville is a ghost town called Cubero, which was named after the Spanish State Governor, Pedro Rodriguez Cubero, centuries ago. Located on a desert plain with a spectacular view of Mount Taylor and its foothills, the town was on the first alignment of Route 66 that ran through the San Jose River Valley.

Wallace and Mary Gunn ran the local trading post, selling gas and goods to travelers, along with Navajo rugs and jewelry. When the road was paved and re-aligned in 1937, the Gunns relocated their business to the new highway and partnered with Sidney Gottlieb to build the Spanish-styled Villa de Cubero Trading Post.

It quickly turned into a popular tourist destination, thanks to the attached DeLuxe Tourist Court of 10 small cabins, each with tiled bathrooms, which meant hot and cold running water. It was the first stopping point west of Albuquerque and one of the few motels in the county.

Although the Villa never served alcohol and never had televisions in the guest rooms, it still managed to become a showbiz hideaway in the early 1950s. Among the guests were Lucy and Desi Arnaz, Ernest Hemingway, Gene Tierney, and the Van Trapp Family.

Cubero is mostly boarded up today. Although the trading post was still open a few years ago, the motor court has long since been abandoned. Nothing remains of it now but memories.

CHIEF'S RANCHO

JUST TWO MILES PAST THE FADED GHOST TOWN OF SAN Fidel was Chief's Rancho, a restaurant, tavern, souvenir store, service station, and motel. The original complex was built by a career lawman named Ely J. House, Jr.

House – known to friends and guests as "Chief" – had been just 19 when he started working as a jailer and deputy sheriff for his father in Kaufman County, Texas. In 1928, when the family moved to New Mexico, House became a police officer in Roswell. Six years later, he became one of the first 10 men to join the newly created New Mexico Motor Patrol. When the New Mexico State Police was formed in 1935, he became the first chief, earning him his enduring nickname. He even designed the agency's black uniform and shoulder patch using his son's crayons.

After retiring from the State Police in 1944, Chief House moved his family to San Fidel and opened Chief's Rancho. In January 1946, Santa Fe Trailways bus driver Charlie Moore leased Rancho's kitchen, and in 1948, the service station was opened by former Texaco agent Ray Wilsford. His mother-in-law, Katherine Harman, took over the restaurant, bar, and souvenir shop. Chief House continued to operate the motor lodge and service station until moving to Albuquerque in 1952. He bought a farm near Los Lunas and settled down to enjoy his golden years.

When Chief House died in February 1960, his funeral procession stopped traffic in Albuquerque for two hours.

There is one odd story that, while unconnected to the Chief, is very strange. Apparently, during Rancho's heyday, a young man named Bud South was driving a 25-ton dump truck

across some railroad tracks when he was struck by a fast-moving train. It hit the truck so hard that it carried it almost a mile down the tracks.

But Bud survived the crash. In fact, he got out of the truck, walked to Chief's Rancho, went into the café, and ordered a hamburger. Then he fell over. He had a broken neck.

Bud survived that, too, though, and later became a state patrolman.

MOTORING TO GRANTS

AFTER THE DUSTY STREETS OF SAN FIDEL, THE ORIGINAL alignment of Route 66 traveled on to the lonely village of McCartys, which was once the center of the farming and trading community of the Acoma Indian Reservation. It had been named after the railroad contractor who had built the local section of the line.

The old section of the highway crossed the rough and barren Malpais badlands in 1926. A decade later, it was straightened and realigned as part of the New Deal's Civilian Conservation Corps program, which was formed during the Depression. The workers from the CCC also constructed a steel truss bridge to carry Route 66 over the San Jose River. Eventually, McCartys was bypassed when the interstate came through in 1956.

Traveling along the desert highway brings motorists to the town of Grants, which was named for three brothers – Angus, Lewis, and John Grant – who built the Atlantic & Pacific Railroad through the area in the 1880s.

Grants grew as a farm community through the 1930s and 1940s and was acclaimed for its carrot fields, which extended as far as 12 miles outside of town. But carrots wouldn't remain the town's greatest source of prosperity.

In 1950, a Navajo rancher discovered a "funny-looking" yellow rock in the nearby Haystack Mountains. The discovery uncovered one of the largest uranium deposits in the world. The U.S. Atomic Energy Commission contracted multiple mining companies and bought all the uranium they could dig up. Grants and the surrounding area became one of the largest uranium suppliers in the world until a recession in the early 1980s closed all the mines.

By then, Grants didn't even have Route 66 commerce to fall back on – it had been bypassed by the interstate years earlier – but the town managed to survive as a tourist destination for those traveling to nearby Bluewater and Ramah Lakes.

Even today, a few of the old Route 66 businesses survive, while others have become legends that refuse to fade away.

MIKE CROTEAU'S TRADING POST IN GRANTS WAS KNOWN as a small but high-quality place that specialized in fine silver and petrified wood jewelry. Mike had operated other trading posts in the past and had made a name for himself displaying handmade Native American items in eastern cities.

When he and his wife, Florence, opened their store on Route 66, they had only a handful of display cases to showcase their jewelry. They were more interested in serving collectors than tourists.

In 1949, though, Mike and Florence decided to expand and enlarge their store. The additional space allowed them to add a large selection of Navajo rugs and an art gallery featuring Mike's paintings. They also added a room of stuffed and mounted animals from the regions.

However, the couple was proudest of the items in the store that were not for sale – their collection of Anasazi pottery. They had gathered the artifacts for their personal enjoyment over a period of decades. They were as fascinated – and as knowledgeable – as any scholar when it came to the Southwest's early residents.

After the couple had both passed away in 1965, the town of Grants was surprised to learn that they had left their collection to the city. The trading post is long gone, but the collection remains on display in the building that houses the regional Chamber of Commerce and the New Mexico Mining Museum.

THE MURDER OF NASH GARCIA

TRUE CRIME

THE ISOLATED TOWN OF GRANTS MADE HEADLINES ACROSS the country when a state police officer was killed there on Friday, April 11, 1952.

New Mexico State Police Officer Nash Garcia was parked on the shoulder of Route 66 east of Grants that day when a pickup truck sped past him, recklessly passing other vehicles. Garcia saw the truck slide onto the shoulder, pass some cars, and then jerk abruptly back onto the highway in a cloud of dust. Narrowly missing several other motorists, the truck continued roaring toward town. Garcia hit the lights and sped off in pursuit of the vehicle.

Obviously spotting Garcia's spinning red lights in his rearview mirror, the driver in the pickup left the highway near the Acoma Indian Reservation, turned onto a dirt road, drove a few miles, and then violently hit the brakes.

Garcia was still a few hundred yards behind the truck and could see little ahead of him on the dusty road. That's the reason he missed the man who slipped out of the cab of the truck with a rifle in his hands.

As Garcia neared the truck, the man lying in ambush opened fire with the rifle. He fired into the police car nine times, hitting Garcia several times. The sniper and the driver of the truck pulled the wounded officer from the vehicle and then stomped on him and beat him with the rifle butt before dragging him back into the cruiser and driving it to a spot near Sandstone Mesa. The car was filled with scrub brush and wood and set on fire.

New Mexico State Police Officer Nash Garcia

Nash Garcia was the first member of the New Mexico State Police to be murdered in the line of duty.

Thanks to the remote highways and isolated spots near the Indian reservations, it wasn't unusual for an officer to be out of contact for a day or so. However, when Garcia failed to check in on Sunday morning, his boss and fellow officers became concerned. When they contacted his wife and discovered she hadn't heard from him since Friday, a search was started.

Word about the missing office spreads through Grants and across the area. A local cowboy contacted the police on Friday to say that he'd seen Garcia chasing a truck that belonged to two brothers, Willie and Gabriel Felipe. More calls followed, passing on the same information.

On Sunday evening, state police officers Dick Lewis and Joe Fernandez contacted the authorities on the Acoma reservation and arrested Willie Felipe, who offered no resistance. Almost immediately, he made a full confession and incriminated his brother. "I knew they'd get me," he said. "They always get them."

The next morning, Willie directed seven vehicles filled with cops to Sandstone Mesa, where the burned-out police cruiser had been partially hidden in an arroyo.

The following day, Albuquerque officer Robert Olona arrested Gabriel Felipe, who, like his brother, didn't resist when he was taken into custody. However, he claimed that he hadn't taken part in the murder and, in fact, tried to prevent it.

But no one was interested in his stories.

The brothers were tried, convicted, and sentenced to death in the fall of 1952. An appeal was filed, claiming they were both drunk and insane at the time of the shooting, but while the appeal was denied by U.S. District Court Judge Carl Hatch, he did commute their sentence to life in federal prison. Both served just 20 years before being paroled.

THE CRASH OF THE "LUCKY LIZ"

IN MARCH 1958, THE MINING TOWN WAS BACK IN THE NEWS again, but these headlines were even bigger, thanks to the celebrities involved.

About 20 miles from the Civil Aeronautics Agency communications station in Grants, a twin-engine Lockheed Lodestar crashed during a storm. Everyone on board was killed instantly, including Avrom

Goldbogen, who was better known by the name of Mike Todd, who'd recently won an Academy Award for producing the film *Around the World in 80 Days*.

More importantly to movie fans, he was also the third husband of actress Elizabeth Taylor.

MIKE TODD – WHEN HE WAS STILL AVROM GOLDBOGEN – grew up in Minneapolis but put his rough and poverty-stricken childhood behind him, earned a fortune in the construction business, and then made a splash as a theatrical impresario at the 1933 Century of Progress Exposition in Chicago. He went on to produce nearly two dozen Broadway shows before becoming a widely acclaimed producer in Hollywood.

Elizabeth Taylor had been Todd's third wife. He married his first wife, Bertha Freshman, when he was only 19, and they had a son together. She died from a collapsed lung while undergoing surgery for a damaged tendon in her finger in 1946.

His second wife was actress Joan Blondell, whom he married in 1947. They divorced in 1950 after Blondell filed for divorce on the grounds of mental cruelty.

A short time later, Todd began a stormy relationship with Elizabeth Taylor, which led to their marriage in Mexico on February 2, 1957. At the time, Liz was 24, and her new husband was 49. A daughter, Elizabeth Frances Todd, was born on August 6, 1957.

She would never really know her father.

On March 17, Todd flew on his private plane, "Lucky Liz," to Albuquerque to promote a screening of *Around the World in 80 Days*. Then, five days later, he took a second flight from Burbank airport, heading for Tulsa, Oklahoma, but he never made it.

Mike Todd and his wife, Elizabeth Taylor, posing in front of Mike's plane, the "Lucky Liz"

The twin-engine Lodestar suffered from engine failure and went down near Grants. The plane had been overloaded and experienced icing at an altitude that was too high for only one engine working under the heavy load. The plane went out of control and crashed, killing all four on board.

The others on board the plane were screenwriter and author Art Cohn, who was writing a book about Todd; Tom Barclay, a replacement for the usual co-pilot; and pilot Bill Verner, a veteran military flyer who had flown Curtiss C-46 Commando cargo planes between India and China.

The Lodestar should have been no problem for him, even though Todd had paid for the installation of two extra fuel tanks in the aircraft, which caused it to weigh more than its official rating when all the tanks were full. Verner had flown the plane overloaded before without incident. During the fatal flight, the tanks had been filled to capacity.

When news of the crash reached Elizabeth Taylor, she collapsed. Todd was stopping in Tulsa on his way to New York to accept the New York Friars Club "Showman of the Year" award. Liz wanted to go with him, but she had a bad cold, and he insisted she stay home.

And she wasn't the only celebrity that narrowly escaped death. Just hours before the flight, Todd had phoned several friends, including Joseph Mankiewicz and Kirk Douglas, trying to get them to come along so he'd have another gin rummy player for the flight. Everyone turned him down, even after he told them, "Ah, c'mon. It's a good, safe plane. I wouldn't let it crash. I'm taking along a picture of Elizabeth, and I wouldn't let anything happen to her."

Although his son wanted his father's body to be cremated after he was identified through dental records, Liz refused, saying Todd wouldn't want that. He was buried at Beth Aaron Cemetery in plot 66, which is part of Jewish Waldheim Cemetery in Forest Park, Illinois.

Actor Eddie Fisher, who was Todd's best friend, attended the funeral and wrote:

There was a closed coffin, but I knew it was more for show than anything else. The plane had exploded on impact, and whatever remains were found couldn't be identified... The only items recovered from the wreckage were Mike's wedding ring and a pair of platinum cuff links I'd given him.

In June 1977, though, thieves went after that ring and pair of cuff links, digging up his grave and breaking into his coffin. They were caught in the act, and Tood's remains were moved to a secret location for reburial.

The location of his new grave remains a mystery today.

OLD CRATER TRADING POST

AS THE HIGHWAY LEFT GRANTS IN THE REARVIEW MIRROR, it rolled past another collection of the old trading posts that once lined Route 66 through the region.

The trading posts of the Southwest, of course, preceded the highway and were once more than just a roadside store. They were part of a time that bound the Anglo and Navajo together when trading posts were the centers of communities and a link between two different worlds.

Few Route 66 businessmen championed the old days of the trading posts more than Claude Bowlin. He worked extensively with the Navajo people and became a highway character who was almost universally respected.

Claude was born in rural Arkansas in 1891, and his grandfather, George, moved his entire family to the Indian Territory of Oklahoma to trade with the Cherokee when Claude was just a toddler. In 1906, Claude's father, James, took his brood to New Mexico, and while he farmed for a while, he eventually opened a mercantile store at Fort Sumner in 1915.

Young Claude's life among the Navajo began three years earlier when he moved on his own to Gallup with a plan to open a trading post. He first found work with the A.B. McGaffey Lumber Company in Thoreau, New Mexico. Most of his customers were Navajo, and he soon found himself overseeing trades in rugs, jewelry, sheep, and wool.

Although World War I took him to England – which led to a foray into ranching following his 1919 marriage to Willa Harding – by 1922, he was in Gallup dealing with the Navajo.

In 1927, Claude moved his family to Grants and bought the Orange Front Soda Shop, a combination of a confectionary and drugstore that served as a Yelloway bus stop. It offered travelers refreshments, along with a selection of Navajo rugs.

Five years later, Claude traded the Orange Front Soda Shop to Ottis Graham for a highway business that was west of Farmington, New Mexico. Known as Shady Corners, it boasted a general store, service station, campground, and cabins that were rented to travelers. Again, most of Claude's regular customers were Navajo, and he'd spend the rest of his career working side-by-side with them.

In early 1935, Claude returned to Gallup and partnered with B.D. Westbrook in a mercantile business called Indian Home Trading Company. However, he only stayed there for a year. In 1936, he sold his interest in the company and built Old Crater Trading Post one mile west of Bluewater on Route 66.

Old Crater – named for an extinct volcano that had become a tourist attraction nearby – was opened on the new, modern, cross-country highway, but it hearkened back to the trading posts of decades past. The enormous two-story structure was built with wooden slabs, and the grounds were filled with sheep corrals, dipping vats, shearing sheds, and other amenities designed for traditional Navajo traders. Inside, a pot-bellied stove brewed a hot kettle of coffee. Metal cups hung on nails along a nearby roof support. Shelves overflowed with denim pants, Pendleton shawls, horse bridles, and canned goods. Any customer – whether they arrived by automobile or on horseback -- received a free can of Clabber Girl Baking Powder with the purchase of a bag of flour.

Also, in the tradition of the old-time trading posts, the Old Crater became a community center. Claude and his family sponsored chicken pulls, wagon races, and card games for their Navajo neighbors.

When Claude built the Old Crater Trading Post, the highway in front of the store hadn't yet been paved, so when progress arrived, he added gas pumps and refrigeration units. He knew the modern age was coming, but even Claude failed to predict the sweeping changes that would follow after World War II. With gas rationing at an end, travelers flooded Route 66 like never before.

The Bowlin family had started dipping their toes in the tourist trade since the Depression when Willa started selling tiny souvenir moccasins and Navajo dolls to supplement the family income. Claude had hired silversmiths and rug weavers to work at Old Crater, hoping to snag highway travelers with Native American art.

But the end of the war turned business along Route 66 upside-down, and Claude jumped in with both feet. With the highway now teeming with souvenir shops, he started looking for other markets. He sent family members south to drive from one city to another, and when they found themselves hungry, thirsty, needing a restroom, or low on gas, they looked for a building to buy. By the end of the 1940s, Claude had opened three additional stores – Continental Divide Trading Post between Deming and Lordsburg, Wagon Wheel near Gage, and Akela Flats, west of Las Cruces. All were operated by family members.

Claude's business chain grew in the 1950s with the creation of the Old West and Jackrabbit Trading Posts near Las Cruces and Running Indian, north of Alamogordo. The Bowlin family even incorporated in 1953.

The new stores were all designed to pull tourists off the road. They all had souvenirs, ice, refreshments, snacks, and at least one gimmick for the eyes. Old West had kachinas that were 20 feet tall.

Claude spent his last years in satisfied retirement. He lived just long enough to see Old Crater Trading Post close in 1973. Killed off by the interstate, the old store had been run by Claude's daughter and son-in-law, Hope and Frank McClure, since 1954.

There's nothing but loose stones and good memories left behind at the site today.

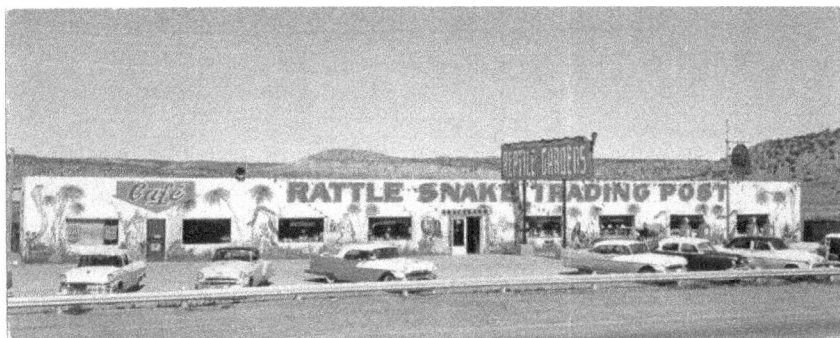

RATTLESNAKE TRADING POST

FOLLOWING THE WINDING CURVES THROUGH THE DESERT landscape, highway travelers soon reached another spot as they continued their westward journey – a trading post operated by one of the free spirits of the road.

John "Jake" Atkinson was the second son of a modest Texas farmer whose life was permanently changed when he contracted polio when he was 10. He was left with severe scoliosis, a hunchback, and trouble walking when he was young due to one of his legs being significantly shorter than the other. Many pitied him as a boy, and even his own family wondered what kind of future lay ahead of him – but Jake surprised them all.

He taught himself to walk and honed his mind to a razor's edge, landing a government job in Texas when he was in his twenties. Then, when his brother, Leroy, sent him a bus ticket to the west, Jake went.

Jake joined Leroy at the Three Hogans Trading Post near Allentown, Arizona, which he managed for Gallup, New Mexico, businessman Jack Hill. Leroy had big plans of someday owning a trading post with his brother – but Jake surprised him again by opening his own modest store in a leased building on the Arizona-New Mexico border.

In 1944, Jake moved to Thoreau, New Mexico, and became the manager of the Beautiful Mountain Trading post. The small store was on Route 66 at the turn-off to the Navajo Reservation. It was there that he met his wife, Maxine, who had come to New Mexico from Missouri. Together, the couple served tourists on the highway, but most of their customers were their Navajo neighbors – who followed them in 1945 when Jake and Maxine bought their own building west of Bluewater and opened the Rattlesnake Trading Post.

They'd bought the place from an eccentric character named Vic Holmes, who'd run it as the Hogan. Holmes had been a scout for Hollywood westerns and somehow had ended up with five old, mangy burros that he kept tied to his gas pumps. When tourists stopped to take pictures of the burros, Vic sold them gas. He also used to have pens of fighting chickens and would host weekly illegal cockfights. When the law came after him, he'd chop their heads off and put them in the kettle. The law came looking for the chickens, but they were already cooking.

Jake wasted no time in making the place his own. He turned the house that Holmes had lived in with his wife into a restaurant, built a larger store, and dubbed the place the Rattlesnake Trading Post, inspired by a nearby piece of land that was teeming with the reptiles. As a gimmick, Jake put an enormous rattler in one of the store showcases and later turned an entire room into a snake museum.

Jake and Maxine initially lived in a trailer on the property but soon built a house on the east side, joining several Navajo hogans into one large living space. The dirt floors were covered with lumber, and Navajo blankets were used as rugs.

Their first child, John, was born shortly after the family opened the Rattlesnake. When business at the new store began to boom, Maxine placed a bassinet behind the counter and rocked her son while she waited on customers.

In October 1946, Jake completed the Rattlesnake Trading Post as he had planned it. Later that month, he announced the grand opening of his new Rattlesnake Night Club. His first night's "Barn Dance" was packed to capacity, and patrons danced the night away to the music of the Dude Wranglers, a popular western swing band.

The tiny town of Bluewater was never the same.

The Rattlesnake not only gained a reputation as a fun place for drinking and dancing but also for nocturnal activities that were just outside of the law. Jake continued to stage the cockfights made infamous by Vic Holmes, and they took place in a pit hidden inside a hogan on the property. They often lasted from dusk to dawn, but unlike Vic – who frequently had to lop the heads off the chickens to hide them from the law – Jake managed to avoid official interference.

He was a personable and likable man who seemed to have friends everywhere – literally. Jake's brother, Herman, once recalled that he was on a trip to Florida one time and stopped at a restaurant to have breakfast. The waitress asked where he was from, and when he told her, she asked if he knew Jake! "That was the kind of fellow he was," Herman said. "He made friends with everyone. I guess he had more friends than Leroy and I put together."

Something about Jake just appealed to everyone – and almost everyone seemed inclined to cut him some slack. When a New Mexico military base wanted to unload a supply of old canvas water bags, Jake talked them into giving them to him for free. He filled them with water from his well and made a profit selling them to tourists.

One day, Jake and a Navajo weaver who worked for another store decided to take a road trip. But instead of taking the weaver on a buying trip – as he'd promised the man's employer – the two men disappeared. The rival store owner eventually located Jake and his employee having a wild weekend in Las Vegas. Any guesses where the weaver started working soon after that?

Jake's carefree ways often frustrated his older brother, Leroy, who felt Jake should act a little more responsibly. Leroy got used to his little brother buying a new car every year, but he was bothered by Jake's habit of buying cars for no reason at all. Once, while driving a new Oldsmobile to town, Jake got a flat tire. Instead of changing the tire, he walked to the dealer and bought a new car. On another occasion, Jake bought a new car simply because the ashtray in the vehicle he was then driving was full.

Then, there was Jake's "Prehistoric Monster," which was even featured in *LIFE* magazine. Constructed from cow vertebrae, pelvis, and skull, the fabricated monster was spread over 48 feet of sand inside the trading post. Jake advertised the fraud on roadside billboards, and people stopped to see the thing in droves.

When the alignment of Route 66 changed through the area, and the road passed through the back of Jake's property, he built a new store behind the one he'd been using, just facing the other way. Later, when the alignment flip-flopped back, he re-opened the original doors.

On an early Thursday morning in March 1951, the Rattlesnake Trading Post burned. No one was injured in the blaze, but three of the buildings were destroyed.

Jake escaped the calamity, too. He'd recently sold the Rattlesnake to Maxine's sister, Pauline, and her husband, Paul Gibbs. They quickly rebuilt the trading post while Jake went off in search of new prospects.

In the years that followed, he built a store near Las Cruces and two outside of Carlsbad, New Mexico. In the late 1950s, he returned to Route 66 and opened a new spot at Correo, New Mexico, where he delved into the leather belt and purse business. He lived in Albuquerque for a while and ended his career in Tucson, Arizona.

His son, John, later recalled that Jake was sharp as a tack to the day he died. "Pop had Lou Gehrig's Disease – what his doctors felt was post-polio syndrome. They put him in a hospital in a respirator. He couldn't talk but he woke up one day. I was there and I told him, 'Pop, we've got some time, but you're going to be on this respirator the rest of your life.' He wrote me a note and what he wrote was, 'Any breath is better than no breath at all.'"

ZUNI MOUNTAIN TRADING POST

THE STORE THAT EVENTUALLY BECAME THE TRADING POST was built by T.B. "Teke" Greer, whose brother, Bert, also operated a roadside store in the area. Teke believed it was the perfect place to tap into tourist traffic and built Zuni Mountain as a store with gas pumps, a café, and a four-room motel. Although Teke opened for business in 1947, he soon rethought his future on Route 66 and found buyers for his new store – Dave and Betty Ortega.

Dave Ortega was part of a family that seemed destined to define the roadside trading post business. His grandfather, Thomas Ortega, operated two stores in Arizona. His uncle, Max, also owned a trading post, while his cousins, Gilbert and Armand, became known as some of the most prominent dealers in southwestern jewelry. Dave's life was only slightly quieter at the Zuni Mountain Trading Post.

But things didn't go smoothly for Dave and Betty at first. They immediately earned the ire of nearby businessman Justin LaFont. Justin and his wife, Odessa, had purchased another, older trading post only a year earlier and had staked their claim to the area's tourist trade.

And they weren't happy about the competition.

They did all they could to run the Ortegas out of business. They had a large restaurant at their trading post, and the post office for the area was located in an alcove outside the LaFont home. Odessa manufactured and sold "squaw" dresses and skirts, which she sold as far away as Albuquerque. They spent a fortune in advertising, always trying to steer business past Zuni Mountain.

Dave and Betty did what they could to fight back and carve out their piece of the highway pie. They always made sure their gas prices were the lowest in the area, and Betty battled the LaFont's fancy restaurant with her own home cooking. She served a popular stew at the café that found devoted fans among the New Mexico State Police.

But the real key to their success turned out to be stocking Zuni Mountain with food and supplies that local Navajos needed. Soon, these neighbors began coming to their place, asking to barter for goods. Dave was happy to accept Navajo rugs in trade.

It wasn't long before Zuni Mountain gained a reputation as the best place to find quality rugs in the region. Dave treated the Navajo fairly and took good care of them as customers. This earned him great respect among the Navajo and brought the Ortegas even more business.

In 1950, when uranium was discovered at nearby Haystack Butte, Zuni Mountain Trading Post shifted gears. They discontinued their tourist souvenirs and even closed the café so they could focus on the handmade goods provided by the Navajo. When the interstate came through, which closed the LaFont trading post, Dave and Betty found a new focus in the southwestern jewelry consignment business, something that Dave had been interested in since he started selling Navajo rugs.

They invested heavily in the jewelry business, and Dave spent his days visiting artisans on the reservations. Big buyers brought their bankrolls to Zuni Mountain Trading Post. One man spent so much money that they closed the store for the day so he could shop in private.

He also held hospitality nights for different companies and for doctors and nurses from local hospitals so they could shop after hours. He was doing them a favor but never took advantage. In all his years in the business, Dave sold things the same way – cost plus 10 percent. During the southwestern jewelry boom of the 1970s, his competition never slowed things down. They could never beat Dave's prices.

On a cold day in January 1980, Dave died from a heart attack in the backyard of his home. He was only 55 years old. Dave's death shocked the community. When the news reached the Navajo, a steady stream of friends made their way to Betty's door. Each wanted to tell her what their friendship with Dave had meant to them.

After Dave's death, Betty leased the Zuni Mountain Trading Post to a series of different entrepreneurs who buried its name under fresh coats of paint. The name may have changed, but its history has not been forgotten.

JOHNNIE'S CAFE

AS ROUTE 66 CONTINUES TO THE WEST, THE TUMBLEWEEDS and shrubs of the high desert began to change to a landscape of pinyon pines and junipers.

The town of Thoreau has faded over the years, far from the thriving small town it once was. In its heyday, motorists along the unpaved early alignment of the highway could find the Red Arrow Cottage Camp, Crownpoint Trading Company, Thoreau Mercantile Company, Anderson Garage, the 66 Café, and others – but little remains today.

At least a few years ago, **Roy T. Herman's Garage and Service Station** was still standing. It was opened in 1937 on Route 66, but it actually had three different locations over the years. Prior to being in Thoreau, the steel building had originally been in Grants, where it operated as a Standard Oil Company station. When Route 66 was re-routed in Grants in 1937, the building was picked up and moved to just outside of Thoreau. At first, it stood next to a trading post on the eastern side of the crossroads outside town, but in 1963, the building was moved to its current location.

After World War II, Roy T. Herman operated it as a part of a small chain of service stations. After the building had been moved for the last time, he stopped selling fuel, and it became a repair garage only.

Thoreau was also home to the **Thunderbird Bar and Trading Post**, which was built by Bill and Charlie Bass in 1947. It had a Texaco station, grocery store, and tavern, but it closed in 1964 after the interstate bypassed the town. The crumbling ruins of the building can still be found today.

The best-known business in Thoreau was undoubtedly Johnnie's Café. When the place was built by John Radosevich, a Yugoslavian immigrant, in 1936, the small café was located on First Street, which was then dusty and unpaved Route 66. Johnnie was the cook and his wife, Anna, did a little bit of everything, including waiting on customers. The cramped little place had a counter with a few stools and only four tables. Food was initially prepared on a wood stove, and dishes were washed in water heated by the same stove. A one-cylinder diesel generator was put into service to provide electricity in the evening.

In 1947, Route 66 was rerouted to the south side of town, and the cafe was moved – building and all – to the new alignment. An addition was made to one side of the building two years later, followed by another addition in the early 1950s.

JOHNNIES CAFE, THOREAU, N. MEX.
GOOD EATS
Reasonable Prices   Tourist Headquarters
U. S. HIGHWAY 66

Mileage from Johnnies Cafe			
WEST TO		EAST TO	
Continental Divide	5	Grants	31
Gallup, N. Mexico	32	Laguna	68
Painted Desert	196	Los Lunas	116
Petrified Forest	118	Albuquerque	135
Holbrook, Ariz	134	Domingo	176
Winslow	167	Santa Fe	203
Flagstaff	230	Las Vegas	277
Maine	350	Trinidad, Colo	413
Grand Canyon	215	NORTH TO	
Williams	266	Crown Point	28
Needles, Cal.	420	Chaco Canyon	60
Los Angeles	779	SOUTH TO	
		Albuquerque	138
		El Paso	444

Over the years, Johnnie's became known for its thick steaks and outstanding chili. As word of the chili spread up and down the highway, there was never a shortage of customers. Area residents often drove from Gallup just to get a bowl of it.

After Johnnie passed away in the 1960s, his son, Jay, continued to operate the place as a tavern for a few years, and later it became a liquor and convenience store.

The last time I passed through Thoreau, the building was still standing, and the store was open. Sadly, though, I couldn't get a bowl of Johnnie's chili. I'm pretty sure he took the secret of its flavor with him to the grave.

TOP O' THE WORLD

THERE IS NO OTHER GEOGRAPHICAL AREA ALONG ROUTE 66 that has managed to defy development like the Continental Divide.

Tourist establishments have been taking overblown shots at success here since the late 1920s. There has been someone at the divide offering drinking, dancing, shopping, and entertainment since the start of Route 66. Skirmishes between buyers and sellers have favored the ones who take the most risk, and if illicit dealings occasionally earned a little extra for the cash register, then that was how things worked out at this lonely spot.

The Continental Divide was first settled by a woman named Alma Gaines, who first arrived in 1925. She soon married a man named Joe Rosenburg, and they started a dance hall and service station on the north side of the railroad tracks that ran along her property. When the highway alignment changed years later, the engineers moved the road to the south side, so Alma and her second husband went over there and built a new place.

The dance hall, gas station, and everything else it was rumored to have offered was dubbed Top O' the World. As one resident later recalled, "Anything you wanted to buy, they had it for sale. And I'm not talking about souvenir ashtrays, neither."

Among roadside attractions, Top O' the World was an enigma. Those who remembered the place years later seldom agreed on what was there. Some remembered a fine dining restaurant, while others recalled hard drinking, fighting, and prostitutes. The truth may be somewhere in the middle, but more likely, everything ever rumored about the place was likely true. As the years passed, "Top O' the World" was the name given to every establishment located there, run by a myriad of owners, with a bar or a hotel or a café at the center of the thing. They operated on both sides of the law because Top O' the World was whatever people wanted it to be.

Alma's initial business, run with her husband, Crow, along Route 66 at the Continental Divide, was little more than a gas station and store. Operations expanded when Alma decided to parcel out pieces of her property, finding an early buyer in B.D. Westbrook, a Texan who'd come to find his fortune in New Mexico. His older brother ran a trading post near the Navajo reservation, and in 1935, Westbrook partnered with Claude Bowlin at the Indian Home Trading Company in Gallup. He liked the looks of the Continental Divide and decided Top O' the World was the perfect place to open a bar.

Top O' the World in the 1920s

The smartest thing that Westbrook did when he opened his business was to hire Tex Hargus, who'd been a rancher before the Depression. When times got tough, though, he discovered he was skilled as a cook. It was his cooking that earned the café at Top O' the World its first taste of fame. Gallup residents started making it a tradition to drive to Top O' the World for Sunday brunch, and tourists on Route 66 raved about the place from L.A. to Chicago.

Westbrook, meanwhile, was working to attract customers in other ways. Aware of the number of roadside zoos along the highway, he decided that Top O' the World was the perfect place for another one. However, I think that anyone would have been hard-pressed to call the mangy bears, the lone mountain lion, the grungy snakes, and the monkey named "Toughy" an actual zoo.

Nevertheless, Toughy the Monkey did gain some notoriety. Tex often made him pancakes, which the monkey would eat and then offer a salute to the cook. He also liked to sit on the bar and smoke cigarettes to the delight of customers – until he decided to flip the still smoldering butts down the front of women's dresses.

As though the atmosphere at Top O' the World wasn't circus-like enough, it took another step in that direction with the arrival of W.S. "Lee" Neal. A long-time carnival man, Lee came to the Continental Divide looking for an audience. He opened a hotel – which was used as proof that Top O' the World was becoming "a popular resort" – but Lee's connections to the carnie world always had him chasing a quick buck.

He began displaying oddities – like a mummy and a two-headed calf – and kept cages with birds in them. He'd remove the eggs from the cages, color them, and put them back, charging admission to the tourists who wanted to see the birds that laid the multi-colored eggs. He also offered three-card monte, dice games, and poker nights that almost definitely were not on the up-and-up.

One of his favorite ways of attracting customers to his various legit – and not-so-legit – operations was to send one of his employees down the highway in his car. He'd turn around and drive back toward the Continental Divide really slow. In those days, it was not easy to pass on the highway, so by the time Neal's frontman made it back to the divide, there would be a line of cars behind him. He'd turn into Neal's place, and since many people behind him had been traveling behind him for so long, they'd turn off, too. He'd lead them inside, and Neal would have a new batch of suckers to fleece.

By the late 1940s, Top O' the World was crowded with a combination of new and old, upstanding and illicit enticements. In addition to the hotel and Westbrook's Buckskin Squaw Trading Post, Nicholas Kalamaris and his wife, Frances, operated a coffee shop, and Bert Greer maintained the Great Divide Trading Post.

The first area rodeo of the 1947 season was held at Top O' the World, and the following year much was made of the new artesian well that had been drilled on the property. The well, newspapers claimed, could shoot water 50 feet into the air and was so close to the Continental Divide that some of its water flowed east and some flowed west. To locals, all this attention meant just one thing – that Top O' the World, for better

TOP OF THE WORLD
Continental Divide, New Mexico

Top O' the World earned a reputation for its illicit entertainment

or worse, was now firmly established as the greatest ongoing show in the region.

And news of the antics that went on there continued to spread. One day, Westbrook's mountain lion got out of his chicken wire cage, and he ran up to the front of the café, where there was music blaring and horns honking. Terrified, he ran into the café, grabbed Toughy the Monkey off the bar and killed him, then took a stroll between the booths where people were eating and plunked down on the floor.

Tex Hargus came out of the kitchen with a lariat, dropped it around the lion's neck, and quietly led him out the back door at the end of the rope. When they got outside, the lion hurried back to his cage – he'd been scared to death.

Tex cried when he found out that Toughy was dead and demanded that Westbrook build a real cage if he was going to keep the lion there. His boss agreed. They brought out some welders and built a real cage for the big cat.

Customers who'd been in the café that day were torn between being scared by their near-death experience and believing that the lion had been trained to make appearances at the eatery – such was the reputation of Top O' the World.

Although the reputation of the place was going to get worse in the years to come – much worse. By the 1960s, Tex Hargus, B.D. Westbrook and even Lee Neal had moved on. Top O' the World wasn't known for cigarette-smoking monkeys anymore but for hard liquor, fights, and prostitution. The rundown buildings attracted a seedier clientele and transients that stayed for weeks and months at a time. Airmen from a nearby base made Top O' the World their designated watering hole, which added to the violence and the notoriety.

Rock bottom for Top O' the World came when the restaurant couldn't make it as a steakhouse and became a topless bar instead. Things were so bad that even that failed.

The Continental Divide is a much more peaceful place today. The buildings that once housed Top O' the World have vanished, along with the ongoing party that marked the spot for so many years when Route 66 was still passing by a few feet from its front doors.

NAVAJO LODGE

IN 1936, MERLE AND DAISEY MUNCY HAD DECIDED THEY'D had enough of cold Canadian winters, and at the urging of Merle's brother, Van, they packed up and moved south to New Mexico. They settled on some land just east of Gallup in a town called Coolidge, which had been named for the former president.

It was there where they built Navajo Lodge – a store, service station, bar, and restaurant that resembled a Spanish hacienda. A year or so after they started, Noble and Hazel Rogers opened a trading post next door, and the two couples worked together to draw business to their section of the road. On Saturday nights, they hosted dances, and the chicken dinners at Navajo Lodge became the stuff of legend. They began advertising the fried chicken on billboards as far away as Albuquerque.

When World War II broke out, the economy took a turn for the worse, and business at Navajo Lodge followed suit. Merle was forced to take a job at Fort Wingate, and the business closed.

Toward the end of the war, the Muncys sold Navajo Lodge to a Chicago couple, Alexander and Melvina Lavasek. They focused on expanding souvenir sales at the shop and building on the reputation of the restaurant. Melvina – or "Grandma Lavasek" as she was known to family and friends – became locally famous for her pound cake and custard pies.

As roadside businesses began springing up along Route 66 around this time, everyone was looking for the right gimmick to appeal to tourists. Al Lavasek decided to purchase two bears – Tillie and Millie – which were kept chained to a tree. They were trained to drink bottles of soda that were given to them by paying customers.

Al and Melvina retired to Albuquerque in the 1960s, and traffic at the Navajo Lodge dropped off, but it dropped off to nothing after the interstate came through. Even so, it managed to survive. In recent years, Roberta and Sherwood Stauder re-opened it as a bed and breakfast.

In case you wondered – after Al and Melvina retired, the bears, Tillie and Millie, were shipped off to the Navajo Zoo at Window Rock. They went to visit them one Sunday, and the bears recognized them. In fact, they got so excited that Al had to go and get them a Coke before they would settle down.

GREETINGS FROM The INDIAN CAPITAL GALLUP NEW MEXICO

LAST STOP: GALLUP

IN 1880, ATLANTIC & PACIFIC RAILROAD OFFICIAL DAVID L. Gallup established an office and pay station to prepare for the arrival of the rail line, which didn't make it to the area for another year. Once it did, the small settlement that sprang up there was named in Gallup's honor. The railroad named the town as a division terminal in 1895, and for the next 40 years, railroads, lumber, and coal mines dominated the local economy.

Gallup's proximity to the Navajo, Zuni, and Hopi reservations made it a significant trading post for Native American crafts and goods in the early 1900s. This connection to Native American culture has been a defining characteristic of the city, earning it the nickname "Indian Capital of the World."

The arrival of Route 66 caused tremendous growth in Gallup, and from the 1930s through the 1960s, it expanded in all directions. Legions of motorists passed through daily and spent their tourist money in local stores, eateries, and neon-lite motels like Bruce Spruce Lodge, Zia Motel, Thunderbird Motel, and other spots.

Many local Route 66 icons still stand today, welcoming travelers trying to recapture the magic of the highway's glory days.

ARROWHEAD & LOG CABIN LODGES

THE MOTELS, MOTOR LODGES, AND TOURIST CAMPS IN Gallup developed at different times and at different places in town. The west side motels were built in the 1950s and beyond and were built only on the south side of Route 66 since the Santa Fe Railroad yard and tracks on the opposite side of the room left no room for development.

Motels on the east side of town, though, started to spring up in 1946 after the railroad made some land available for construction sites within city limits. These locations, located on a narrow strip of land between Route 66 and the railroad tracks, attracted dozens of investors hoping to cash in on the post-World War II tourism boom. Soon, the night sky above Gallup was glowing with the light of neon signs.

Log Cabin Lodge
West "Y"   Highway 66
GALLUP, NEW MEXICO

TONY AND FRANCIS LEONE OPENED THE LOG CABIN LODGE in Gallup in 1937. It was meant to evoke a feeling of frontier life, consisting of six log cabins and a single-story office. Both the cabins and the lobby were decorated with taxidermy animals and Navajo rugs and decorations.

A fireplace in each cabin provided ambiance and heat for cold desert nights. Each cabin initially had its own kitchenette, too. However, once the owners realized how much longer it was taking to clean up after a guest's overnight stay, additional beds replaced the appliances, making more room for guests.

During the 1940s and 1950s, the Log Cabin Lodge was part of the Best Western chain, and two double log cabins were added, as well as a new wing built in adobe style with side-by-side rooms and attached garages.

Tony and Francis retired in 1959 and sold the motel, but the new owner was unable to keep up with the payments, so the property was reverted back to them. Multiple owners followed, but time took its toll on the place. Little maintenance occurred, and repairs were non-existent. If something broke in a room, the room was closed because no one wanted to waste money fixing anything. Eventually, the Log Cabin Lodge – despite being added to the National Register of Historic Places in 1993 – fell into a state of disrepair.

Not long after it was listed on the register, the lodge served its last guest and began its slide toward an inevitable end. Home to transients, drug dealers, prostitutes, and worse, the motel was beyond restoration. Deemed an eyesore by the city of Gallup, one of the most distinctive motels on Route 66 was torn down on May 14, 2004.

Nothing remains of it today.

THE ARROWHEAD LODGE WAS ONE OF THE NEWLY BUILT motels on the east side of town, and it was advertised as "ultra-modern." It opened in 1948 and boasted "unsurpassed comfort in large roomy accommodations, featuring Serta Springs and Mattresses and carpeted floors." The ads also touted "tiled combination tub and

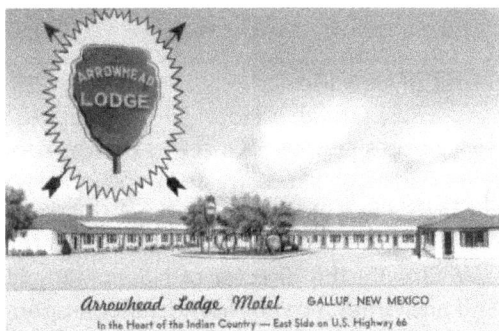

Arrowhead Lodge Motel   GALLUP, NEW MEXICO
In the Heart of the Indian Country — East Side on U.S. Highway 66

shower baths, air conditioning, and individual panel ray heat."

The 25-unit motel was designed in a U-shape with a small, landscaped courtyard in the middle, which eventually became a children's playground. The office is on the east side of the building, steps away from Route 66.

For some unknown reason, the owners replaced the original arrowhead-shaped neon sign with a more modern-looking one. While I prefer the original, even the replacement has a cool retro look to it today.

Arrowhead Lodge became a popular place for both traveling businessmen and tourists to stay. Thanks to its proximity to the El Rancho Hotel (coming up next), folks on a budget could stay at the Arrowhead and still take advantage of the El Rancho's fine restaurants and bar – something that was a key to the Arrowhead's long success.

As of a few years ago, the Arrowhead Lodge was still in operation as a roadside motel, but it had definitely seen better days. So, unless you're really a diehard nostalgia buff, it's safe to give this one a pass.

HOTEL EL RANCHO

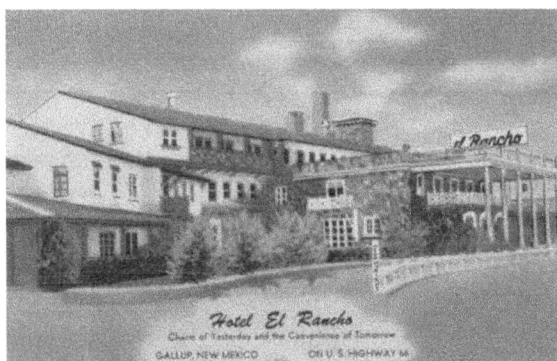

Hotel El Rancho
Charm of Yesterday and the Convenience of Tomorrow
GALLUP, NEW MEXICO   ON U.S. HIGHWAY 66

UNLIKE THE MOTOR LODGES THAT SPRANG UP IN GALLUP to profit from the arrival of Route 66, the El Rancho is something special. This place transcends highway nostalgia and offers more history than most people expect to find in this corner of New Mexico.

R.E. Griffith's Hotel El Rancho was built in 1937 as a haven for Hollywood's famous. "Griff," as he was known, had come to Gallup a few years earlier to film a western and quickly fell in love with the area. He returned a few years later to open the hotel – and turn it into a movie set and a desert escape for actors and directors, like his well-known brother, D.W. Griffith, the director of classic early films such as *Birth of a Nation*. Griff and other director friends encouraged using El Rancho as a base for crews and stars on location because of its access to Western landscapes and the rustic elegance of the hotel. From the 1940s through the 1960s, the Gallup area became a popular film location. It became the backdrop of dozens of Hollywood productions like *Billy the Kid, The Sea of Grass, Ace in the Hole, Escape from Fort Bravo, The Grapes of Wrath, Streets of Laredo, Fort Defiance*, and literally dozens of others.

El Rancho in the 1940s offered elegance in the desert with superior service and food, comfortable rooms, a beauty parlor, a barber shop, a coffee shop, and gaming tables and liquid refreshments in the tradition of the Old West.

Stars arrived in Gallup in the insulated atmosphere of Sante Fe Railway trains. But soon, they learned about the frontier during a journey to the El Rancho by wagon, carriage, or buggy that met every Santa Fe passenger train. If the train wasn't suitable for a star, they arrived from Hollywood in a chauffeur-driven limousine on Route 66.

Inside the El Rancho... the home to Hollywood stars in Gallup

Among the famous guests at the El Rancho were Alan Ladd, Betty Grable, Burt Lancaster, Dana Andrews, Doris Day, Errol Flynn, Fred MacMurray, Gene Autry, Gregory Peck, Humphrey Bogart, James Cagney, Jean Harlow, John Wayne, Katherine Hepburn, Kirk Douglas, Lee Marvin, Lucille Ball, Rita Hayworth, Robert Mitchum, Spencer Tracy, Tom Mix, Troy Donahue, and dozens more. It became *the* place to stay in the Southwest, and autographed photos of the stars lined the walls of the second-floor balcony that overlooked the magnificent main lobby.

Although Gallup locals were just as in awe of the Hollywood actors as the rest of the country, contact with them in a hometown setting created a more natural relationship. The locals worked as stand-ins, extras, location employees, delivery boys, guides, stock suppliers, and interpreters. Retailers sold everything from toothpaste to Indian jewelry, as well as, of course, proper cowboy hats. Gallup and the El Rancho became a working holiday away from the Hollywood photographers and gossip rags.

Rumors spread wildly in Gallup, but the stories never went any further than the city limits. Stories were often told about the quantity of

alcohol that flowed night and day when some actors were residents of the hotel. According to El Rancho night employees, Errol Flynn worked all day and drank all night. John Wayne usually headed straight for Monument Valley, so the only rumors about his actions circulated on the reservation in the Navajo language.

Gallup local Howard Wilson could have translated those stories, but he didn't. Howard and another man, Bert Cresto, were indispensable when it came to attracting Hollywood studios to Gallup and the El Rancho. Not only did they provide general transportation, extras, location and housing arrangements, and interpret the Navajo language, they also provided equipment, advice, and filled in as actors on occasion.

When Leone Rollie, the stand-in for Marilyn Maxwell in the Western *New Mexico* in 1950, was assigned to ride a stagecoach in a chase scene along the base of the red rocks, Bert Cresto offered to ride with her. The hair-raising ride at breakneck speed, with Navajos in pursuit, can be seen in the film, and the stagecoach careening along the edge of the Rio Puerco is seen today as a classic western pursuit. With Bert's help, it was shot in just one take.

El Rancho was linked to Hollywood and the movie industry through the mid-1960s. By then, brilliant technicolor vistas were replacing the stark, dramatic images in black and white, and the mystery of the west – along with Route 66 – was about to be replaced by a more modern, faster-moving world. Hollywood lost interest in Westerns for a while, but as it turned out, the Western – like the El Rancho – refuses to die.

During the 1960s and 1970s, the hotel changed hands several times, and the lack of steady ownership led to its decline. The interstate bypass sounded the death knell for the El Rancho, and it closed in 1987.

But this wasn't the end. In 1988, Armond Ortega, who had admired the hotel as a boy, bought the El Rancho and began a mission to restore it to its former glory. He went to work tracing the location of many of the hotel's original furnishings, and he successfully recreated what he couldn't find. He brought back the classic ambiance of the yesterday.

The El Rancho operates today and is a modern throwback to the days when it was the western home and playground to scores of moviemakers. Don't miss this place when you make your next trip to Gallup.

LOOKOUT POINT TRADING POST

IT TURNS OUT THAT THE EL RANCHO IS NOT THE ONLY Gallup location with a connection to Hollywood. After R.E. Griffith made the area popular for Westerns, location scouts started showing up in town with remarkable frequency. Driving out of town to check the light at high noon and framing mountains and mesas between outstretched

thumbs, the advance men for the Hollywood directors came back to Gallup again and again.

So, it wasn't much of a surprise in early 1950 when a car carrying scouts from Paramount Pictures rolled around the face of Devil's Cliff west of Gallup, passed by two Gulf Oil gas pumps, and stopped in the parking lot of the Lookout Point Trading Post. They'd found the perfect spot on the rocks behind the trading post and wanted to lease the trading post and build a cliff dwelling on the rocks. It was there, they explained, where they planned to film a movie called *Ace in the Hole*.

Lookout Point was located outside Gallup and roughly three miles west of Manuelito. It had once been owned by a Zuni family, but by the late 1940s, it was being operated by Wane Russell, his mother, Alma Sue, and her current husband, Dan. But after Dan hit the highway one night and never came back, a neighbor named Leroy Atkinson bought the place and kept Wayne and Sue as employees.

As Wayne Russell admitted many years later, the trading post was "simply a tourist stop." It was a small place, built from two-by-fours covered with plywood and adobe. Inside, there was a modest selection of souvenirs and Indian jewelry for tourists. There was an upstairs living area and a corner downstairs that was stocked with canned goods that local Navajo shopped. A small restaurant fed motorists and had a daily special of whatever the cook felt like making that day. Wayne recalled that most were fond of the chiliburger.

Paramount Pictures liked the atmosphere of the place and paid Leroy to close the trading post to the public while filming was taking place.

The arrival of the film crews brought attention to the trading post, which had already received some unwanted attention the previous year during what locals dubbed "The Big Buffalo Hunt."

The incident began when the Atkinson kids from the nearby Box Canyon Trading Post inadvertently aggravated the buffalo that were there on display. Two of the boys were walking past the buffalo pen while wearing spurs, and the sound they made apparently upset the two animals. One of them charged at the gate and smashed it open, and both escaped.

The buffalo round-up that followed took several days. Alma Sue, who had a reputation as a skilled horsewoman, saddled up and joined the Navajo who were chasing the two beasts. Sue and the others ultimately cornered the animals in Box Canyon. They built fires to contain them, but the next morning, the buffalo broke free. The hunt ended tragically with the deaths of both animals, but even so, just for a few days, the West was wild again at Lookout Point.

Paramount's story for *Ace in the Hole* had nothing to do with buffalo. Inspired by the 1925 entrapment of a man named Floyd Collins in a cave in Kentucky, the film featured Kirk Douglas as a failing newspaper reporter trying to turn the story of a man trapped underground into big news. Richard Benedict played the doomed Indian trader, and Lookout Point Trading Post was his store. An entire carnival – complete with a towering Ferris wheel – was trucked in from California, and Hollywood set builders created the phony cliff dwelling into the post's backyard bluff.

Before and during the filming, Gallup was chaotic. While casting director William Poole worked out the filming schedule at the El Rancho, the McKinley County Courthouse became a casting office. School Superintendent Charles Owens weeded through birth and baptismal certificates, trying to decide which local children were qualified to receive work permits. A call for extras appeared in the newspaper because so many were needed for the crowd scenes. Extras were paid 75 cents an hour for a 10-hour day, but they could receive an additional $3 if they brought an automobile to the set.

Shooting began on July 14 and was just as strange as Gallup locals assumed it would be. On one occasion, a Navajo woman was scolded for improperly handling her own sheep. First Assistant Director C.C. Coleman barked orders over a loudspeaker while director Billy Wilder entertained reporters under a massive beach umbrella. Kirk Douglas and co-star Jan Sterling visited the Zuni Pueblo with a photographer to spread a little Hollywood goodwill.

Since the trading post was closed, Wayne Russell ran his concession stand during the filming. He shipped in ice, soda pop, and ice cream, selling the refreshments to the crew and extras. He made enough money from concessions during the filming to be able to buy his first car. He even ended up onscreen at one point, making the rounds on the Ferris wheel.

After filming was finished, Paramount left Lookout Point with its fabricated cliff dwelling. The post then became a showplace for Rex Bollin, Leroy Atkinson's brother-in-law. Rex had been operating a museum at the Box Canyon Trading Post, but after the film was completed, he hired Navajo to lay a flagstone floor for a new and bigger museum next to the cliff dwelling movie set, knowing it would draw a tourist crowd.

Leroy called the revamped trading post El-Morro, and it was advertised as a place to see the "Authentic Replica Cliff Dwelling built at a cost of $30,000 by Paramount Pictures." He also started offering Indian dances that were staged every half-hour.

But this new enterprise didn't last long. He sold the store in 1953, and the new owners decided to call it the Cliff Dwelling Trading Post. It closed a decade later in 1963.

Today, visitors to Lookout Point will find very little of the trading post or the cliff dwelling. A few photos remain from the production at the El Rancho Hotel, showing both Kirk Douglas and the cliff dwelling, taken at a time when Gallup was still Hollywood's go-to spot for a western.

BOX CANYON TRADING POST

ROUTE 66 HAS ONE MORE STORY TO TELL BEFORE WE LEAVE New Mexico, and it's the story of a man who understood the tourist business – and the story of a man who let no one push him around.

"This is still America, not Russia."

Leroy Atkinson said that in 1953 while facing down the State Highway Commission about the Box Canyon Trading Post. Leroy believed in America – and the American dream. He'd had the dream, and he'd lived it.

When Hollywood first came down Route 66 to turn John Steinbeck's great American novel, *The Grapes of Wrath*, into John Ford's great American film, he'd done what any great American would do. He allowed them to film at the Three Hogans Trading Post, and he'd even furnished some of his sheep as extras.

Leroy's love for America was intertwined with his love for his family, especially his wife, Wilmerine. Although the pair met and fell in love in a small town in Texas, Wilmerine was related to Gallup Indian trader Tobe A. Turpen. When the Depression worsened and her parents decided to follow Tobe west, Wilmerine refused to go without Leroy. They married in Gallup and found jobs managing the Three Hogans Trading Post near Allentown, Arizona.

Once he was secure, Leroy turned his attention to the well-being of the rest of his family, first bringing his younger brother, Jake, then youngest brother, Herman, to work at the Three Hogans. In time, Leroy helped both brothers build their own highway stores, but he did it first when he built Box Canyon Trading Post between Gallup and the Arizona border.

The store would always be remembered by travelers not only as the last stop out of New Mexico – or the first, depending on what direction you were coming from – but also as one of the most impressive trading posts on Route 66.

It opened in 1943, and Leroy built the place from army ammunition boxes that he covered with stucco and painted a pristine white. He installed three gas pumps for the Chevron Oil Company and later added a fourth. Gas was cheaper in New Mexico than in Arizona, and it became the drawing card for a spot that was just one mile east of the border.

With success came improvements, like the restaurant that was added to Box Canyon's east end that could seat and feed 40 people at a time. On the west side of the store, a modest motel was added. The Atkinson family itself lived in a complex of hogans that were adjacent to the trading post. The four Navajo dwellings served as bedrooms, a center living room, and a kitchen.

Leroy's years at the Three Hogans had left him fluent in the Navajo language. Native friends called him *Hosteen clah nez* – Navajo for "big left hand." During the war years, when a shortage of traditional jewelry pushed Indian crafts to a premium, Navajo silversmiths worked at Box Canyon, tinkering in a long room on the store's north side. When demand went down after World War, the room mostly stayed empty, although the actors and film crew from the movie *Ambush* used it as a lunchroom in the late 1940s.

Leroy came to understand the need for oddities to entice the tourists into his store. To the east of Box Canyon, he placed two large figures of cavemen. Motors installed inside them caused them to raise and lower their clubs to the delight of tourists, who steered their cars into his parking lot. Corrals were built east of the store that contained two buffalo – the ones that later escaped and were the source of the "Big Buffalo Hunt" incident.

As the success of Box Canyon Trading Post grew, Leroy took the time to help his brothers with their stores, and he also employed Wilmerine's brother, Rex Bollin. Rex managed to purchase the stuffed corpses of a steer and a bucking bronco and installed them outside the store. When tourists sat in the saddles that had been placed on them, Rex snapped photos, developed them instantly, and charged the folks just $1 for an authentic souvenir of the Wild West.

Later, Rex started a museum at the trading post where he displayed Anasazi pottery, antique guns, and old Navajo rugs. But he was really looking for something bigger. A trading post in nearby Manuelito had done well exhibiting an exhumed mummy, so Rex wanted a mummy of his own. Eventually, he and Wayne Russell – the young man who worked for Leroy at the Lookout Point Trading Post – found one and brought it back to the museum. We likely don't want to know where it came from.

By 1951, Box Canyon Trading Post had almost become a destination in itself. Buses dropped off tourists at the front door of the store each day, while local Navajo used Box Canyon as a hub to travel into Gallup. Sales were brisk at the store, meals were flying out of the kitchen of the café, and night after night passed without any vacancies at the motel.

But in 1952, Leroy Atkinson and the Box Canyon Trading Post found themselves at the center of a controversy. Portions of Route 66 in the county were scheduled for straightening and widening. However, the State Highway Commission had cited Box Canyon Trading Post as the reason for withholding money for the project. They stated that Leroy's restaurant, gas pumps, and most of the souvenir store encroached on the road's right-of-way. Leroy was ordered to remove these problems so that work could begin.

Leroy said no. And he continued to say no, regardless of who asked him and how threatening they became with him. He dug in his heels – no one was telling him how to run his business or what he was going to do with his property.

The legal battle raged back and forth for over a year. In January 1953, Sheriff Kelsey Presley came to the trading post and sat down to coffee with workers from Cresto Plumbing, who were there on orders from Standard Oil Company to remove the store's gas pumps. When the business emptied of customers, Sheriff Kelsey padlocked the doors.

When he left, Leroy got his tools, removed the locks, and opened them back up again.

One week later, Emmett B. Wall – chairman of McKinley County's county commissioners – gave the County Road Superintendent permission to proceed with demolishing the trading post with bulldozers. Realizing the battle was lost, Leroy spoke to the newspapers. He spoke emphatically for himself and for others who had been in his same situation – "This is still America, not Russia."

Leroy and Wilmerine sold what was left of Box Canyon to Bud Wilson of the Minnetonka Moccasin Company, and they moved to Tucson, Arizona, where they started over again in the tourist business and made a name for themselves all over again.

It turns out that part of living the American dream is knowing when the fight is over, getting back on your feet, and starting over again.

ARIZONA
US
66

ARIZONA
The Grand Canyon State

GREETINGS from ARIZONA
THE GRAND CANYON STATE

ROUTE 66 CAME TO ARIZONA IN 1926, SPANNING JUST OVER 400 miles and taking the place of the Santa Fe Railroad when it came to bringing travelers to the region. The highway started in Lupton (sort of) in the east and ran to Topock in the west, following ancient trade trails and routes used by the California gold miners across the empty desert.

Very little of Route 66 in Arizona was paved before 1933, when the state received federal funds to upgrade the surface. Even then, the Arizona stretch of the road was always wild, with hairpin turns and some of the steepest hills along the entire highway, sometimes soaring to elevations of 3,500 feet above sea level.

Route 66 across Arizona was always one of the most picturesque sections, passing through many kinds of fantastic scenery, including green pine forests, volcanoes, the Petrified Forest, meteor craters, snow-covered mountains, Navajo reservations, the Painted Desert, and even side trips to the Grand Canyon.

Arizona also had some of the most extreme weather conditions along the route, from winter snows to blazing summer heat. The scarcity of water along the highway meant that travelers usually had to carry water containers with them – for their cars and themselves.

Route 66 turned Arizona into a major tourist attraction, as thousands of Americans kept looking west for the romance of the cowboys and the mystique of the Native Americans. The explosive increase in traffic on Route 66 after World War II kept Arizona's towns buzzing with activity – and even today, the nostalgia of the road has kept many of those towns alive.

The Arizona stretch of the highway was ultimately bypassed by the interstate, with Williams, Arizona, as the very last town on Route 66 to be bypassed. The highway was finally decommissioned in 1985.

BETWEEN THE BORDER AND THE PAINTED DESERT

ROUTE 66 MAKES A DRAMATIC ENTRANCE INTO ARIZONA from New Mexico, even though the highway is truncated and chopped into pieces by the interstate from a point just east of the state line all the way to Seligman.

At the border, towering stone walls on the north and south transform the broad valley into a grand entryway, and the roadside is peppered with the ruins of tourist traps, trading posts, and a few lonely spots where services have been offered to travelers for decades.

The towns between the state line and Holbrook had never really amounted to much more than a store of a trading post, a service station or two, and maybe a garage, so the bypass of Route 66 wiped out all of them. The trading posts, cafes, and service stations – except for a lucky few that were near an interstate exit – fared even worse.

Along this stretch of road, Route 66 could be as deadly as it was scenic. It was unpaved for years, crossed narrow, antiquated bridges, and was filled with steep hills, sharp curves, and abrupt drops. And, of course, there was the weather. If it wasn't blowing snow, then it was blowing sand

that was causing near-zero visibility on some parts of the open road.

Horrendous multicar accidents were commonplace, as were fatalities when cars left the roadway or were caught in torrential summer rains that turned dry arroyos into raging rivers within minutes.

Just one example of a tragedy that haunted eastern Arizona occurred in January 1962. Eugene Wildenstein and his family were returning to El Centro, California, following a family Christmas holiday in Las Vegas, New Mexico, when an eastbound truck crossed the center line and crashed into their car. A contributing factor to the wreck – which killed six of the seven family members – was the narrow roadway they were on, which had no shoulder.

Death came calling far too often on this stretch of road.

JUST ACROSS THE BORDER WAS THE APTLY-NAMED **STATE Line Station**, which was on property owned by Harry "Indian" Miller and his second wife, Margaret.

In April 1933, the Millers leased a 100-by-200-foot section of land along Route 66 to Carmen Ferrari of Gallup. They allowed him to rent the land with the agreement that he would open an establishment that served food and drink to complement the Millers' tourist business at the Cave of the Seven Devils (back to that soon).

By the early 1940s, Jake and Leroy Atkinson had established a roadside trading post at the site and it was touted as the last stop out of Arizona, or the first, depending on which way you were traveling.

THE **INDIAN TRAILS TRADING POST** WAS A LITTLE CLOSER TO the dusty town of Lupton, and it was opened in June

1946 by Max and Amelia Ortega. Their son, Armand, went on to become one of the world's largest dealers in handcrafted Indian jewelry.

Indian Trails primarily served local Navajo, who often arrived by wagon to stay the night.

THE **THREE HOGANS TRADING POST** WAS OWNED BY Gallup trader Jack Hill and sat on Route 66 in the tiny community of Allentown. In the 1930s, Jack sent his apprentice, Leroy Atkinson, to manage the store for him.

In those days, most of the stores in the area used "trade money." They minted coins that looked like nickels, dimes, and quarters, as well as $1, $5, $10, and $20 pieces. When Navajo came to barter for goods, they'd get trade money in exchange for whatever they brought. They used it to buy groceries, gasoline, or whatever they needed. Traders typically accepted each other's trade money. Leroy's brother, Herman, remembered that they received a lot of trade money from Mike Kirk's Trading Post in Manuelito, and when they built up a stash of it, Leroy would take it and trade it back to Mike, and vice versa.

THE **WHITE MOUND TRADING POST** WAS THE SUCCESSOR TO the old Houck Trading Post, built by James D. Houck – a mail carrier between Prescott, Arizona, and Fort Wingate, New Mexico – in 1877. White Mound was planned specifically to take advantage of the new highway that was coming through the village of Houck in 1926. It was established by Joe Grubbs and has since disappeared, just like the other tourist stops on this stretch of the road.

QUERINO CANYON TRADING POST SAT ON ROUTE 66 NEAR the edge of Querino Canyon and was once operated by A.C. "Chappy" White. In 1945, he sold it to Claude and Clara Lee, who came into the roadside trading post business more prepared than most. As a husband-and-wife team, they had run trading posts at Hunters Point and Burnt Water, Arizona. Clara had been born in Zuni, New Mexico, and enjoyed a natural rapport with their Navajo customers.

A few years after settling into Querino Canyon, Claude and Clara decided to expand. They bought the nearby Big Arrow Trading Post from carnival showman "Slim" Brazier and sent their daughter, Arlene, and son-in-law, Jay Crone, to operate it.

In the 1950s, the section of Route 66 that looped through Querino was abandoned for a newer and straighter alignment between Lupton and Holbrook. The new route abandoned Querino and Big Arrow. The Lees adjusted by closing Querino and building a larger Big Arrow along the new highway. The family continued to run the post until the late 1960s.

Claude and Clara's son, C. Arthur Lee, once told a story about his mother and their store: "Querino Canyon Trading Post was once robbed at gunpoint. The two thieves herded our family into Querino's wareroom. They escaped to Concho, Arizona, before they were finally caught. After they were sentenced, my mother started referring to them as 'two wayward boys.' She brought them candy and cigarettes in jail, and she'd tell them, 'You boys come and see us after you get out but leave your damn guns at home.'"

CAVE OF THE SEVEN DEVILS

SITTING ALMOST DIRECTLY ON THE INVISIBLE LINE THAT separates New Mexico from Arizona is the Cave of Seven Devils, a spot that Harry "Indian" Miller believed was inhabited by ghosts.

He found the cave to be a place of unearthly inspiration – not only for his personal search for the Seven Lost Cities of Cibola but for the future of all mankind. In the cave's wide mouth, Harry experienced visions – specters that gave meaning to his own life and perhaps even foretold the end of the world.

Harry was an "interesting" character. He was a full-time showman, an accused rogue, an aspiring artist, and a would-be archaeologist. At the time of his death in 1951, he considered himself a bona fide prophet. In his final years, he wore a thick, white beard that hung down over his chest and tended to wrap his words in religious metaphors, so it was hard to see what

HAUNTED

SEVEN DEVILS CLIFF DWELLINGS
NEW MEXICO NEAR LUPTON, ARIZONA

his early life had been like. It was all there, though – from his spiritual awakening among Malayan headhunters to a gunshot that put his rival in the grave – shaping a man who remains a mystery even today.

Harry was born near Roswell, New Mexico, in February 1879. He was the eighth child in a family of 10. When he was only five years old, he wandered away from home and became lost for days in the desert. He later wrote: "When I was finally captured, I had gone wild. I fought my captor viciously." Harry blamed the incident for an affliction that returned to plague him as an adult – incessantly walking and talking in his sleep.

Harry grew up in Eugene, Oregon, where his father, William, died of tuberculosis. His mother, Sara Ann, passed away from cancer. After all that suffering, he looked at his life and decided his existence would be served best by becoming an artist.

He was pursuing this goal in May 1898 when he answered President McKinley's call to fight in the Spanish-American War. Harry joined the Second Oregon U.S. Volunteer Infantry from Portland. Six months later, he found himself fighting in the Philippines. The countryside around where Harry was stationed was teeming with headhunters, and Harry slept each night in a lighted guard house to prevent himself from sleepwalking, unarmed, into the jungle. Although Harry excelled as a soldier – his military records were filled with medals and commendations – there were also weeks lost in the local hospital, injuries suffered in the line of duty, and bloody acts of violence that would haunt his dreams for years to come.

With chaos all around him, Harry withdrew from his friends and comrades, spending most of his time in the company of his dog, writing letters and sketching. By the time Harry was made a constabulary officer and assigned to service in Northern Luzon, he had started to question the western world's definitions of "savage" and "civilized."

Harry "Indian" Miller

Finally, he resigned from the service, took his dog, and went to live in the village of Pingad, where he befriended members of the local indigenous tribes. He formed an especially close bond with an elder named Olowan, or the "Old One." Olowan had two-and-a-half lines of X's tattooed on his face, each representing the head of an enemy that had been taken. The modern world would consider him a "savage," but in the old man, Harry found respect and honor and a man at peace.

Harry moved into a small grass and wood hut on the edge of the village, and each night – to curb his sleepwalking – he tied a rope to his ankle and secured the other end of the rope to a bar under the floor.

But one night, even though he had tied himself securely to the bar, Harry was surprised to awaken standing in some thick woods on the side of a mountain. He would later claim that he stood there for nearly an hour, too confused to move. Slowly, though, he began to realize that he was there, but his physical body wasn't with him. He had made the journey as his spirit alone. His physical body was still lying in his hut.

Whatever happened that night, Harry never walked in his sleep again. Several years later, he left the Philippines and returned to America with a wife named Ena, with whom he had four children – Kentis, May, Bender, and Lulu. Ena rarely wore shoes, smoked a pipe, and dressed in her native clothing. Her people kept their family and tribal history tattooed on their arms. That way, if an enemy ever took their head, they could still be identified.

Harry and Ena realized that Americans paid well to see people from other cultures, and with this in mind, the couple developed a small sideshow to tour the United States. Harry imported several of his Filipino friends to appear in the show. Onstage, they dressed in traditional clothing and exhibited their "savage" customs. Among the show's headliners was old Olowan, always amused by the shocked looks on the faces of his audience.

Life back in America held other adventures for Harry, including a foray into the Hollywood world of silent films. He acted alongside cowboy star William S. Hart and many Native American actors. One of them was Chief Joe Sekakuku, a member of the Hopi tribe, and the two of them became close friends.

By the late 1910s, Harry, his family, and his performers were in Pirtleville, Arkansas, working at a smelter during the off-season. One day, Olowan went after a man who stole from him with his hunting knife. The incident ended without bloodshed, but Harry started to wonder about the longevity of his sideshow. The show did continue – managed later by his daughter, Lulu – but Harry began to spend more and more time away from the stage. He started spending a lot of that time at the Walnut Canyon Cliff Dwellings, east of Flagstaff, Arizona.

Archaeologist Harold S. Colton later described how he found Harry at Walnut Canyon in the early 1920s, living in a shelter made from the brush behind the old log ranger station. At the time, the National Old Trails Highway passed in front of the station. Harry displayed his drawings in his Indian museum, which also included cliff-dweller skulls, clay jars dug from area graves, and other relics.

During this time, Harry also dabbled in the self-publishing business. *The Moccasin* was billed as "a monthly magazine edited by Indian Miller" with articles attributed to "Indian Miller" or "Crazy Thunder" – nicknames that dated back to Harry's show business days. He printed the magazine through the Flagstaff newspaper and sold copies for 25 cents. Paying customers were assured the editor and authors were full-blown Apache. Although Harry's ancestry was Dutch and Scottish, he always wore Western-style clothing, and his hair was long and braided in Plains Indian style.

Through *The Moccasin*, Harry found an outlet for his artwork, his budding interest in archaeology, and his growing urge to criticize the "civilized" world. The first issue in August 1923 harmlessly dissected the myth of the "Munchies," a white indigenous people that folklore claimed lived in a secret mountain valley. But the second issue, which didn't come out until May 1924, went after the Southwest's first Spanish explorers, calling them "murderers" and describing how they had forced Native Americans into "slavery in its ugliest form." He also wrote about the

Seven Lost Cities of Cibola for the first time, never imagining how that subject was going to come back to haunt him later in life.

Harry remained at Walnut Canyon for several years. In early 1925, he left and ended up at another roadside home at Canyon Lodge – 38 miles east of Flagstaff – and at a point when the National Old Trails Highway bridged Canyon Diablo. He came there with plans to enlarge his tourist zoo and called the new place "Fort Two Guns" as a nod to the 1914 William S. Hart silent western *Two-Gun Hicks*.

In the mouth of a cave in Canyon Diablo, Hartry built a village of fabricated cliff dwellings. Chief Joe Sekakuku signed on to operate a souvenir store and perform Hopi dances for tourists, for Two Guns seemed destined for success.

Well, until the murder.

On March 3, 1926, Harry shot and killed his Canyon Lodge landlord and business associate, Earl Cundiff. Harry was cleared of any wrongdoing by the authorities – there was evidence that Earl had shot at Harry first – but the dead man had many friends in nearby Winslow, and they all had opinions about whether Harry had broken the law or not – he had, they agreed.

Unfortunately for Harry, the local sentiment that was attached to him in the wake of the shooting may have served to aggravate the traumas he'd brought home from the war, and he began to believe that people were plotting against him, trying to ruin his business. As he became more and more paranoid, he finally decided to leave Canyon Diablo and look for a new home. He soon found one, about 28 miles east of Holbrook, where his nephew, Paul Jacobs, had built a service and highway trading post.

Desert View Station sat on Route 66 along the rim of the Painted Desert. The small complex included a tower that travelers could climb to get a view of the sea of colored sand that surrounded them. Harry soon moved his animal menagerie from Fort Two Guns to the Painted Desert.

After getting settled, Harry bought highway frontage east of Lupton that included enough land he would be able to section off parcels to be sold or leased at a profit.

On the property was a shallow cave that straddled the Arizona-New Mexico line, and Harry decided to make it his permanent home. At the entrance, he went to work building another roadside zoo.

Harry was hard at work on July 21, 1931, but was also apparently distracted because when he entered the cage of his pet bobcat, Tony, the

cat attacked him, ripping apart his right hand, wrist, and arm before Harry could fight it off. Blood poisoning set it and nearly killed him.

Delirious and near death, Harry suffered at Desert View Station in a sweltering room for a week. Four doctors cared for him, applying ice packs and poultices since antibiotics didn't yet exist. They stopped the infection but could do nothing about Harry's spirit.

Within months of this latest near-death experience, Harry experienced the first of his life-changing visions one night inside of his cave. He believed that he'd been spiritually guided to the cave in 1930, where he was greeting tourists within three months of the attack. The zoo that he completed at the cave was his best one yet. Arranged in an L-shape, it featured a duck pond that was fed by a natural spring.

As he'd done at Canyon Lodge, Harry built fabricated cliff dwellings at the cave's entrance. To most people, the fake ruins looked like just another bit of Harry Miller showmanship – a gimmick to pull tourists off the road. But to others, the design of the ruins hinted at something darker. The cliff dwellings had been constructed with peepholes in the outer walls – peepholes that Harry often peered through to make sure that no one was coming for him. As a local named Frank Yellowhorse said, "Maybe you'd say he'd gone paranoid, but a lot of people were after his hide."

The difficulty with understanding what was happening to Harry at this time comes from the fact that he seemed to be so successful in his professional life. Harry painted an enormous portrait of a Navajo chief on a natural rock projection on the exterior of the cave. It could be seen from a distance, and it attracted tourists who were thrilled to stop and take pictures of it. The roadside zoo had expanded, and many considered it the best in the Southwest. It boasted a horned owl, coyotes, Arizona quail, wolves, porcupines, bobcats, foxes, and four lions. One pair of lions – called Big Sugar and Little Sugar – were so tame that Harry often went into their cage and played with them, much to the delight of the tourists.

But more and more – after the tourists were finished for the day and night had fallen on the desert – Harry wrestled with his twin demons: religion and his trauma from the war. They haunted his sleep, and one night, Harry dreamed they came to him as seven supernatural creatures – the seven devils that gave his cave its name.

Harry had been toying with mysticism since his days in the Philippines, but in the Cave of Seven Devils, he came to believe that his past was a form of spiritual training. His vision of the seven devils confirmed this belief, and for the rest of his life, Harry regarded the cave as a magical place that guided the direction of his life.

Harry slowly began to retreat from his role as a roadside showman. Although visitors were welcome to the Cave of Seven Devils for years to come, Harry closed his zoo to the public. He grew his beard long and spent nights with his second wife, Margaret, sleeping on the roof of his house. His behavior sent local rumors flying, and his reputation grew larger than life.

Joe Atkinson, who grew up at the Box Canyon Trading Post, had vivid recollections of Harry from when he was a kid. "We were scared to death of Indian Miller. We used to make up stories about him, trying to scare ourselves. We would sneak around on the mesa above his cave. One time, he caught us and took us in. Of course, he was a very nice man. He gave us a bunch of Apache devil-dancer masks. He made us a kite out of goatskin. It was so thin; I don't know how he did it."

Harry experienced visions in his dreams at night, while sleeping, and while he was inside the cave, but his most vivid occurred when he dreamed that he looked out the window from his bed and saw seven glittering cities – the Seven Lost Cities of Cibola.

Harry had been fascinated with the legend of the lost cities since his days at Walnut Canyon. He knew how a 1539 report of Friar Marcos de Niza had launched dozens of Spanish expeditions from Mexico, all looking for the cities with golden roofs and gates of turquoise where kings drank from jeweled cups. Historians had since dismissed the lost cities as a myth, but Harry believed he was destined to prove the skeptics were wrong.

Harry spent the majority of the 1930s exploring and looking for clues that might lead him to the lost cities. He amassed what he believed was credible evidence that the Seven Lost Cities had once existed in an area around nearby Lupton. Among his discoveries were petroglyphs that no Navajo or Hopi could read, large holes that had been artificially opened in cliff walls, three cisterns carved into Battleship Mountain, and three crosses carved into a sandstone ledge near the initials "M.N." Harry believed Friar Marcos de Niza had made these last inscriptions.

Even though some people – including *Holbrook Tribune* editor C.C. Anderson – lauded Harry's discoveries, widespread recognition continued to elude him. As Harry tried in vain to interest scholars in further excavation, most dismissed his finds.

Through a print shop in Gallup, New Mexico, Harry published *Songs of the Navajo Sea* – a collection of 35 volumes that he wrote between 1946 and 1951. In the books, he defended his archaeological discoveries and charged his critics with narrow, unimaginative thinking.

Harry Miller died there in his cave. After a December storm, Margaret walked to Box Canyon to break the news. Harry had told her that he didn't feel well and then simply fell over dead. Joe Atkinson later recalled that his uncle, Rex Bollin, and Wayne Russell went to the cave. Harry and Margaret had 24 cats, and when they arrived at the house, all the cats were sitting around him. "The cats were sitting all over the bed – all around him in that little room," Joe said. "It was very eerie."

Today, the Cave of Seven Devils still exists just across the Arizona state line. If you ever get a chance to visit, listen closely as the sun slowly

sinks behind the nearby hills. The stories say you might hear voices – frightening and ancient – calling out to you from the land where so many have lived and died over the centuries.

LUPTON AND HOUCK

IN THE FAR DISTANT TIME OF 1930 – OKAY, MAYBE NOT THAT long ago – a guidebook described the town of Lupton as "a western cow town, named for a pioneer." It had a population of 75. The pioneer was George William Lupton, who worked for the Atchison, Topeka, and Santa Fe Railroad, which had reached the little town in 1881.

Lupton, located adjacent to the Cave of the Seven Devils, is little more than a handful of trading posts today, including the **Yellowhorse Trading Post**. Located on the Navajo reservation, it was founded by the Yellowhorse family in the 1950s, selling Navajo rugs and petrified wood to highway travelers. In the 1960s, Juan and Frank Yellowhorse added Shell gas pumps and advertising signs, cementing their place on Route 66 for years to come.

The Yellowhorse family still runs the trading post today, selling authentic Native American jewelry, pottery, and artwork.

THE SETTLEMENT OF HOUCK WAS FOUNDED BY A MAIL carrier named Houck, who started a trading post there around 1880. But it wouldn't be the trading post that earned a reputation for the little town – it would be **Fort Courage**, the Army post that was carved out of the wilderness in the 1860s.

If you're reading this and are old enough to have watched the television show, *F Troop,* then that name might ring a bell.

For those who didn't see the show when it aired or catch it in reruns, *F Troop* was on the air from 1965 to 1967 and was set in the fictional Fort Courage. The bumbling troop – which included actors Forrest Tucker, Larry Storch, Ken Berry, and Jim Hampton – got into all kinds of hijinks during its two seasons before going off the air. However, the show's legacy lived on as a roadside attraction... sort of.

Built in the 1970s, the replica fort was not officially affiliated with the TV show, but the owners never let this potential legal problem slow them down. They sold official merchandise and proudly displayed actual *F Troop* props. Because there was only so long

The cast from F Troop... despite the sign out front, the TV show had no connection to Fort Courage

F Troop nostalgia could be considered even vaguely financially viable, there was also a general store that sold groceries and Native American arts and crafts.

There was an Armco gas station on the property and a pancake house, which were, like the fort itself, eventually abandoned. When I last passed through the area, there was a small eatery that may or may not have been a Taco Bell many years ago. I spotted a sign hanging above the door, but that was all there was to go on.

There are still some faded signs for Fort Courage along the interstate today, although, at one time, there were many more. With all those signs, it seems like there should be more history available about a place that was obviously once an entertaining tourist trap, but there seems to be little information out there to find.

LOG CABIN TRADING POST

NO ONE KNOWS FOR SURE HOW THE TOWN OF SANDERS got its name. Some historians insist the name belonged to a railroad office engineer named C.W. Sanders. Others believed it was named for Art Sanders, who operated a trading post in the area. The railway station in town was given the name Cheto to avoid confusion with another Sanders that had already been established along the line.

Cheto, founded along the Atchison, Topeka, and Santa Fe Railroad, gained a post office in 1896, but it only lasted a few years. The town had a hard time keeping enough of a population to need a post office, so it came and went for years. Finally, in 1932, the name was changed back to Sanders, and this time, it stuck.

Trading posts were the primary source of supplies for travelers in the early days and would also come and go over the years. The Cedar Point Trading Post was one of the longest-lasting along Route 66 in town, opening in 1928 and remaining open until 1980.

But the most notorious trading post in town was undoubtedly the Log Cabin Trading Post, which was owned and operated by Al Berry for more than 25 years.

Al hailed from Texas and came to the parched stretch of Route 66 outside Sanders in 1929. He had come to Arizona to become an Indian trader and was soon doing business with the local Navajo, initially buying and selling rugs from his living room. A short time later, he built a small store on the south side of the highway.

In the 1930s, Al decided to build a bigger store on the north side of Route 66. He called it the Log Cabin Trading Post and built it using pine logs cut from a forest about 20 miles away. He installed gas pumps and built living quarters on the back side of the trading post.

Al's south side store was passed on to Alvie "Sonny" Turpen, and the two men decided to split the business at this spot on the road. Sonny focused strictly on Navajo trading, and Al leaned towards roadside souvenirs and entertaining the tourists.

Al's decision to focus on souvenir and curio sales demanded that he snag as many tourists off the highway as he could. With this in mind, he excavated some ancient stone ruins on the east side of his property, which he surrounded with a shed and charged visitors a small fee to visit them. They soon became a popular attraction.

By now, Al had also realized that kids were the key to stopping cars filled with vacationers, and he decided to stop them with

animals. He advertised his animal menagerie as the "Largest Free Zoo in the Southwest," and this wasn't a simple boast. He consciously fashioned his zoo after those he'd seen in large cities with monkeys, snakes, llamas, bears, and much more. The animals lived in their own heated houses. Paths connected one attraction with another. A donation box took coins from folks who felt the need to pay something, and a wishing well provided a spot for parents to take family photos. The well, of course, accepted its own share of change.

But it wasn't souvenirs and zoos that lined Al's pockets. The Log Cabin Trading Post also became quietly known for its illicit gambling rooms. There were slot machines and gambling tables where travelers on Route 66 could hope to increase the size of their vacation bankroll – but usually found they left more money behind than they took with them. Al likely made his share of money with the gambling room, but he lost some, too. In 1947, three slot machines were seized in a government raid, and Al was fined $1,500.

This didn't slow Al down, in any case. Situated on the edge of the Navajo reservation, the Log Cabin never lost its link to the community. Navajo made up most of Al's employees. Some stepped into the kitchen to cook when Al wasn't giving the job to hitchhikers and drifters who needed a break and a little money for the road.

During the time he operated the Log Cabin, Al ran other highway stores, too, like the Covered Wagon Trading Post in Gallup, New Mexico, and in 1948, bought the Chamese Lodge on Route 66 west of Sanders. It

had been opened originally as a combination bar, café, and motel, and locals loved the place because of its dance floor. The owners, though, had depended on liquor sales for their success and went bankrupt. That was when Al Berry bought it, and he renamed it the White Elephant Lodge.

He didn't keep it for long. In the early 1950s, he traded the lodge to Skeet and Maude Eddens in return for a guest ranch near Durango, Colorado. He sold the Log Cabin Trading Post after this and settled down with his wife, Sue, to enjoy life in the Rockies.

In 1967, Al was killed in a car accident on U.S. Highway 550 south of the New Mexico-Colorado state line. He left little behind that has survived on Route 66. The White Elephant Lodge eventually burned, and the ruins of the Log Cabin Trading Post lie today in the shadow of the newer store that was built east of the site. Anyone who stops at this place in search of authentic Navajo jewelry might still find some stones and an abandoned wishing well from the "Largest Free Zoo in the Southwest."

BUT THE RUINS OF THE LOG CABIN TRADING POST ARE NOT the only thing to watch out for on this stretch of road. Since the days of Route 66, travelers have reported a hitchhiking ghost along the side of the road. Legend says that he was a drifter who was run over and killed at this spot in the 1940s.

Drivers report they have pulled over to offer the man a ride, but the figure disappears when they slow down. Others state that it's only after they pass the man by – and look in their rearview mirror for him – that he vanishes. Everyone who has seen him swears he is not an optical illusion but what appears to be a live person in clothing that's long out of date.

HAUNTED

The lesson to be learned here is that you might want to be careful who you pick up along Route 66.

WEST TO CHAMBERS

FOUNDED BY CHARLES CHAMBERS AT SOME POINT BEFORE the railroad arrived in the area in 1881, the small community finally got a post office in 1908. It became a popular stopover spot in the 1920s after Route 66 came through, and, naturally, service stations, cafes, and trading posts followed.

Chambers today is a scattering of houses with a gas station and a motel that opened in the 1970s after the interstate bypassed the old highway. It's still in business today as the Best Western Chieftain Inn, serving as a gateway to the nearby Petrified Forest.

The **Cedar Point Trading Post** was once a thriving business in Chambers. Owned by Charles Garrett Wallace from North Carolina, it specialized in Zuni silverwork. Wallace – an Indian trader who also operated a store in Gallup, New Mexico – had come to Arizona in 1918 and helped to develop a market for carved fetish necklaces.

In 1971, Wallace sold Cedar Point to Bruce and Virginia Burnham, who bought the place with their own ideas about encouraging Native American artists. They closed the trading post in 1975, and little remains of it today.

The **Chambers Trading Post** still stands, although it hasn't been a roadside store in many years. It now has offices for Apache County, but during the heyday of Route 66, it was owned and operated by Robert and Laura Jane Cassady.

Robert was born in West Virginia and came west in the early 1900s to serve as a U.S. Indian Service Agent at Laguna Pueblo for 12 years. In 1914, he and his wife, Laura, opened their first trading post at Sunrise Springs, Arizona, before opening the Chambers Trading Post in 1928.

The couple eventually sold the trading post to Alf and Bertha Riggs. Alf was the Standard Oil distributor in Chambers, but one day, he drove to Sanders to pick up a customer's load of fuel and accidentally drove in front of a train. He was killed on the spot.

Frank and Alice Young operated the store in later years, but when a new alignment of Route 66 bypassed their store, they closed it and built the Chieftain Motel off the new highway.

THE PETRIFIED FOREST

THE PETRIFIED FOREST NATIONAL PARK WAS THE ONLY national park on Route 66. It bisected the main park highway and was the first paved road in the region. It followed the path of the railroad, following the National Old Trails Road, and a variety of motor courts, cafes, and other tourist businesses lined the route. Traces of the old road and a line of weathered telephone poles still mark the path of the highway today.

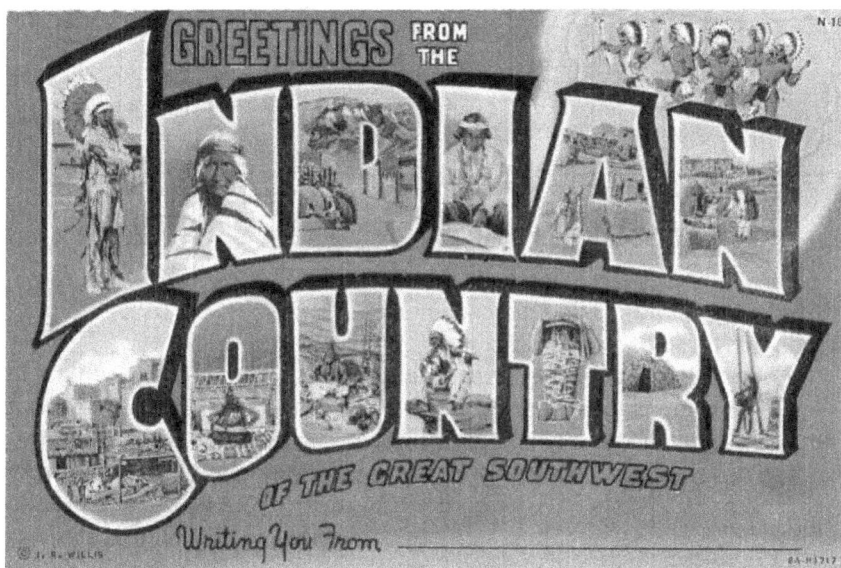

GREETINGS FROM THE INDIAN COUNTRY OF THE GREAT SOUTHWEST

Writing You From _____

The Petrified Forest area was designated as a National Monument in 1906. The Painted Desert was added later, and in 1962, all 93,000 acres received National Park status.

But when I first visited here as a kid – maybe 10 or 11 years old – I was incredibly disappointed. When my parents told me that we were going to be visiting "a petrified forest," I was thrilled. Who wouldn't want to see an entire ancient forest that had been turned into stone? So, you can imagine my dismay when we arrived, and I discovered the trees were lying all over the desert as broken pieces of quartz. But I overcame my disappointment and marveled at the story of how this place came to be.

More than 200 million years ago, massive trees were uprooted by floods, washed down from high regions, and later buried by the sand of the floodplains. Water seeped through the wood and replaced the organic material with multicolored silica. As the land was eroded over time, it began to reveal the long-buried petrified wood – now turned into almost solid quartz. Each piece is like a crystal, often sparking in the sunlight. The colors that give the Painted Desert its name come from impurities in the quartz, such as iron, carbon, and manganese.

Explorers and travelers who came to the region in the mid-nineteenth century carried off pieces of petrified wood as souvenirs.

Wagons were often filled to capacity and hauled away to be sold as keepsakes.

When the Petrified Forest was named a National Monument in 1906, it became illegal to remove any of the wood from the park – and it remains illegal today. Even though thieves can end up with hefty fines, this has never stopped tourists from removing their own pieces of history from the park. Visitors have often thought that no one would ever notice if they took just one little rock, but they sometimes found out that stealing bits of petrified wood wasn't such a great plan after all.

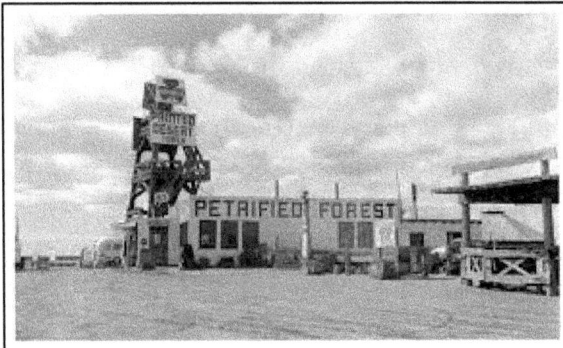

Starting in the 1930s, visitors to the Petrified Forest began to report that after taking a piece of wood from the park, they suddenly began experiencing a run of bad luck. Rangers called it a "curse," and it allegedly continues today. There is even a room at the Rainbow Forest Museum at the park that's dedicated to the hundreds of "cursed" thieves who stuck just one little rock in their pocket or rucksack during their visit. Letters – and now emails – of confession tell stories of car problems during their trip, job loss, house fires, medical conditions, and more. Envelopes and sometimes boxes of stolen rocks continue to be received at the park on a regular basis.

The display at the museum – dubbed the "Mystery of the Conscience Wood" – offers a bench where guests can sit and read through a binder that contains letters from all over the world written by travelers asking for forgiveness—the earliest "conscience letter" dates to 1935.

But the idea of a curse started long before that. The Navajo traditionally refused to touch petrified wood because they also believed it would bring bad fortune. In their legends, pieces of the wood – or yei-bits-in – were the bones of a fierce and mighty giant called Yei tso.

But don't worry if you're visiting the park today and would like a souvenir. Tourists can purchase plenty of petrified wood that has been collected legally, and the good news is that these keepsakes don't come with a curse attached to them.

At least, I hope they don't.

PAINTED DESERT INN

BUILT FROM PETRIFIED WOOD AND OTHER NATIVE STONE, the Painted Desert Inn was created by Herbert David Lore, who operated it as a tourist attraction during the early days of Route 66. Visitors could stop for meals in the dining room, purchase Native American crafts from local artists, and cool off with a cold drink in the downstairs taproom. Six small motel rooms with private entrances were available to travelers for $2 a night, and Lore would even throw in a tour of the Painted Desert and Petrified Forest below the inn.

HAUNTED

But the inn was an isolated place. It was not connected to electrical lines; it depended on a lighting plant at the site for electricity. Water had to be hauled in from the Puerco River.

After a few years, Lore wanted to sell the place but also wanted it to be protected and preserved for the future. In 1931, the Petrified Forest National Monument purchased the inn and a large section of land.

After structural problems were discovered with the building, the inn was restructured in a more Southwestern style. Working by plans provided by architect Lyle Bennett, workers from the Civilian Conservation Corps (CCC) used Ponderosa pine and aspen poles cut from Arizona forests for the roof and cross beams. Light fixtures were handmade from punched tin. Wooden tables and chairs were carved in Native American designs.

Skylight panels were hand-painted by two CCC workers and were based on prehistoric designs from various archaeological sites in the region. Even the floors were painted with patterns taken from Navajo blanket designs.

The Painted Desert Inn had been given a new life, and it once again began attracting Route 66 motorists with meals, souvenirs, and overnight stays.

At the start of World War II, the CCC was disbanded as young men were sent off to war and highway travel ground almost to a stop, thanks to gas rationing. This led to the closing of the inn in 1942.

Five years later, it was rescued by the famous Fred Harvey Company, and the inn was refurbished and reopened once again for Route 66 travelers. It thrived for almost two decades, but wear and tear on the building led to another closure in 1963. The foundations had cracked, rain had damaged the interior, and most believed the days of the Painted Desert Inn were numbered. Finally, the park scheduled it for demolition in 1975.

However, a concerned public rallied to save the inn, and the campaign led to its inclusion in the National Historic Register in 1987. After years of preservation, the building became a museum and information center in 2006.

And that was about the time when the ghost stories about the Painted Desert Inn began to be told.

The incident that inspired the ghostly tales of the former inn occurred on April 9, 1953, when a fire broke out in the building. A park ranger was one of the first on the scene, and crawling on his hands and knees, he made his way through the building to look for the hotel manager, 59-year-old Marion Mace. He found her unconscious in her bedroom and carried her outside to safety. He then bravely went back inside to save the historic building by putting out the flames with a fire extinguisher.

The inn survived, but the same couldn't be said for the unfortunate Marion Mace. She died from smoke inhalation before an ambulance could make it to the secluded inn.

No one knows for sure what started the fire, but it was generally believed to have been started by a cigarette – and it started in the manager's bedroom. It was noted that Marion had been rarely seen over the years without a cigarette in her hand.

Since Marion's death – although this wasn't widely talked about until much later – those who worked and stayed at the inn often reported strange happenings like footsteps on the stone floors when no one was present, whispered voices in empty rooms, and the lingering smell of cigarette smoke, even when no one was around.

And the occurrences continue today, years after the old inn had been turned into a museum.

After locking up one evening, a park ranger looked back through the windows and saw someone inside the museum walking from one room to another. Exasperated by a tourist who was where they shouldn't be, the ranger unlocked the door and went back inside. As soon as she entered the building, she detected the unmistakable odor of cigarette smoke. Needless to say, smoking was not allowed in the museum. Now more irritated than before, the ranger hurried from room to room, searching for the smoker, until she realized there was no one else in the building but her.

It seems that even a fire – and her subsequent death – wasn't enough to convince Marion Mace that she needed to give up cigarettes.

PAINTED DESERT TRADING POST

TRY AND IMAGINE THE LONELIEST, MOST SUN-BAKED SECTION of the Arizona desert that you can – a place where a single lizard might be the only living thing, besides yourself, for miles around. Can you do it?

P.D.25—Trading Post on Rim of Painted Desert Park, Arizona

Now, look to the north side of the highway, and there, in the middle of all that lonely sand and rock, you'd once have found the Painted Desert Trading Post.

Opened by Dotch and Alberta Windsor in the early 1940s, the trading post sold Indian souvenirs, cold drinks, and sandwiches, as well as gasoline and water for radiators with the potential for overheating.

It was the only glimmer of civilization in the surrounding region, but you could never forget how isolated it was. The trading post had no telephone, so calls had to be made from the Painted Desert Park, which was several miles away. The appliances ran on electricity that was generated by a windmill.

An incident that occurred at the trading post in 1947 attests to the remoteness of the area. In April of that year, Alma Shelnutt was traveling with her husband from Colorado Springs to Pasadena, California. Shortly after stopping at the trading post, Alma suffered a heart attack and collapsed. Since there was no telephone and Holbrook was the nearest community with a hospital, it was more than an hour before medical help arrived. By that time, Alma was dead.

The Windsors continued to operate the trading post together until 1950 when a woman named Joy Nevin – who ran a veterinary supply business in Holbrook – met Dotch while passing through on a business trip. He and Alberta soon divorced, and Joy and Dotch were married and had a daughter together in 1952. The pair then ran the trading post together until they also divorced in 1956.

The section of Route 66 that ran past the store was relocated, widened, and turned into an interstate in the late 1950s, and the trading post has been empty and forgotten ever since. The skeletal remains of the building were visible alongside the abandoned roadway for many years, but it's since been reclaimed by the desert, which created the need for it to exist in the first place.

Greetings from PAINTED DESERT ARIZ.

MURDER AT GOODWATER

THE DISTANCE BETWEEN TOWNS AND SERVICES ON THIS PART of Route 66 was often difficult for travelers but turned out to be ideally suited for killers, bandits, and murderous hitchhikers. With the highway being the most direct connection between the Midwest and Los Angeles, criminals of every kind often shared the road with vacationing families. This becomes clear as we recall a meeting between a killer and a family of travelers in Goodwater, Arizona, that ended in tragedy.

With only a service station and a small café, Goodwater, located on the western edge of the Painted Desert, was once nothing more than a name on the map, but in December 1953, it was the scene of a horrific crime that shocked the Southwest.

Raymond Allen was traveling from Pennsylvania to California to start a new job and was accompanied by his wife, Betty, and his 10-

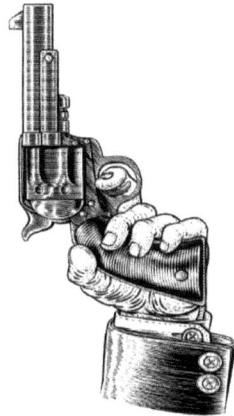

TRUE CRIME

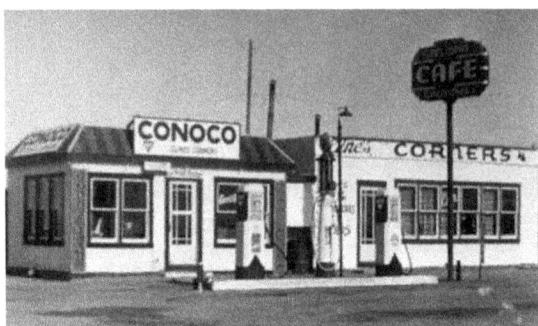
Carl Folk first encountered the Allen family at this service station in Cline's Corners, New Mexico

month-old son. With an old truck and an overloaded trailer, it was a slow trip but a steady one, and part of the trailer's load included camping gear, which allowed them to save some money by not paying for motel stays along the way.

Tragically, they would soon encounter another traveler – Carl Folk, a dangerous man with a lengthy criminal record. In 1930, he was convicted in Indiana for attempted robbery and rape. He'd surprised a young couple, robbed the man, tied him up, and then tried to rape his girlfriend. In the struggle, Folk dropped his gun and fled. After serving five years in the state prison, he headed west and became involved in an array of violent incidents, although none of them had ended with a conviction. Finally, he was convicted of rape in Albuquerque in 1949 and was locked away in the New Mexico State Asylum – but for less than a year. By February 1950, he was on the loose again – and on a collision course with the Allens.

According to later testimony, Folk first encountered the Allens at a service station in Clines Corners, New Mexico. He struck up a conversation with Raymond, asking questions about their trailer, roadside camping, and problems with towing. It was from this point that he began to stalk the family secretly. He would pass them on the highway, stop at a café or motel, and then follow behind them after they passed.

On December 1, 1953, the Allens stopped at the café in Goodwater around 9:00 P.M. After eating, they continued west for a short distance and found a place to pull off the road for the evening. They planned to drive to Kingman the next day.

Folk had passed the family west of Gallup and then had noted their vehicle and trailer at the café in Goodwater as he drove past. After waiting for them for a while on the road ahead, he realized they'd likely stopped, so he backtracked and found their truck and trailer. Just before midnight, he parked his car on a ranch road just off the highway, crept up on the camp, and surprised the sleeping family.

Gun in hand, he told them he was only interested in money. After ordering them to lie down on their stomachs, he tied them around the ankles and wrists with their hands behind them. After making sure that Raymond was securely tied, he raped Betty and then drove the truck and trailer to where he had parked his car. After dragging Raymond out of the trailer, he began to torture and repeatedly rape Betty. An autopsy later determined that she died from strangulation. Her child was unharmed.

By early morning, Raymond had managed to free his ankles, stagger to the highway, and flag down a passing truck driver. Though his hands and feet were horribly swollen due to lack of circulation, once the truck driver had cut away the ropes on his wrists, Raymond ran toward his vehicle. The driver followed behind him after taking a moment to grab the gun that he kept under his seat and handing it to Raymond.

Folk heard them coming. He stepped out of the trailer, and Raymond immediately opened fire, striking the man twice. Folk went down, but he survived the shooting.

After a trial and conviction, Folk was later executed at the Arizona state prison – which was a cold comfort to Raymond Allen and his son, whose lives were never the same again.

"THE TOWN TOO TOUGH FOR WOMEN AND CHURCHES"

IN 1881, THE ATLANTIC AND PACIFIC RAILROAD BEGAN construction in northeast Arizona, laying a track through an area known as Horsehead Crossing. A station was opened there the following year, followed by a name change to Holbrook in honor of H.R. Holbrook, the railroad's first chief engineer. In September 1882, the town became official when the first post office opened.

Holbrook became a vital railroad shipping point for cattle in the region, which turned it into a rough-and-tumble cowboy town awash with liquor and prostitution. One of the roughest places in town was the infamous Bucket of Blood Saloon, which earned its name with nightly brawls and shootings that stained the wooden floor with blood. Holbrook became known as "the town too tough for women and churches."

By the end of the 1880s, Sheriff Commodore Perry Owens was credited with bringing law and order to the town, and things calmed down considerably. The violence was long over by the time Route 66 arrived in town.

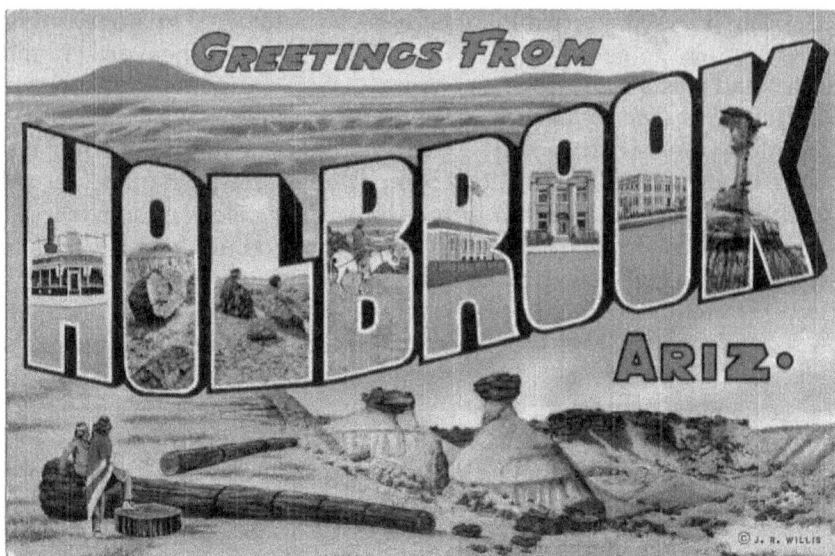

In the 1950s, West Hopi Drive in Holbrook was lined with motels, cafes, and service stations, all cashing in on the steady flow of traffic that was passing through town. With the Painted Desert, Petrified Forest, and Indian reservations all nearby, it was seemingly always full of Route 66 travelers.

Holbrook enjoyed the benefit of being one of the last towns on the highway to be bypassed in 1981. Once it was, though, it never really recovered. Within a year of the new interstate, 45 local businesses closed. The town had struggled economically ever since.

"HAVE YOU SLEPT IN A WIGWAM LATELY?"

FRANK REDFORD HAD ALWAYS BEEN A TRAVELER, EVEN AS A child. His parents traveled extensively and always took him along. On one trip to California, Frank couldn't believe his eyes when he saw a snack stand that was shaped like an ice cream cone. Later, on a trip to South Dakota, he saw his first wigwam.

Over the years, the two ideas blended, and inspired by the similar shapes of the two structures, he dreamed of building a roadside business – like a café or a filling station – inside a structure that looked like a wigwam.

By the time he turned 30, Frank had found a tourist spot in Horse Cave, Kentucky, bought a piece of property, and began building a diner and filling station to match the image he'd long held in his imagination. It was completed in 1933, and unsuspecting tourists who came to visit nearby Mammoth Cave were startled to find giant teepees along the highway.

For years – long before Disneyland or any other theme park – wild and colorful roadside attractions like the one that Frank built got a lot of attention. No one had ever seen a service station housed in a 60-foot-high wigwam, accompanied by two smaller ones that served as restrooms.

Despite pushing Native American stereotypes and little thought for indigenous cultures – this was a much different time – Frank's idea brought in plenty of customers. This led to him expanding beyond just a service station and into the motel business. If people would fill up their gas tank at a giant teepee, then why wouldn't they spend the night in one, too?

Frank's teepees were nothing like the

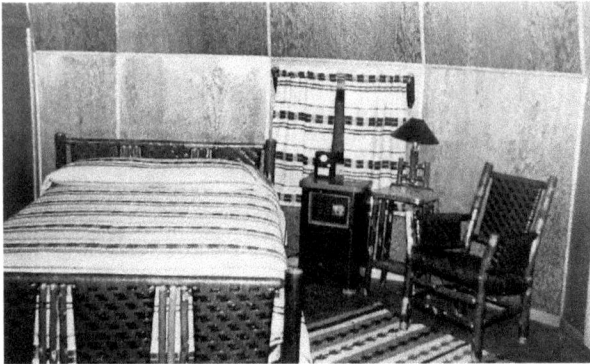

Inside one of the wigwams in 1950

real thing, of course. The primary framing was engineered to be very sturdy, using metal poles that poked out of the top of the cone to provide the effect of lodge poles. On the outside, the steel skeleton was covered with industrial-strength tarpaper and a layer of stucco.

Frank painted the teepees white and accented them with red zigzag edging at the top. Another red line circled below, leading the eye to a diamond-shaped window. Builders hung standard doors in an entryway and sculpted a surround out of concrete mortar to look like a rolled-back flap of animal hides.

The strangest thing about the wigwams was that, in their original form, they featured a swastika symbol directly above the door. The sacred religious symbol was known to the Navajo as one of good luck, but after Hitler and the Nazis rose to power later in the 1930s, its use was, of course, stigmatized. Swastikas quickly fell out of use, and they were removed everywhere, including at the Wigwam Villages.

Sleeping in an authentic Native American teepee wasn't going to provide the level of comfort modern travelers were used to, so roadside wigwams had to be reimagined for the tourist trade. The teepees were given insulated walls, knotty pine paneling, and decorative molding. Ceramic tiles covered the walls and floors of the bathrooms. Overnight guests had all the comforts of home, including a sink and shower with hot and cold running water and a flush toilet. A campfire wasn't needed – steam-powered radiators provided the heat.

Specially selected furnishings continued the stereotypes of the Wild West. Frank had beds, chairs, and nightstands crafted from hickory with the bark still in place. To keep the theme going, the rooms also had real Apache blankets and Navajo rugs.

After Frank's first Wigwam Village opened, he soon had investors eager to franchise, and in 1937, he built a second location in Cave City, Kentucky. Three more villages followed in New Orleans, Orlando, and

Birmingham. Two Wigwam Villages sprang up along Route 66 – one in San Bernadino, California, and the other in Holbrook.

After visiting Frank's second Wigwam Village, Chester Lewis returned home to Holbrook with plans to build his own. After purchasing the rights to Frank's design, Chester negotiated a royalty agreement for the use of the Wigwam Village name, which was, well, a little strange. Chester installed coin-operated radios in each teepee, and the dimes collected from customers were sent to Frank.

Chester's Wigwam Village opened in the summer of 1950 with 15 wigwams in a U shape. It became an immediate success, especially with kids. The motel captured the imagination of the traveling public and made the village the top place to stay in Holbrook. Perhaps sleeping in a wigwam was a small part of the Wild West that tourists could still be part of, even if the wigwams were made of steel and concrete.

When the interstate bypassed Holbrook, business at the Wigwam Village waned, just as it did in the rest of the town. It wasn't long before the place had seen what was thought would be their final overnight guest.

Chester passed away in 1986, but his family decided not to let his dream die with him. Two years later, each wigwam was completely renovated and, by 2002, was listed on the National Register of Historic Places.

The Wigwam Village continues to thrive in Holbrook today, ensuring that we'll all be able to take part in a Western adventure for many years to come.

GERONIMO TRADING POST

IN THE DAYS OF THE OLD WEST, TRADING POSTS WERE AN essential service for settlers, travelers, and Native Americans alike. Furs and handmade goods were exchanged for items like salt, coffee, clothing, and more.

But during the heyday of Route 66, trading posts gained a new role – to separate tourists from their cash. Instead of salt and dry goods necessary for survival, they offered Indian trinkets, moccasins, souvenir spoons, glasses, cowboy hats, spears with rubber points, postcards, and every other kind of curio and souvenir you could imagine.

The Geronimo Trading Post – located between Holbrook and Joseph City – was one such modern trading post. The store was established around 1950 by local personality "Doc" Hatfield, who named

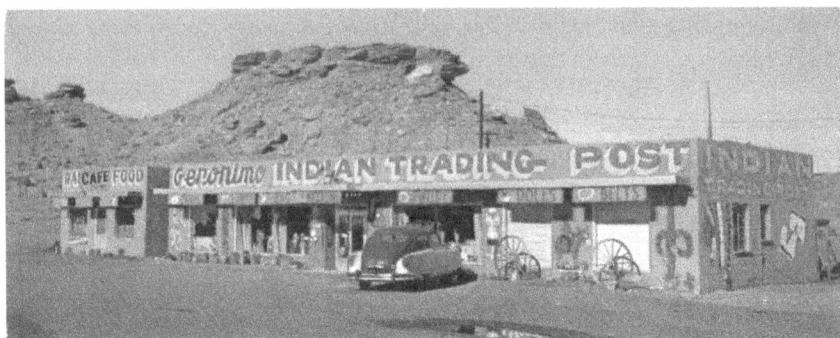

it for the Apache warrior captured nearby and sent to prison by train from Holbrook.

Carl Kempton purchased the Geronimo in 1967 and, seven years later, built the structure that houses the store today. The landscape that surrounds the trading post looks like something out of a Hollywood western, and the wigwam on the premises lends the whole thing an air of authenticity.

For the past few decades, the store has attracted customers by advertising the "World's Largest Petrified Tree." The enormous log – placed at the edge of the parking lot – was pulled from a gravel pit behind the store by Carl himself, and it boasts a weight of 89,000 pounds.

The Geronimo holds one other distinction. Located as it is on the shortest of old Route 66 loops – and with its own exit from Interstate 40 – it may be the only old highway business ever aided by the arrival of the modern interstate.

As Carl said in an interview: "A man named Chubby Autrey was leasing Geronimo when the interstate came through. It worried him, and therefore, I was able to acquire the store. Chubby didn't realize what a wonderful interchange it would be. In our case, the interstate did us a favor."

APACHE FORT

ONE OF THE MORE UNUSUAL ROADSIDE STORES ON THIS stretch of the highway was called Apache Fort, and while its uniqueness didn't come from the trading post itself, or even what it sold, but from the man who built it.

Otis Baird was an old-school lawman who'd pinned on the badge of a Deputy Sheriff for Navajo County long after the frontier lawmen of early Arizona had become the stuff of legend. However, his no-nonsense notions of right and wrong hearkened back to the old days, although instead of wagon trails, Otis kept busy fighting crime on the modern highways of the 1940s.

Unlike so many entrepreneurs who built tourist businesses along Route 66 in Arizona, Otis was no transplant from the east. He was born in the Grand Canyon state in the mid-1930s and grew up near Snowflake on an honest-to-goodness western ranch. His father, Thomas, was a cattleman and he also often wore a lawman's badge.

In 1948, the Baird family moved to Joseph City – west of Holbrook – and there, Otis got a taste of highway life. He took a job with Ella Blackwell, who owned a trading post on Route 66, and soon, he was traveling the reservations alone and working as a supplier for other stores in the region. The Navajo appreciated the fairness that Otis showed them and pressed him to open his own trading post.

Otis took their advice in the early 1950s and built a highway trading post on Route 66 between Holbrook and Joseph City. Otis, his brother, Brantley, and a group of Navajo friends constructed the building from cheap lumber that cost little and looked simple and tough. Otis then surrounded the store with a western stockade and coated the finished project with old motor oil to make it look weathered and aged.

Back home, the Baird family ranch sat near Apache Butte – a stone landmark that was named for the past clashes between the U.S. Calvary and the Apache. Otis decided to pay tribute to that history by calling his trading post Apache Fort.

After he opened the store, Otis quickly realized that his rendition of the "Wild West" wasn't a nostalgic illusion. It seemed like a peaceful place on the surface. The store sold a variety of leather goods, moccasins, and turquoise jewelry and offered a snack bar for hungry and thirsty travelers. But, thanks to his other job as a deputy sheriff, Otis was well aware of the

Apache Fort during its heyday

uptick in Route 66 crime – from robberies to hijackings – and he made sure that Apache Fort always maintained a no-nonsense aura about it. Bars protected the windows, police cars were often in the lot, and an old-time gallows stood at the edge of the lot with a mannequin dangling at the end of a rope – just as a warning, of course.

Otis' second job as a deputy sheriff kept him busy. When neighboring highway businesses experienced trouble, Otis got the call. He frequently traveled south to aid overwhelmed authorities in Maricopa County as well as in other hot spots.

On one occasion, when word got out that a motorcycle gang with bad intentions was on its way to Joseph City, he created his own band of deputies by rounding up some of the old cowboys who lived in the area and making sure they were well-armed. Once, during a knife fight, his arm was slashed from wrist to elbow. His toughest arrest, he always said, was of a 15-year-old girl who fled from a juvenile facility in Flagstaff. When he caught up to her, she bit and took a hunk out of his arm. He carried a scar from her teeth marks for the rest of his life. Once, when a highway drifter was harassing and scaring people in front of the trading post, Otis nicely asked him to leave. When he refused, he sent the man on his way with help from an electric cattle prod.

But beneath his gruff exterior, Otis had a soft spot for kids, animals, and the tourists who stopped at Apache Fort. He opened a small zoo on the premises that offered travelers a look at prairie dogs, guinea hens, and a one-eyed timber wolf that had once appeared in a Walt Disney nature film. Inside the store, Otis kept a baby mountain lion as a pet. It rolled around and interacted playfully with the customers, and while it got a lot bigger as it got older, it remained playful, as though unaware it was no longer the size of a kitten. One day, just for fun, the lion jumped onto the back of a tourist, almost scaring the man to death. Otis immediately got the cat off and explained that he was only playing, but they couldn't keep the lion in the store after that.

Many of the customers were also surprised to find that Apache Fort housed a collection of native snakes – which Otis realized were the best security system he could ever have. If he suspected anyone who'd dropped in that day of being a shady character, he'd put some of his largest rattlesnakes inside the jewelry showcase at closing time. The living deterrents spent the night there, and apparently, this system worked. Apache Fort never saw a break-in during all the years that Otis was there.

In the early 1970s, Otis met and married Cindy Calahan, and the two of them moved to Arkansas in 1973. They left Apache Fort in the care of Otis's mother, Irabelle, who was not a fan of the trading post's snakes. She got rid of them, along with the occupants of the small zoo.

Otis subsequently sold Apache Fort to Paul Hatch and started a new life away from Route 66 and away from law enforcement. He and Cindy moved to Utah and built a new roadside trading post in Orderville that was an almost exact replica of Apache Fort. Route 66 enthusiasts are glad that he did since the original store outside Joseph City burned down in 1984. Otis' son, Malachi, still operates the Utah store today.

After Otis died in 1996, responsibility for carrying on the family's western traditions fell to his brother, Brantley, who opened Rock Art Ranch about 17 miles south of Joseph City. It offers visitors not only a chance to experience cattle drives and round-ups but also features excavated Anasazi dwellings, a Navajo hogan and sweat lodge, and some of the most well-preserved examples of petroglyphs carved by American natives in the Southwest.

"HERE IT IS!"

THE FADED TOWN OF JOSEPH CITY WAS SETTLED IN 1876 BY colonists from the Church of Jesus Christ of Latter-Day Saints – the Mormons. The band of 73 missionary travelers was led south from Utah by Captain William C. Allen

The famous Jack Rabbit Trading Post

and Joseph City – named for the church's martyred prophet Joseph Smith – and became one of four Little Colorado River colonies. The others in Arizona were Brigham City, Sunset, and Obed, although only Joseph City survives today. The only real bustling period in its history was during the heyday of Route 66.

Even though there isn't much left in town these days, one of the most iconic signs in Route 66 history can be found along the road in Joseph City. It's a sign for a place that many travelers had known was coming for hundreds of miles before they reached Arizona. During the glory days of Route 66, the black silhouette of a jackrabbit painted on a yellow billboard could be found across the western states and as far away as central Missouri. After seeing those signs for days, travelers finally made it to Joseph City and spotted the large welcome sign that exclaimed, "Here it is!"

They had just arrived at the famous Jack Rabbit Trading Post.

The original building that housed the iconic store was built and used by the Santa Fe Railroad and later was home to the Arizona Herpetorium. In 1949, James H. Taylor converted the former snake farm into one of the most legendary and successful businesses along Route 66. He lined the walls and counters with curios and souvenirs – offering rubber snakes, toy tomahawks, bows and arrows, cowboy hats, and Indian headdresses, as well as authentic native jewelry, beadwork, and more.

After browsing the shirts and souvenirs, travelers who wanted to make the most of the stop sampled the trading post's "world famous" ice-cold sherry cider, which became the spot's trademark item.

In 1961, Taylor leased the Jack Rabbit to Glenn Blansett, who eventually purchased the trading post in 1967. Glenn's son, Phil, and his wife bought the business in 1969 and ran it for 26 years before passing it on to their daughter, Cindy, and her husband. The Blansett family, one way or another, has owned and operated the Jack Rabbit ever since, proudly keeping the legend alive.

JUST A SHORT HOP (SEE WHAT I DID THERE?) DOWN THE road from the Jack Rabbit, modern travelers will catch a glimpse of a Route 66 ghost. It's not a specter but what's left of **Howdy Hank Indian Trading Post**, which was once operated by a friendly Texan whose name is only remembered as "Hank." Those who visited the store told stories of the congenial owner and the efforts he made to entertain the kids who stopped in with their parents.

It was a bustling trading post – for a time. It was known as a haven for travelers seeking souvenirs and supplies for their trip, and it lured in tourists with a wooden teepee that was built into the side of the building.

But after opening up, Joseph City residents learned that Hank had a love for children that was anything but innocent. Former Jack Rabbit Trading Post owner Phil Blansett later recalled, "It turned out he was a lot friendlier with children than he should have been. Howdy Hank got run out of the county."

Later, the Howdy Hank became the site of Sitting Bull's Indian Store and then was a store for hay and cattle feed. However, today, the building – with its wooden teepee still intact – stands silent and weathered, a reminder of the heyday of Route 66 and how small-town justice often occurred in secret.

JUST A SHORT DISTANCE FROM WHERE HOWDY HANK STOOD A traveler can find another almost forgotten piece of the highway's history – the sign for the **Red Arrow Camps Campground**. The campground itself is long gone, but the sign still stands, a proud reminder of a time when families piled into their station wagons and set off on cross-country adventures.

A few years ago, you could still see the remains of some of the wooden picnic tables and the fire pits where folks gathered to share stories and roast marshmallows under the desert stars. Even though the campground is gone, the memories still linger.

ELLA'S FRONTIER TRADING POST

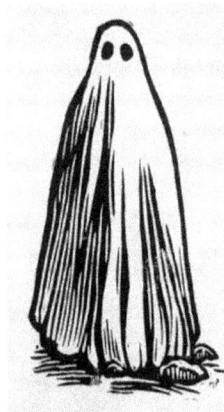

HAUNTED

THE RUINS OF ELLA'S FRONTIER TRADING POST REST ALONG an abandoned section of Route 66 just outside the western edge of Joseph City. The once thriving business was owned and operated by Ella Blackwell, who ended up with the property in 1955 after divorcing her second husband, Ray Meany, who had also owned the Hopi House Trading Post west of Winslow.

A former student at the Julliard School in New York City, Ella kept a piano in the store and was known for impromptu recitals for tourists and travelers. Locally known as an eccentric and oddball, she became well-known as one of the entertaining characters of the road. She loved to tell stories about her former life back east and also loved to brag to customers that her store had been established in 1873, making it the oldest trading post on Route 66. And while it had been known as the Last Trading Post – and had been in business for years before she bought it – her claims were met with a lot of skepticism, especially considering some of her other strange behaviors, like having conversations with people and animals that no one else could see.

Despite Ella's odd reputation – or more likely because of it – her

Frontier Trading Post became a must-stop location for travelers. More of the items she sold at the store – moccasins, feathered headdresses, bows and arrows with rubber tips, and toy six-shooters – were simply souvenirs to adults, but they were treasures to kids traveling out west for the first time.

When Ella died in 1984, Theo Hunsaker, who was executor of her estate, discovered that she had acquaintances all over the world – people who had stopped at the trading post and then stayed in touch with her. When he cleaned out her home, he found bags full of letters and postcards.

Although other businesses used the building that was once home to Ella's Frontier Trading Post after Ella died, it was later abandoned and fell into ruin on the side of the old road.

For years, stories circulated that the ghostly sounds of a piano were sometimes heard coming from inside the empty building, even though Ella's piano was sold after her death. It became widely believed that the tinkling keys were a manifestation of Ella's ghost, unwilling to leave the trading post that she had loved so much during her life.

GHOST OF THE COTTONWOOD WASH

ON SEPTEMBER 11, 1926, ONE OF THE FIRST FATALITIES ON Route 66 in Arizona occurred when a beautiful young actress plunged to her death in a flooded river just six miles east of the town of Winslow.

Her name was Leorena Shipley, and she was born in Iowa in September 1897, the second daughter of Leo and Della Shipley. Her musical talent blossomed almost as soon as she began to walk. She played the violin in kindergarten and mastered the clarinet the following year. The Shipleys moved west while Leorena was young and made their home in Winslow. She became active in sports, drama, and school plays. She graduated from Winslow High School in 1916 and won a scholarship to the University of Arizona in Tucson, where she studied theater and the arts. After graduating with a teaching certificate, she taught school for two years in Winslow.

With World War I behind the country, Leorena decided to follow her dreams of stardom and went west to California. She adopted the stage name "Norma Deane" and

HAUNTED

A publicity photo using Leorena's stage name of "Norma Deane."

became a popular stage star with terrific reviews. She toured with a traveling production around the west, and there was even talk of her appearance in one of the silent films that steadily gained audiences across the nation.

Tragically, though, Leorena's stardom came to a crashing end in 1926. She was back home in Winslow, visiting friends and family, and decided to explore the Petrified Forest with her mother and two friends.

That afternoon, the area was pounded by heavy rains, filling the washes and riverbeds. Driving slowly in the storm around 10:00 P.M., heading for Winslow, the Shipley car met up with a vehicle driven by Vance Wilson, a family friend. Vance was driving, and Leorena's father, Leo, was in the passenger seat. He had become concerned about the safety of his wife and daughter in such bad weather. Fearing that the heavy rain flooded Manila Wash near Winslow, he and Vance had set out to meet the others and assist them across the torrent of water that was surely flooding the washes.

Crossing the first wash was no problem. Both vehicles easily passed through the rising waters. The two cars then continued toward Cottonwood Wash, with Vance Wilson's auto leading the way about 50 feet ahead. The first car made it across without any difficulty, and they assumed the second car would be safe.

Even so, Leo looked back to watch as the car with his family started across the wash. Suddenly, he saw the second car fall backward. The bridge had collapsed. The headlights of the car were shining straight upward as it fell into the fast-swirling water.

Jumping out of the car before it came to a stop, Leo dashed back to the scene, where he found the second auto lying on its side. The entire vehicle was submerged except for the front corner of the driver's side.

The window on the door was open. The driver, Tug Wilson, had managed to escape and was dragged up to the road. Leo and Tug then pulled Della Shipley and her friend, Mrs. Ingledew, from

The Route 66 bridge over Cottonwood Wash

the vehicle, passing them up to Vance Wilson, who had turned his car around to aid in the rescue. Tug shouted that Leorena was still missing and trapped inside the car.

Vance Wilson was lowered on a rope into the churning, muddy water, and he frantically searched inside the car, finding Leorena trapped behind the driver's seat. He tried desperately to free her but failed. She had been knocked unconscious by the crash, it was believed, and her body had been pinned by the seat.

The other two women were taken to receive medical treatment in Winslow, but Tug remained at the scene, waiting for more volunteers to arrive and aid in the rescue. Dozens of men were soon at the scene, but it took two days for them to retrieve the vehicle from 15 feet of quicksand.

They found Leorena's body still inside.

Grown men wept as her corpse was wrapped in blankets and transported back to town. Their sadness was matched by the locals who loved and admired the talented young woman. Thousands of flowers, shipped in by train, covered her casket during the funeral. The final paragraph in her newspaper obituary read:

"A great soul of light was gathered into the Soul of the Supreme Light, shining on forever."

Leorena was buried at Winslow's Desert View Cemetery, but legend has it that she didn't rest there in peace. The stories claimed that her uneasy ghost began making appearances at the site of the new bridge that replaced the one that collapsed on that terrible night.

Local stories claimed that Leorena was there as a warning to other drivers to slow down and avoid the kind of highway tragedy that had claimed her life. There were reports from drivers who said they saw a pretty girl with brown curly hair, wearing a white dress, who darted into the road near Cottonwood Wash, forcing them to slow down.

But when they looked into the rearview mirror of the car after they passed the site, they always discovered that the young woman had disappeared.

"STANDING ON A CORNER..."

Well, I'm standin' on a corner
In Winslow, Arizona
And such a fine sight to see.
It's a girl, my Lord, in a flatbed Ford
Slowing down to take a look at me.

Eagles, 1972

THE COMMUNITY OF WINSLOW, ARIZONA, REAPED THE rewards of Route 66 for decades. The road seemed to provide an endless number of tourists and travelers. They rolled in from the east and west, cash in hand, eager to experience the "Indian country" of the Southwest, dine at the last Harvey House restaurant, and be amazed by the Meteor Crater, the Painted Desert, and the Petrified Forest.

But as this town that was created by the Atchison, Topeka, and Santa Fe Railroad eventually learned, all good things come to an end. Route 66 went dark at the end of 1977 when the highway was rerouted around the town. A switch had been flipped, and Winslow became the next victim of the interstate.

For the next 13 years, Winslow was just another doomed town, unable to reclaim the prosperity it once had. Across Route 66 states, tourism died. Communities, small and large, tried to reinvent themselves, but nearly all of them failed. One by one, businesses along the once thriving highway hung up "closed" signs and boarded up their windows. No one could imagine what could be done to restore the business Route 66 had once provided.

But the highway refused to die. In 1990, the first signs of new life emerged when author Michael Wallis published a book called *Route 66: The Mother Road*. More books, films, and events followed, and eventually, there was a groundswell of interest in old Route 66 – not just as a road used to get somewhere else but as a destination in and of itself.

By the mid-1990s, the nostalgia for bygone America that had started small had grown into a monster. Soon, tourists from all over the country – and even the world – began seeking out a lost America from a simpler time. More books appeared, money was raised, and historical groups started rebuilding and restoring. Tourism returned to towns that had been given up for dead years earlier.

In 1999, Winslow came up with their own tourism idea when they created Standin' On A Corner Park, a spot that was inspired by the classic Eagles song, "Take It Easy." Written primarily by Jackson Browne, the song told the story of a young man's brief encounter with a woman in a pickup truck. He wrote the lyric, "Well, I'm standin' on a corner in Winslow, Arizona," but then had no idea of

Eagles when "Take It Easy" became a huge hit

A bronze statue of Glenn Frey takes it easy while standing on a corner in Winslow, Arizona

where to go from there. His friend, Glenn Frey, who became one of the founding members of the Eagles, played around with it and added the next few lines about the girl in the flatbed Ford.

After that, the rest of the song pretty much wrote itself, and "Take It Easy" became the opening cut on what was to be the band's first album, with Glenn Frey providing the vocals. Although it only ever made it to number 12 on the *Billboard* charts, it eventually made the Rock and Roll Hall of Fame's list of the top 500 songs that helped shape America.

After hearing the song played countless times on the radio over the years, Winslow became engrained in the consciousness of a generation or two, and they wanted to connect tangibly with the band they loved so much. Winslow was happy to help them, creating the park on a corner where it wasn't hard to imagine a girl in a flatbed Ford driving by.

In September 2016, a lifelike bronze statue depicting Glenn Frey in his younger days was installed at the park. Sadly, Glenn never got to see it. He passed away in January of that same year at age 67.

The devotion to the song, love for the Eagles, and dedication to Route 66 have formed a potent mixture of pop culture in Winslow. Every year, more than 100,000 visitors come to Winslow to experience the corner for themselves.

HAUNTS OF LA POSADA HOTEL

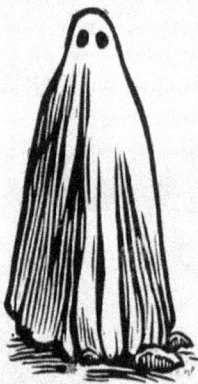

HAUNTED

LA POSADA HOTEL, A ONCE GREAT RAILROAD HOTEL, IS NOT the usual kind of lodging a traveler expects to find on Route 66. Built in 1930, it wasn't constructed to appeal to motorists but to passengers who traveled via the Santa Fe Railroad. The north side of the building faced Route 66, but this was originally the back door. The front door faced the railroad tracks on the south.

La Posada was the last of the Harvey House Hotels designed for the Fred Harvey company. Harvey Houses were renowned throughout the west

H-4224 LA POSADA, FRED HARVEY HOTEL, WINSLOW, ARIZONA

during their heyday. They had large staffs of dedicated female employees who provided first-rate service. They were known as "Harvey Girls," and they wore distinctive black dresses and white aprons – usually.

Mary Colter designed La Posada, and she felt the standard Harvey Girl uniform was too severe for her place, so she substituted colorful aprons with green, blue, or red backgrounds with quilted cacti, donkeys, and cowboys on them.

Mary, by the way, is just one of the many spirits whom staff members and visitors to La Posada have encountered. She has been seen and felt by those who work in and explore the beautiful lobby, dining and banquet rooms, and long hallways.

But if Mary does haunt the hotel, she is not alone.

During its heyday, famous guests at the hotel included Gene Autrey, Bob Hope, Howard Hughes, John Wayne, President Franklin D. Roosevelt, Clark Gable, Gary Cooper, Amelia Earhart, James Cagney, and, of course, literally thousands of ordinary train and highway travelers who have spent countless nights within the hotel's walls.

How many of those visitors – or staff members – have lingered behind at La Posada? Many guests have found items in their rooms moved from one place to another or have awakened at night thinking someone was in their room, only to realize that it was a ghost.

METEOR CRATER OBSERVATORY

AT SOME POINT AROUND 50,000 YEARS AGO, AN IRON AND Nickel meteor fell out of the sky and slammed into the Arizona desert with the explosive force of about 20 million tons of dynamite.

Meteor Crater was a huge attraction for Route 66 travelers

It left a very big crater behind.

Thousands of years later, a young artist showed up on the rim of that massive crater, and he turned it into an attraction that would be seen by scores of Route 66 travelers in the years that followed.

That artist's name was Harry Locke, and he was born in Oregon in October 1888, but he spent his early years in Colorado. He spent a few years as a police officer but knew it wasn't what he wanted to do with this life. He wanted to draw, and he wanted to learn to fly. He conquered his desire to soar into the skies first, flying around the country in several early single-engine propeller plans. He satisfied his other itch by drawing pictures of the places he visited and sending them home to wide-eyed family members.

During World War I, Harry served as an army mechanic. When he came home, he married a woman named Hope and went back to buzzing around the country until 1920. That was when the couple decided to land in Gila County, Arizona, where Harry drew postcards – and fell in love with Meteor Crater.

Harry wasn't the only one. It had been fascinating people for ages. The Hopi had a legend about the massive hole, located about 20 miles west of Winslow, that claimed it was the home of an outcast god who had fallen from the sky in a fiery blaze. The first white man recorded the crater in 1871. His name was Charles Franklin, and he was a scout for General George Custer. For a while, the crater was known as Franklin's Hole.

By the time Harry first took an interest in the place, it was called Barringer Crater, named after a determined Colonel Daniel Barringer, a Philadelphia mining engineer who had taken up residence nearby in 1903. Barringer had concluded that a cataclysmic meteor crash had formed the crater, but scientists dismissed this idea. They believed the hole had been caused by volcanic activity, and Barringer was widely criticized and ridiculed.

Intent on proving his meteor theory, Barringer filed four 160-acre mining claims on the crater and surrounding land and spent the next 26 years searching for the buried meteorite. But on April 11, 1922, Barringer's rotary drill bit jammed, the cable broke, and the drill was lost. Barringer was down but not willing to accept failure – yet. In 1929, he finally called off the search and died later that year in Haverford, Pennsylvania, never knowing that his theory would eventually be proven correct. It was just that the meteor itself had vaporized on impact. A single, sizable fragment was never found.

Harry Locke was one of Barringer's most devoted disciples. He subscribed to Barringer's theory long before it was universally accepted, and when he moved to Arizona, he made himself the crater's caretaker. Harry and Hope homesteaded 640 acres of land several miles north of Barringer's Crater. Their property was crossed by the road to the crater and by Route 66. On the southeast side of this intersection, the Lockes built a service station they dubbed Meteor Station.

When the station opened, Harry and Hope sold gas and started regaling motorists with the story of Arizona's enormous meteor. In the late 1920s, many travelers didn't even know what a meteor was. Harry educated them using a large relief sculpture that covered one wall of his store.

Visitors who were entranced by his stories were thrilled to find that Meteor Station sold fragments of the space rocks that had been collected on private land around the crater.

Harry was often amused by the reaction that tourists had to the crater itself. Their amazement sent him back to his real-life drawing board, where he started creating postcards that depicted the massive hole.

Harry and Hope operated Meteor Station for years, slowly finding themselves more interested in talking about meteors than pumping gas and changing tires. By the early 1930s, they had decided to build a large-scale meteorite museum on property east of the store.

In August 1933, they leased Meteor Station to "Rimmy Jim" Giddings, who would have wrangled his way into Western lore whether he operated the station or not. Born in Texas in April 1873, the cowpoke rode into Arizona in 1910 and found work at a cattle and mercantile company in Seligman. One day, the foreman's son asked Jim what type of saddle he used. Jim replied that he rode a "Rimfire" or a "Rimmy-rig" – a double-cinch saddled made in Texas. The amused boy dubbed his new friend "Rimmy Jim," and his legend was born.

Rimmy partnered with Milt Powers in the cattle business, running herds on the Little Colorado River. One day, Rimmy was in Flagstaff and entered the store of William Switzer, a hardware man who had placed a leather worker in the store to serve local ranchers. Conversations about cowhide turned into a friendship, and Switzer all but adopted Rimmy into his family.

Years later, Switzer's daughter, Ruth, recalled in an interview: "I don't think Rimmy had much family of his own, but he was like an uncle to me. Every Thanksgiving, my mother baked two turkeys – one for our family and one for Rimmy Jim. Rimmy joined the Oddfellows Lodge with my father. He was always at our house."

In 1927, William Switzer became a charter member of Flagstaff's National Order of Boneheads, an anti-club dedicated to silliness of any kind. Members met at the Monte Vista Hotel and spent their time petitioning Congress to repaint the Painted Desert and pestering the State Fish and Game Commission to stock local streams with smoked herring. The Boneheads had a special place in their hearts for Rimmy Jim, who liked to tell tourists that he kept a graveyard across the road from Meteor Station and buried traveling salesmen there if they dared to knock on his door.

He also once bought an early version of an intercom system and installed it in the two-hole outhouse behind his building. When a woman would go to the outhouse, he'd wait for her to get settled and then come on the intercom and say, "Pardon me, madam, would you mind switching over to the other hole? I'm trying to finish painting under this one."

Harry Locke also had a soft spot for Jim. With his thick, sandy mustache, stereotypical Western wear, and eyes that twinkled with both humor and hellfire, he turned him into a cartoon. In the late 1930s, he drew a series of postcards with him as the main character.

Jim's lease with the Lockes called for $30 a month in rent – plus $1,000 upfront to cover the rent for two years. The Lockes needed the advance money because the museum they had planned was going to be grand. At its east end, Harry envisioned a tower so tall it could offer a glimpse of Meteor Crater, even though it was a few miles away.

Construction had only just started when tragedy struck. One day, Hope complained of stomach pains, and Harry helped her into the car and sped toward Winslow. By the time they reached the hospital, though, there was nothing the doctors could do. Hope had died from a ruptured appendix.

Heartbroken, Harry turned his despair toward building the museum. Day after day, he carved flagstones out of the countryside. He packed bricks together with his own mixture of adobe and concrete. Slowly, the building took shape.

Harry was still hard at work on the museum in 1936 when he married his second wife, Attie Treat, a Winslow postal worker. She had a young daughter from a previous marriage, Marguerite, who saw her new stepfather as something of a hero – a man who built castles.

Meteor Crater Observatory opened to the public around 1938. Harry offered formal lectures to visitors and formed a business relationship with the Hayden Planetarium in New York, selling them meteorites on consignment. He also sold meteorite jewelry to tourists, but within a few years of opening Meteor Crater Observatory, Harry realized his dream would never support his family. Depression-era customers often refused to pay for lectures, and few were interested in buying souvenirs. One night, Harry forgot to retrieve his telescope from its place in the tower and awoke the next morning to find the expensive item had been stolen.

Saddled with the debt of

AMERICAN METEORITE MUSEUM - U.S. HWY. 66
SITES METEOR CRATER - H. H. NININGER, DIRECTOR M-1

building the place in the first place, Harry lost Meteor Crater Observatory to foreclosure. Although Rimmy Jim took over Meteor Station and the observatory and owned it for some years afterward, Harry's dream would only be realized after both men had died under the direction of Dr. Harvey Nininger.

Dr. Harvey Nininger

DURING HIS YEARS AT METEOR JUNCTION, DR. NININGER often recalled for visitors the exact moment that he realized the power of meteors – it was November 9, 1923, at exactly 8:57 P.M.

Harvey, a biology professor, on that particular night, had attended a function at the small Kansas college where he taught. As he was walking home with a faculty friend, they saw a ball of fire streak across the sky and vanish behind a pine tree. The next morning, Harvey climbed to the top of that pine tree, figuring out the bearings of where the meteorite might have crashed. And this began his lifelong obsession with hunting rocks that fell from space.

Harvey's first years as a meteorite hunter were hampered by his professor's salary. He solved that problem by offering natural history lectures at schools in areas where meteors had recently fallen. He acquired his first large meteorite by making a Sunday morning appeal to a church congregation. When services were over, the minister led him to an odd-looking rock that had fallen from heaven into his yard.

In the years that followed, Harvey found meteorites used as doorstops. Another held down the lid of a general store's pickle jar, and one covered a rat hole in a basement.

As Harvey's assets and reputation grew, he moved to Denver in 1930 and became the curator of the Colorado Museum of Natural History. He installed a meteorite saw – special blades were needed to cut the nearly indestructible iron – in a general store owned by a friend, and he dubbed the place Nininger Laboratory.

Like Harry Locke, Harvey considered Arizona's Meteor Crater ground zero in his search and often visited the area. During one trip, he noticed Harry's old  Meteor Crater Observatory. He discovered the building was available for lease and moved in. He renamed the building the American Meteorite Laboratory and set about finishing what Harry had started.

From the beginning, fortune seemed to smile on his plans. On October 9, 1946 – the day he moved his collection of meteorites into the building – he saw the night sky explode with a spectacular meteor shower. He counted 91 meteors falling in one minute – the greatest celestial display he'd ever seen.

Harvey opened the American Meteorite Museum 10 days later, and while Harry Locke had once found visitor enthusiasm dampened by the Depression, Dr. Nininger found postwar visitors eager to learn. During its first year in operation, the museum saw 33,000 paid admissions, and he estimated he and his staff had provided more than 2,000 hours of educational talks.

By the late 1940s, Harvey had turned the museum into one of the most active meteoric research centers in the world. The museum tested any rock specimen sent to determine its origins for free. His location on Route 66 encouraged travelers to quickly notify him of new meteor falls.

Harvey looked to the day when a fully equipped and well-staffed laboratory and observatory would supplement his museum facilities. He longed for a landing strip and a plane to use for quick trips to newly reported falls. All this seemed destined to happen until 1949, when a new alignment of Route 66 passed north of the museum. Cut off from the new section of highway, Harvey abandoned Harry Locke's building and moved to Sedona, Arizona, where he founded a new American Meteorite Museum.

Dr. Nininger continued watching the skies until his death in March 1986.

A HEAVY BLOW WAS DEALT TO HARRY LOCKE WHEN HE WAS forced to give up Meteor Crater Observatory and the dream that it had represented for him. He ended up in Phoenix, working for Porter Brothers Men's Wear, where he tooled leather wallets on the sales floor. Attie, meanwhile, had gone back to work at the post office.

At that point, Harry didn't realize that his artistic work with leather was going to lead to bigger and better things. He soon became affiliated with El Sahuaro Studios, where his artwork evolved into a new comic strip that featured creatures of the desert. Harry called it *Desert Cuties*.

Harry developed the comic during World War II. Appropriately, the first panels of the strip incorporated wartime themes, like having horned toads looking suspiciously at alarm clocks like they were ticking bombs and Japanese beetles carrying enemy flags. Mostly, though, he concentrated on giving faces and personalities to saguaro cactus. Harry wandered out into the desert, studying the bumps and curves of the cactus and letting his imagination run wild.

As the fame and popularity of *Desert Cuties* grew, Harry took to motoring between Winslow and Phoenix with his menagerie of desert animals. He showed up for appearances with snakes, horned toads, and cactus owls, but his favorite was a Chuckwalla lizard named Chucky, named for one of the comic strip's main characters. Harry fashioned little costumes for Chucky – usually a tiny caballero hat – and dressed him up for events. The public loved it.

By late 1942, Harry was on the verge of becoming a national celebrity. His writer, Oren Arnold, predicted he might rival Walt Disney. Children followed him everywhere he went when he was home in Winslow. Harry was just waiting for the end of the war. A New York publishing firm had offered him an exclusive contract for *Desert Cuties* once peace returned.

Then, in early 1943, Winslow's under-sheriff resigned, leaving the local lawmen in a bind. Aware of Harry's past as a cop in Colorado, the Winslow City Council asked him to join the force temporarily.

Harry agreed – and 11 weeks later, he was dead.

He died on May 26 in the fireman's quarters at City Hall after tussling with a drunken prisoner. He was only 54 years old.

LESS THAN A MONTH LATER, AN AILING RIMMY JIM Giddings walked into Wright Hospital in Winslow, complaining about chest pains. He promptly passed away.

Rimmy left equal shares of Meteor Station and Meteor Crater Observatory to William Switzer and a Flagstaff orphanage. The orphanage needed the money more, so Switzer bought their shares. He subsequently sold Meteor Station to his daughter and son-in-law, Ruth and Sid Griffin. They stayed there for more than 20 years, even after the new alignment of Route 66 slid north of the store. They simply moved the building to the new road, finally closing when the interstate came through.

Parts of the Meteor Crater Observatory are still standing today, the crumbling ruins still visible in the distance to travelers who rush past on Interstate 40.

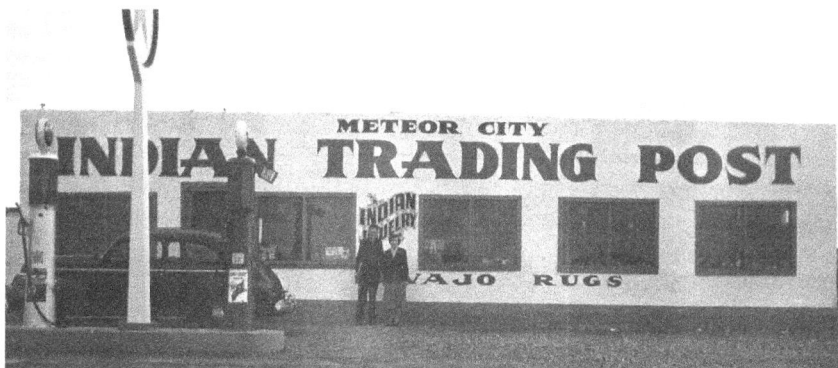

"THE WICKED WITCH OF ROUTE 66"

DESPITE ITS NAME, METEOR CITY WASN'T A TOWN – IT WAS a trading post located a stone's throw away from Meteor Station and the nearby crater. It started as a service station, opened by Joe Scharber in 1938, serving scores of Route 66 travelers every day.

In 1941, the property was purchased by longtime bachelor Jack Newsum, who added a small store to the station so tourists could buy food, drinks, and meteor souvenirs. In 1942, he erected a large sign along the highway that exclaimed, "Population 1." He ran the Meteor City Trading Post alone and quite successfully for several years. The popular spot grew larger over time and offered the usual array of curios and souvenirs, along with food and gas.

But Jack always seemed sad to his friends. They started calling him "Lonesome Jack," and after a while, he took it to heart. When he returned home after a trip to

In 1979, the concrete dome was added to Meteor City and a few years later, the location achieved notoriety thanks to its appearance in the movie, "Starman."

Alabama to visit his family, he returned with a surprise – a new bride named Goldie. The couple, both in their 40s, never had children, but together, they operated Meteor City for almost a quarter of a century.

When Jack started suffering from health problems in the late 1950s, he decided to resign from his long-held position as the local justice of the peace. Goldie took over for him with full approval from her husband. However, the tiny, otherwise friendly woman soon became the terror of the nearby stretch of Route 66, handing out stiff penalties to speeders and traffic violators.

She earned the nickname "the Wicked Witch of Route 66."

Jack died in 1960, and a short time later, the trading post burned, forcing Goldie to move to another building. She and her mother continued to live there and run the trading post until Goldie died in 1967.

The trading post building went through many changes in the years that followed. In 1979, the structure was replaced, and the large concrete dome that was added soon gained fame as the highway restaurant in the 1984 film *Starman*. However, that shop also burned in 1990 and was rebuilt as a souvenir shop for visitors to Meteor Crater. Sadly, it closed in 2012.

As of a few years ago, the dusty and rundown-looking building was still sitting empty along this stretch of the old highway, hoping for someone new to come along and keep the legend alive in the new century.

TRAGEDY AT TOONERVILLE

IT SEEMS HARD TO BELIEVE THAT A PLACE NAMED FOR A cartoon could become known for the kind of tragedy that Toonerville did.

Never more than a trading post located on a slice of desert just east of Twin Arrows, Arizona, the name was inspired by a comic strip that ran from 1908 to 1955 called *Toonerville Folks*. The fictional Toonerville had a "Toonerville Trolley" and was populated with "Toonerfolks" who had names like Terrible-Tempered Truman and Little Woo-Woo Wortle. Its popularity prompted a Phoenix baseball to call itself the "Toonerville Merchants," and many cities called their trolley cars "Toonervilles."

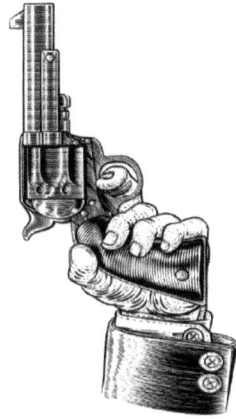

TRUE CRIME

Despite the name, there is nothing funny about the events that took place at the trading post.

Established by Earl Tinnin and his wife, Elsie, in 1935, the trading post provided a dependable income for them during the Depression, as well as a home for their family that grew to include a son, George, and a daughter, Helen.

The first Toonerville tragedy occurred in August 1947 when 14-year-old George accidentally shot himself in the face with a .32-caliber pistol and died.

Earl and Elsie continued operating the trading post until 1954, when they moved to Flagstaff to manage a motel and sold Toonerville to Merritt McAlister, a man with a well-earned reputation for violence with a quick temper. At age 21, he'd been involved in a fight at a roadhouse that

Toonerville Trading Post - U.S. 66 - between Flagstaff and Winslow, Ariz.

ended in a shooting. Several reports of threats, including him brandishing a gun, had been filed during the time he was manager at the Vermilion Cliff Lodge.

However, by most accounts, Merritt had put his violent past behind him by the time he took over the trading post. By 1971, he turned 60 and was quietly running the place with his third wife, Pearl. The interstate had recently bypassed Route 66, and they were thinking of selling the property.

Then, on a hot summer's day near the end of August 1971, Pearl called the manager at the Twin Arrows Trading Post a few miles down the road and said that their store had been robbed and that she and Merritt had been shot. The manager from Twin Arrows arrived within minutes and found Merritt dead on the floor with a gunshot wound to the chest. The trading post had been ransacked, and Pearl was bleeding badly from a gunshot wound to the head. Luckily, she survived.

When the police arrived, Pearl was only able to tell them that there had been three assailants and they were traveling in two cars: a blue sports car and a sedan. The leads went nowhere, and the robbery and murder remain unsolved to this day.

But this was not the last Toonerville tragedy.

More recently, it became the residence of Mary Smeal, a Route 66 advocate and preservationist. Mary led an effort to restore the nearby Twin Arrows Trading Post and planned to resurrect Toonerville as a roadside attraction. She was widely known for her friendliness, willingness to help, and enthusiasm for the highway.

Then, on November 16, 2016, Mary was fatally shot by her boyfriend, Jeffrey Jones, in her Toonerville home. Jones then turned the gun on himself.

The Toonerville Trading Post now stands in mournful silence, hoping for a day when the string of tragedies will be firmly in the past and life on this stretch of Route 66 can return to normal.

TERROR AT TWO GUNS

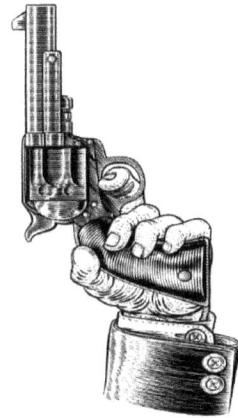

TRUE CRIME

ONE OF THE BLOODIEST STOPS ON ALL OF ROUTE 66 – OR on any highway really – was Two Guns, Arizona. In 1925, Earl Cundiff opened a filling station, garage, café, and rental cottages at Canyon Diablo to accommodate tourists traveling along the National Old Trails Highway. He called this lonely desert spot Canyon Lodge.

Harry "Indian" Miller – whom you might remember from the "Cave of the Seven Devils" section – had his own place south of Canyon Lodge, but progress was not kind to Harry as the path of the new Route 66 bypassed his business by miles. Wanting to take advantage of the new highway, Harry made a deal with Earl Cundiff and, in March 1925, leased a piece of land nearby and opened a store he dubbed Fort Two Guns. The spot boasted the standard souvenir shop, constructed from desert stone, and a roadside zoo showcased mountain lions, wild cats, javelina, and Gila monsters for the tourists.

He also reopened a cave at the site that had a blood-soaked past that Harry was quick to take advantage of. As with most legends, details differ, but the story is true.

In 1878, Navajo pueblos in northern Arizona were attacked repeatedly by Apache raiders from the south, who inexplicably disappeared after each attack. They were, it turned out, hiding in a small cave in Canyon Diablo. After one of their raids, the hideout was discovered by a Navajo scout, and they laid siege to the cave. To smoke the Apache out, the Navajo built a raging fire at the

cave's entrance and kept it burning through the night.

The doomed Apache killed and stacked their horses at the cave's opening, desperate to block out the smoke, but by morning, all 42 had been asphyxiated. Following the massacre, the Apache raids came to an end. In the years that followed, the Navajo warned white settlers that Canyon Diablo was cursed, and it's been said that those who camped there often reported hearing the death chants of the dying Apache drifting out of the cave and into the narrow canyon.

Harry was the first to exploit the massacre and the spooky elements of the cave, and tourists flocked to see it, listen to the gruesome tales, and experience a shiver or two as they stepped into the darkened interior.

Both businesses thrived in Canyon Diablo for the next year, but over time, Harry Miller learned his landlord had a bad temper. A disagreement occurred between them on March 3, 1926, and in the heat of the argument, Earl grabbed Harry's pistol from the table and fired at him. The bullet harmlessly punched a hole through Harry's shirt. In the ensuing scuffle, Harry ended up with the gun, shooting Earl twice.

Both men had their supporters, and the trial in Flagstaff was highly publicized. Testimony eventually revealed that a tryst between Earl's wife, Louise, and Harry's business partner, Joe Sekakuku, was what started the argument. The verdict was returned, finding Harry – "not guilty."

After the trial, bad feelings between factions persisted. Harry's highway billboards were often vandalized, and he was charged with defacing Earl's tombstone, which had been inscribed with the words "Killed by Indian Miller" when it was placed in the cemetery. Harry eventually tired of all of it and moved to the Cave of the Sevin Devils in 1934.

In 1963, Benjamin Dreher purchased Two Guns and kept things running the way that Harry Miller had for years. But then, on August 1, 1971, a catastrophe struck when several gasoline tanks burst into flames, destroying Two Guns in a fiery blaze.

Two decades later, the land where the ruins of Two Guns were still standing was sold to Howard and Marilyn Armstrong, who planned to restore the place to its former glory using vintage photos as reference. The plan never really got off the ground, though, and it's been abandoned ever since.

From the Apache massacre in the 1870s to the death of Earl Cundiff in 1926 to the fire in 1971, Two Guns has seen more than its share of mayhem. Maybe the story of the curse of the Apache Death Cave is not just a legend. Maybe there's something to it after all, and perhaps it's for the best that Two Guns has remained silent for the last few decades.

TWIN ARROWS

HEADING WEST FROM TWO GUNS AND CANYON DIABLO, travelers soon reached the iconic site of the Twin Arrows Trading Post. First opened in 1946 as the Canyon Padre Trading Post, owner Ted Griffith offered a store, service station, and café. The café was a small 10-stool diner designed by the Valentine Manufacturing Company, which made prefabricated diners during the 1940s and 1950s.

Unfortunately, Ted was seriously injured by a passing truck in 1955, and the business was subsequently sold to the Troxell family.

Jean and William Troxell renamed it the Twin Arrows

Trading Post and placed two huge "arrows" in the parking lot to draw the attention of Route 66 motorists. The arrows were made from colorfully painted telephone poles that were adorned with wooden feathers. They became icons of American roadside architecture and were even featured in a car commercial in the mid-1990s.

The Troxells stocked all the usual roadside stuff – Navajo rugs, moccasins, jewelry, glassware, state spoons, and more – and had a thriving business for decades. Even after the interstate came through in the late 1960s, an exit to the Twin Arrows saved it from certain demise.

Even so, the trading post closed in the early 1990s, only to be revived again by Spence and Virginia Reidel. Advertised as "The BEST Little Stop on I-40," the shelves were stocked once more with souvenirs, and the gas pumps were again dispensing fuel. Unfortunately, this rebirth didn't last, and the place closed for good in 1995.

The buildings are now abandoned and crumbling, although the twin arrows were restored in 2009 and are still attracting tourists with cameras from all over the world.

ONE OF THE HIGHWAY'S MOST DANGEROUS BRIDGES

LEAVING TWIN ARROWS, THE OLDEST ALIGNMENT OF ROUTE 66, once traveled north of the modern-day interstate and crossed Padre Canyon, which dramatically split the relatively flat plains of the high desert. Predating the creation of Route 66, the 1914 Canyon Padre Bridge on the old Flagstaff-Winslow Highway became one of the most dangerous on the Mother Road.

Several serious accidents occurred here, mainly because drivers were required to navigate six hazardous approach curves as they descended into the canyon, crossed the narrow bridge, and climbed out the other side. At the time, it was the only way for the many Depression-era travelers, and later, tourists taking vacations, to make their way westward.

But dangerous or not, the bridge was something special. It was one of only two Luten Arch bridges along the entire route. These bridges were designed by Daniel B. Luten and were concrete structures that were created to not only be lighter than most bridges but also reinforced in strategic ways to address load tension on the surface.

Recognizing the traffic volume and the dangerous aspects of the road, Route 66 was realigned with a new bridge in 1937 in the same place that it is today. This bridge, too, was replaced when I-40 came through, but the foundation of the original bridge can still be found under the westbound lanes of the interstate.

"DON'T FORGET WINONA..."

IT WAS BOBBY TROUP'S SONG THAT PUT WINONA, ARIZONA, on the map more than anything else did.

Initially, the place was called Walnut, predating its settlement in 1912. It got its start when Billy Adams was making his way from Moody, Texas, to Long Beach, California, by bicycle. He was on his way there to visit his brother, but his trip got cut short.

Peddling his way across Arizona, he came up to a spot – about 13 miles east of Flagstaff – that would become Winona. He liked the place, and after traveling on to Flagstaff, he bought a train ticket and returned to Texas. He married a girl named Myrtle, and they soon returned to that "perfect spot," where they built the Winona Trading Post and started offering modern necessities like fan belts, tools, tires, cold drinks, sandwiches, and dry goods. They also began exchanging supplies and groceries with the Navajo and Hopi Indians for blankets, jewelry, and other native crafts.

Though Route 66 was not yet established, automobiles were making their way westward on the Flagstaff-Winslow Highway, passing right by the Adams' trading post. Seeing the opportunity, they soon established one of the first tourist camps in Arizona in 1920. Billy built 12 one-room cabins and overnight camping for those who couldn't afford the $1 per night cabin fee. A Texaco service station was also added around this time.

Billy's trade was as a barber, and after he got the tourist camp going, he traveled to Flagstaff to work while Myrtle ran the store and tourist camp. Before long, several ranchers had settled in the area, and a post office was needed. It was established in the **Winona Trading Post**,

Winona Trading Post

and in 1924, Myrtle became the first female postmaster in Arizona. To make mail pick-up easier, she would hang the mail sack outside so that railroad men could hook it as the train rolled by.

The couple continued to live upstairs in the trading post through the 1920s when they moved across the highway. There, they homesteaded a piece of land, and Billy began ranching, a career he continued, increasing their landholdings until they wound up with a sizeable spread, and he retired in the late 1960s.

In 1925, Billy added the two-story Winona Motel to the property. It had 14 rooms upstairs and a small lobby below. Throughout the 1940s, it was a beehive of activity, especially during World War II when convoys of troops came through the community.

Winona grew as people began to travel Route 66 again after the war, winding up with a population of just over 100 people. However, the small town's Route 66 heydays would be short. In the early 1950s, the highway was routed south of the town, bypassing the trading post altogether.

Billy and Myrtle sold the store to a couple named the Pills, who added a garage offering mechanical work. When Mr. Pill retired, his son, Bill, took over the operations. It then sold two more times and is currently in operation today as a Shell Station. It still stands today, although the motel, campground, and trading post vanished years ago.

Unlike so many other small towns along Route 66, Winona never really prospered and was never incorporated as a town. It gained its greatest notoriety by being mentioned in Bobby Troup's song – not because there was anything substantial there, but because he was able to make it rhyme.

MURDER OF A GOOD SAMARITAN

ANYONE WHO KNEW HIM CALLED ARY BEST A GOOD MAN. He was the type of man you could always count on, always willing to lend a hand to someone, whether they were a friend or a stranger.

But his last act of kindness took place about 12 miles east of Flagstaff on Route 66.

On July 31, 1959, Patrick McGee, an alcoholic and itinerant farm worker with a criminal history that dated back 25 years and included charges of vagrancy, burglary, driving under the influence, public drunkenness, and assault and battery, was driving from Oklahoma to California with a woman named Millie Fain.

TRUE CRIME

When the car they were riding in broke down near Flagstaff, McGee steered to the shoulder of the road and lifted the hood, hoping someone would stop and help.

And someone did – Ary Best. The older man, who'd been suffering from arthritis for years, stopped, climbed out of his vehicle, and limped over to see if he could offer help. In return for his kindness, McGee attacked him from behind, stabbed him twice in the back, and then stabbed him two more times when he collapsed to the pavement. Millie Fain then grabbed the knife and stabbed Ary twice in the throat. Together, the pair rolled him into the ditch, emptied his pockets, and stole his car.

Witnesses later reported seeing them in Flagstaff purchasing gas and beer and driving Ary's car. In Williams, they went on a drinking spree and were well remembered because they had loudly purchased rounds of drinks for the house at several taverns. They were last spotted buying tickets and boarding a train for Los Angeles.

After Ary's body was found along the highway and his car was found abandoned in

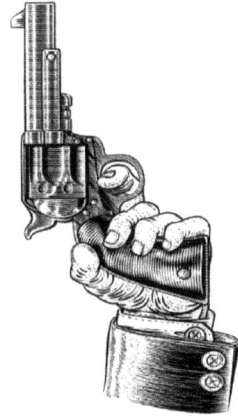

Ary Best's killer, Patrick McGee

Williams with McGee's fingerprints all over the interior, the couple was arrested in L.A., extradited to Arizona, and charged with murder.

The nine-day trial was anticlimactic. McGee claimed that he'd killed Ary Best after the older man attempted to assault Millie, but during the trial, she claimed that Ary had been murdered after their request for money – and then a request for money in exchange for sex – was denied. Both McGee and Fain were found guilty. McGee died in the gas chamber at the Arizona state prison on March 8, 1963. Fain was given a life sentence but was eventually paroled.

FLAGSTAFF

LOCATED ALONG AN OLD WAGON ROAD TO CALIFORNIA, the first white settler in the region was likely Edward Whipple, who opened a saloon next to a roadside spring in 1871. A few years later, another man, Thomas F. McMillan, settled north of the present-day city. Soon, more and more people began arriving in the area, which was plentiful with water, game, and lumber. Others began cattle and sheep ranching.

There are several versions of how Flagstaff got its name, and all of them have to do with stripping a lone pine tree and turning it into a flagpole on July 4, 1876, in honor of the nation's centennial.

Subsequently, they dubbed the area "Flag Staff," and in 1881, the two words were combined into one, and Flagstaff was born. A year later, the Atlantic and Pacific Railroad rolled into town, and its future was secured.

Fire destroyed the city in 1886 and 1888, but it was quickly rebuilt each time. In 1894, Dr. Percival

On the wy into Flagstaff in the 1920s

Lowell was attracted to Flagstaff thanks to its clear skies. He established the world-famous Lowell Observatory, where Pluto was discovered in 1930 – whether it's a planet or not.

In 1899, the University of Northern Arizona was established, and Flagstaff soon became the cultural center of Northern Arizona. By the early 1900s, Flagstaff began touting its connection to the natural "Seven Wonders" of the region – Coconino National Forest, the Grand Canyon, Oak Creek Canyon, Walnut Canyon, Wupatki National Monument, Sunset Crater National Monument, and the San Francisco Peaks.

Flagstaff's location on the Colorado Plateau gave it the honor of being the highest point on Route 66, and as this – and the "Seven Wonders" – became well known, tourism became Flagstaff's biggest industry, and the city continued to grow at a slow and steady pace.

When Route 66 arrived in Flagstaff, several motor courts, service stations, and diners sprouted up along the new highway. Today, the city still sports several vintage cafes and motor courts along its historic downtown district. There are several that are still open today, such as the **Wonderland Motel** nestled up against the pine-covered hills, the **Frontier Motel** with its quiet yellow lantern, the **Saga Budget Inn Motel** complete with a bright blue neon sign, and many more.

One of the most famous motels in town is no longer a motel today, but for nearly 40 years, it was a popular stop in Flagstaff.

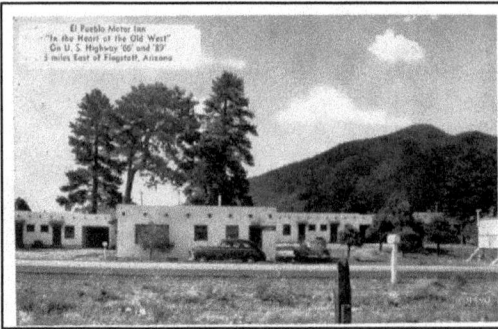

Phillip Johnston opened the **El Pueblo Motor Inn** in 1936. Johnston was the son of a Navajo missionary and is best known as the man responsible for developing the Navajo "Code Talkers" program during World War II. Growing up on the reservation as a child, he learned to speak fluent Navajo, and the complex code that he developed based on this unwritten language stumped the enemy during the war and saved countless American lives.

The El Pueblo was located east of downtown "in the heart of the Old West." This was an area that was considered "out in the country" when the motel was built, and it was quite successful due in no small part to the fact that it was one of the first auto courts travelers saw when approaching Flagstaff from the east. The rooms were set back from the road in a wooded area that was dense with pine trees. Picturesque mountains formed the backdrop, allowing Johnston to use advertising phrases for the place, like "modern comfort in the pines" and "your home away from home."

Johnston died in 1978, but the motel lived on despite time, the elements, and a string of neglectful owners taking a toll on the place. Most recently, it has been turned into apartments, but it still stands as a prime example of a classic Southwestern 1930s-era motel.

In 1968, the interstate bypassed Flagstaff's stretch of Route 66, making it the first Arizona city to lose the tourism lifeline. Thanks to its size and the many things it continued to offer, Flagstaff has continued to thrive over the decades and remains an attraction for nostalgia buffs who still flock to the area.

HAUNTS OF THE MUSEUM CLUB

ONE OF THE ICONS OF ROUTE 66 IN FLAGSTAFF IS THE Museum Club, which began its life as the boyhood dream of taxidermist Dean Eldredge in 1931.

The Dean Eldridge Museum, which became the Museum Club

When Dean discovered a petrified frog as a boy growing up in Wisconsin, he became committed to a lifetime of collecting and preserving rare artifacts, curios, and oddities. His passion for collecting and preserving led to a career in taxidermy in 1918, and his pursuit of unusual items turned him into a sportsman, adventurer, and collector.

Throughout the 1920s, Dean spent a lot of time in Mexico and the Southwestern United States. In the 1930s, he had the opportunity to purchase a piece of federal land just east of Flagstaff on Route 66. He soon hired unemployed lumberjacks to cut trees, haul them to his property, and build what he dubbed "the biggest log cabin in the world" – although he later revised that to "the biggest log cabin in the nation" and later, "the biggest log cabin in Arizona."

HAUNTED

The interior of the Museum Club was filled with Native American artifacts, Navaho rugs, and, of course, hundreds of taxidermied animals

In any case, he finally had a showplace for his collection of stuffed animals, six-legged sheep, Winchester rifles, Native American artifacts, two-headed calves, and more than 30,000 other items. On June 20, 1931, he opened the place as a museum, taxidermist shop, and trading post, and scores of Route 66 travelers began stopping to visit Dean and see his collection of oddities and unusual artifacts. Navajo rugs were hung from ceiling beams and walls and covered the floors. Every possible square inch of the building was utilized for museum pieces and gift shop items – from souvenirs to Navajo and Hopi pottery, baskets, and rugs. Examples of taxidermy were everywhere, and before long, locals dubbed the museum "The Zoo," a name that has stuck with the building to this day.

Unfortunately, the Museum Club operated for only five short years. It closed after Dean died from cancer, and his massive collection was sold. The building was purchased by a Flagstaff saddlemaker named Doc Williams. In 1936, Williams, taking advantage of the many travelers of the Mother Road and the end of Prohibition, opened a nightclub that was an immediate success.

Over the years, the building passed through several owners and served as a nightclub and recording studio. By the 1950s, the club had deteriorated into a rough, beer-drinking, fist-throwing roadhouse that was patronized by a crowd that liked a little blood with its beer.

But then, in 1963, Don Scott, a steel guitarist who'd played with Bob Wills' Texas Playboys, bought the club and moved to Flagstaff along with his wife, Thorna. They wasted no time cleaning the place up and turning it into a country music dance hall. With help from friends like Bob Wills, Waylon Jennings, Wynn Stewart, Wanda Jackson, and Willie Nelson, the Museum Club became a hot country and western showcase and a favorite stop for both big-time and aspiring performers on their way to Las Vegas.

Living in an upstairs apartment in the building, Don and Thorna Scott were active in running the successful club until 1973 when a tragedy occurred. After a long night, the couple closed

The Museum Club eventually transformed into a roadside tavern and later, into a popular music venue

the club, and Thorna went upstairs, leaving Don downstairs to finish things up. On the way up the steps, though, she tripped and fell from near the top of the staircase, falling and breaking her neck. She lapsed into a coma and died a few weeks later.

Don became despondent after her death, suffering from loneliness and traumatic memories of Thorna's death. After two years of unendurable pain, Don took his own life, shooting himself in front of the fireplace in 1975.

Three years after this tragic event, the club sold again, this time to Martin and Stacie Zanzucchi. They began extensive restorations and restored the original feel of the club by adding taxidermy mounts, antlers, period decorations, and, of course, Route 66 memorabilia. Today, the club continues to host the rising stars of country music and the new sounds out of Nashville.

The Museum Club continues to hearken back to an era when music filtered out from under the doors and out the open windows of every town between Chicago and L.A.

But apparently, it's not just country singers and their fans who are hosted at the Museum Club – it seems the ghosts of the former owners are still around, too.

SIGNS THAT DON AND THORNA SCOTT HAVE REMAINED AT the club they loved – and where both of them died – are frequently noticed by staff members and guests. Footsteps and creaks are often heard coming from the second floor where their apartment was located. Lights tend to flicker on and off, chairs rock back and forth, bar items move around, and flames spring up in the fireplace when no one is around.

Thorna herself often makes appearances, frequently being spotted on the back stairway and the back bar, where confused patrons sometimes mistake her for a bartender. She has also been seen in a dimly lit corner booth and occasionally, customers buy her a drink only to find she has vanished when they return.

One man, who lived in the upstairs apartment for a time, claimed he was pinned to the floor by a friendly female ghost. Evidently, Thorna has a sense of humor after death because she told the man while sitting on his chest, "You only need to fear the living." Then, the apparition disappeared. Wasting no time, the tenant broke through the upstairs window, ran across the roof, and disappeared, never to return.

On another night, as a bartender was starting her shift, she was surprised to see the bar shelf was in a state of disarray. Beer bottles were switched around, drink mixes were at the wrong end, and some liquor bottles had been knocked over. Because the bar area had been straightened up the night before, she had no choice but to blame it on the mischievous former owners.

Once located on the outskirts of town, this old highway watering hole is a Route 66 throwback that's now surrounded by present-day Flagstaff. If you get a chance to stop in and enjoy some live country music, be sure to keep an eye out for Don and Thorna and raise a glass to the memory of the couple who made sure the Museum Club is still with us today.

GHOSTS OF THE HOTEL MONTE VISTA

LOCATED ALONG ROUTE 66 IN FLAGSTAFF, THE HOTEL Monte Vista opened on New Year's Day 1927, and it continues to serve travelers today. Almost with hosting numerous celebrities over the years like John Wayne, Big Crosby, and Harry Truman, it's also home to several ghostly residents of the past.

In 1924, tourism was turning into a significant business in Flagstaff, but the city had

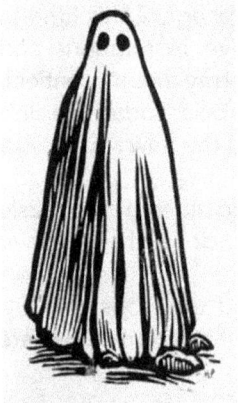

HAUNTED

a problem – not enough hotel rooms to keep visitors in town and spending money. So, that year, a man named V.M. Slipher started a local fundraising campaign to build a new hotel.

His efforts resulted in a city-voted ordinance that established a municipal bond to build the Monte Vista.

After it opened, the hotel was popular not only with tourists but also with locals, who quickly coined the phrase, "Meet me at the Monte V." In its first year, the hotel hosted Mary Costigan's daily three-hour radio show from room 105. Costigan was the first American woman to be granted a radio broadcasting license.

Even though the hotel opened in the middle of the Prohibition era, the Monte Vista lounge largely ignored the law and offered Flagstaff's most popular speakeasy. However, the owners pushed their luck in 1931, and it was closed by local officials. Business resumed two years later when Prohibition was repealed. For five years between 1935 and 1940, the hotel lounge and lobby also offered its many guests a wide range of slot machines to choose from, the only ones ever in Flagstaff.

During the 1940s and 1950s, when Western films were all the rage, more than 100 movies were filmed in nearby Sedona and Oak Creek Canyon. The Hotel Monte Vista hosted famous guests like Jane Russell, Gary Cooper, Spencer Tracy, John Wayne, and Bing Crosby. One scene from the film *Casablanca* was shot in one of the hotel's rooms.

Interestingly, John Wayne was one of the first to report a ghost at the hotel in the late 1950s. He described the spirit as "friendly" after it made a brief appearance in the movie star's room.

Western star John Wayne encountered a ghost at the Monte Vista in the 1950s

It's unknown who this ghost might have been, and, in fact, most of the resident spirits have managed to avoid being identified – although no one doubts they're around.

One of the ghosts might be a bank robber who died in the hotel in the 1970s. Three bandits robbed a nearby bank, and one of the men was shot during the escape. Trying to lie low – and to celebrate the successful robbery – the men ducked into the Monte Vista Lounge for a drink. However, the wounded man's gunshot injury was more serious than he knew, and before he could finish his first drink, he died in the lounge.

Today, staff and guests feel as if this dead bandit is one of the many spirits that haunt the building. One manager reported that he often heard an eerie voice that said "Hello" or "Good Morning" when he opened the bar each morning. Others have told stories of feeling a ghostly presence while enjoying a drink in the cocktail lounge. This might be the ghost of the gunman, but the hotel has such a history of shootings, cowboys on horseback in the lobby, and drunken brawls that no one could know for sure.

It's not just the lounge that is believed to be haunted. The entire hotel seems to be plagued by strange noises, furniture that moves around, objects vanishing, and ghostly figures that make sudden appearances. The telephone in the lobby often rings, but when answered, there is no one on the other end of the line. Both employees and guests have heard band music coming from the second-floor lobby when no band is playing. Reportedly, the staff has become so accustomed to the odd occurrences that it has become more amusing than frightening to them.

The entire second floor seems to be the hub of the hotel's haunted activity. In Room 210 – the Zane Grey room – many guests have been awakened at night by a phantom bellboy who knocks on the door and calls out that room service has arrived. However, when guests open the door, they find the hallway empty. Others have reported seeing the image of a woman who wanders the halls outside this room.

An inordinate amount of activity is reported in the hall outside Room 220. Evidently, in the early 1980s, this room played host to an eccentric long-term guest who died in this room, although his body was not discovered for several days. Today, guests often complain about hearing coughing and other noises from the otherwise empty room. Once, after a maintenance man made several repairs to the room, he turned off the light and locked the door. Then, realizing he'd left a tool behind, he returned to the room just five minutes later and found the light was back on, the bed linens were stripped off, and the television was playing at full blast.

In the Gary Cooper Room, many guests have reported the unnerving feeling that they're being watched. Reportedly, two prostitutes were murdered in this room many years ago when they were thrown out the window. The two ladies have also been reportedly sighted in the pool hall and the lounge.

In yet another room, Room 305, the ghost of a female apparition is often reported sitting in the rocking chair. At other times, the chair simply rocks by itself. It's also said that if the cleaning staff moves the chair, it will always reappear next to the window the following day.

If you're ever making a nostalgia drive on Route 66 and you're looking for a place to stay where you can "sleep with the spirits," the Hotel Monte Vista may be just the place for you.

THE SHOW STILL GOES ON

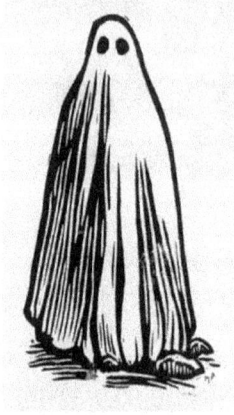

HAUNTED

ONE OF THE MOST INFLUENTIAL OF FLAGSTAFF'S EARLY residents was John Weatherford, who built the Hotel Weatherford, which opened on January 1, 1900. This old hotel has welcomed both presidents and gunslingers and continues to operate today after extensive restoration.

But in 1911, Weatherford also opened the Majestic Opera House, which introduced the first moving pictures to Flagstaff residents. Unfortunately, in the wee hours of January 1, 1915, the Majestic House's roof and walls collapsed under more than five feet of snow. Undeterred, Weatherford was able to rescue the projector from the ruins of the place, and he started building a bigger and better venue, the Orpheum, which opened in August 1917. It continued to operate until the late 1990s when the owners locked the doors and left town. The theater went dark for the next three years.

After months of extensive renovations, the Orpheum was restored and revitalized, and its doors were reopened to entertain a new generation of Flagstaff residents and visitors as Northern Arizona's premier performing arts venue.

Since the theater reopened in the early 2000s, stories have spread that claim the Orpheum is haunted. The stories started with an account from a janitor who saw a shadowy figure that moved across the old balcony after hours one night. As far as he knew, there was no one else in the building. As the janitor watched the figure move back and forth in the dim light, he decided to go up to the balcony and investigate. He quickly discovered he was right – the building was

empty. Whatever the specter had been, it was gone.

On another occasion, employees at the concession stand witnessed a ghost in the lobby during the last performance of the night. A roll of paper towels hanging on a wall dispenser began to unravel onto the floor of the concession stand. One of the staff members was brave enough to stop it, but as soon as he removed his hand, the paper towels started unrolling even faster than before.

Employees and theater patrons have reported hearing unexplained footsteps in the lobby and have experienced eerie events in the men's restroom, like cold chills, electric shocks, and an all-over feeling of uneasiness. One night after the theater was closed, the crew that was cleaning up for the night heard toilets flushing and sinks running at full blast in the men's room.

So, if you've got the nerve, buy your ticket, grab some popcorn and a cold drink, and take your seat at the Orpheum. Just remember that the person sitting in front of you may not be there at all.

PARKS IN THE PINES GENERAL STORE

LOCATED A SHORT DRIVE WEST OF FLAGSTAFF IS THE TOWN of Rhodes or wait a minute... the town of Maine. Or, oops, the town of Parks. Confusing, right?

Originally founded as Rhodes, the small community changed its name to Maine in 1898 in honor of the famous battleship that was sunk in Havana harbor that year during the Spanish-American War. Unfortunately, there was a town already called Maine in the Arizona Territory, so the U.S. Postal Service forced this one to find a new name. As it happened, a man named Parks operated a general store and an early post office in town, so it was agreed to change the name to Parks in his honor.

Not only did the town have three names, but it was also once located two miles east of its present location. It was moved in 1921 when the National Old Trails Highway was completed and started to see its share of tourist traffic. Soon, there was a need for a good road to reach the Grand Canyon, and Flagstaff and Williams fought to have the new road begin in their town. It was decided to split the difference. With Parks between the two other communities, the road was started from there and was completed in June 1921.

A few months later, Art Anderson and Don McMillan filled a growing need for services for the travelers now streaming through the area by

opening a general store and a service station at the intersection of the Old Trails Highway and the new road to the Grand Canyon. The Parks in the Pines General Store was opened and was soon doing brisk business. Things picked up even more in 1926 when the Old Trails Highway was designated as Route 66.

Two years later, in 1928, a flamboyant promoter named C.C. Pyle organized a footrace to promote the new Route 66. Dubbed the "Bunion Derby," the races started on March 4 at the Ascot Speedway in Los Angeles and followed Route 66 all the way to Chicago before then continuing to Madison Square Garden in New York. The athletes ran an average of 40 miles each day through whatever towns Pyle could convince to "sponsor" the race by paying a small fee. Parks became one of those towns. Andy Payne, a farm boy from Oklahoma, won the race, reaching New York on March 26 and winning the $25,000 prize. Promotional photographs of Payne were distributed afterward, showing him running directly past the Parks in the Pines General Store.

The historic building still stands today, and little has changed there since the store opened in 1921. The old wooden floor creaks and groans with every step, and the vintage furniture would tell tales of a bygone era if it could speak.

Stop in if you're passing through and help the owners continue the century-old tradition of service to locals and travelers alike.

THE LAST TOWN TO BE BYPASSED

WILLIAM SHERLEY WILLIAMS.
While he had the misfortune of being given the same first and last name by his parents, William Williams was a famed mountaineer, and this small Arizona town was named after him. Founded in 1876, the railroad arrived six years later, allowing Williams to grow into a thriving center for lumber and cattle. In 1901, the Santa Fe Railroad built a 60-mile spur line

Greetings from WILLIAMS ARIZ.

GATEWAY TO GRAND CANYON

to the Grand Canyon, giving the town a nickname that it's had ever since – "The Gateway to the Grand Canyon."

But in those days, there wasn't a great incentive for tourists to hang around town. Williams, like many western railroad towns at the turn of the last century, had a dangerous reputation for streets that were lined with saloons, brothels, opium dens, and gambling parlors. But one would be hard-pressed to find any evidence of that shady past today. In fact, it was mostly gone before Route 66 made it to town.

Williams hasn't changed much since then. It's regarded as one of the best preserved and picturesque towns on the highway, with a dozen restored motels, diners, and cafes. In the 1930s, Williams was often referred to as "Little Las Vegas" because of its abundance of neon signs in town – most of which survive today.

WILLIAMS, ARIZ. -329-

The preserved state of Williams is often credited to the

fact that it was the very last town on Route 66 to be bypassed by the interstate on October 13, 1984. A huge event was held to commemorate the event, featuring Bobby Troup as a special guest. And yes, he performed his iconic song for the crowd.

FRAY MARCOS HARVEY HOUSE

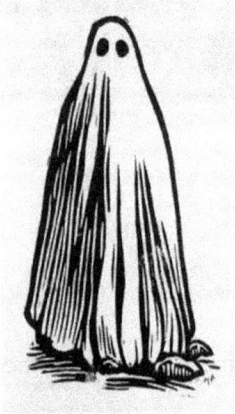

HAUNTED

FRED HARVEY OPENED HIS EATERY IN WILLIAMS WHEN HIS company took over an eatery that had been in town since 1884. In addition to the new restaurant, Harvey also opened a hotel, both located at the local train depot. It opened on March 10, 1908, and was named to honor Spanish missionary Fray Marcos de Niza, the first European explorer of Arizona and New Mexico. This facility served as the southern depot of the Grand Canyon Railway and as a station for the Santa Fe Railroad until 1954.

Built in the Spanish Mission style, the Fray Marcos offered 22 guestrooms and 10 Harvey Girl dorm rooms when it opened in 1908, all fitted with private bathrooms and hot and cold running water. On the ground floor was a baggage room, a ladies' waiting room, a men's waiting room, a ticket office, a souvenir shop, a newsroom, the hotel lobby, an office, and, of course, the famous dining and lunchroom facilities.

The hotel and restaurant were immediately successful, leading to a two-addition with 21 new guestrooms after Route 66 came through Williams in the 1920s.

Travelers found it the perfect place to stay while en route to the Grand Canyon by train or car.

But it wasn't just the convenience and amenities of the hotel that attracted the tourists

– it was the Harvey Girls. Each young woman who worked for the company signed a contract that committed them to work at one location for six months. After that, they were free to go back to their hometowns or marry a local they met on the job. However, most renewed their contracts or transferred to another Harvey facility, excited by the chance to see a new part of the country and another slice of the Wild West. The town of Williams – a rowdy town filled with railroaders, cowboys, and lumber mill workers – must have seemed rough and untamed to the Harvey Girls, but none of them shied away from bringing some refinement to the rambunctious community.

Harvey Girls

(Below) The lobby interior of the Fray Marcos

The Harvey Girls at the Fray Marcos lived above the kitchen on the second floor of the west wing. Each of the girls shared a small, comfortable room with one of the other girls. Their work schedules kept them busy, and when they were off duty, they were carefully chaperoned by company staff members. Even with a 10:00 P.M. curfew, many of the girls still managed to meet their admirers and future husbands and invented creative ways to divert their chaperones. On their days off, the girls made use of railway passes to visit the Grand Canyon and other Arizona cities, visited friends, and traveled around the area in automobiles.

The Harvey Girls were tasked with keeping the Fray Marcos lunchroom counter and dining room tables spotless and always ready for the arrival of the next train. When they weren't feeding hungry travelers, they were polishing silver, cleaning glasses, and keeping the famous Fred Harvey coffee hot and freshly brewed.

Today, the building that housed the Fray Marcos restaurant and hotel is the bustling Grand Canyon Railway ticket office, museum, and gift shop. Furnishings in the depot and gift shop offer a look at vintage train travel. The hotel rooms where weary travelers once slept are now used as offices and storage space.

However, the architecture, museum relics, and furniture are not the only things that remain from the heyday of the Harvey House. With the Fray Marcos being a place where so many young women loved to work, it's not that surprising that at least one of the Harvey Girls seems to have remained on duty at the former hotel and eatery in Williams.

Many of the current employees have encountered the spirit they've dubbed "Clara." Not all of them have seen her. Some have simply felt her presence in the building in the late afternoon or evening. They catch something out of the corner of their eye or hear a movement in an empty room, and they know that Clara is around. As one employee put it in an interview, "We feel Clara senses we are getting ready to close the shop for the night, and she's just tidying up the Harvey House, too."

Gift shop staffers have reported books being rearranged and souvenirs that move around or are mixed-up on the shelves. Cashiers have heard the light footsteps of a woman's shoes clicking on the original tile floors as they count down the cash register drawers at the end of the day. Expecting to see a customer who was left behind in the building or a fellow employee, they are surprised to discover the depot is empty.

Well, they were surprised the first time it happened. After that, they just accepted the fact that it must have been Clara.

A clerk at the Grand Canyon Railway counter once saw a young woman lingering near a doorway. She smiled warmly for a few moments and then just faded away. The clerk described the woman as "resembling a Harvey Girl dressed in a uniform like she had seen in the museum's photograph collection."

After several different maintenance workers reported seeing a black-and-white-uniformed Harvey Girl standing near the top of the second-floor stairway, they refused to go upstairs alone. The second floor had been, of course, the old Harvey Girl dormitory, so perhaps Clara was just on her way downstairs to greet the next train as it pulled into the station.

She's still hard at work, even after all these years.

"THE OLDEST LIQUOR LICENSE IN ARIZONA"

WHEN ROUTE 66 CAME TO WILLIAMS IN 1926, AMERICA WAS in the middle of Prohibition, an era when it was illegal to buy, sell, or manufacture alcohol anywhere in the country. But, not surprisingly, Prohibition failed to stop most people who still wanted to have a drink. As one man put it at the time, "If you can't find liquor, then you ain't trying."

Many previously law-abiding business owners found themselves in the position of providing the product that their customers wanted, and across the country, thousands of speakeasies opened, secret establishments where booze could be obtained whether it was legal or not. Nearly every town in America, big or small, offered at least one speakeasy for thirsty customers – and Williams was no exception.

HAUNTED

The famous Sultana Bar in Williams claims to have the oldest liquor license in the state of Arizona, and it proudly sits on the southwest corner of Third Street and Route 66 today. It's the perfect place for road trippers to mingle with the locals and enjoy a burger while bellying up to the bar.

The building was constructed in 1912 and once housed a saloon, billiard hall, and silent movie theater with 600 seats. The first "talking picture" shown in Arizona was played in this theater in 1930.

During Prohibition, the Sultana provided liquor and gambling for patrons by secret password only. It's no surprise that it was once the social center of the town. Evidence of the bar's lawless past can still be found in the rear of the saloon, hidden in a janitor's closet, where a trapdoor leads down to a series of tunnels that Chinese railroad workers originally built in the 1880s. During Prohibition, the passageways were used for storing and running booze and stretched throughout the downtown area.

Williams had always been a busy ranching and railroad town, and the Sultana was a rough-and-tumble place. Arguments were often settled with fists, blades, and bullets, but the most violent incident that occurred at the Sultana occurred on April 15, 1947.

A 22-year-old service station attendant named Lee Skinner had been drinking in the bar all evening with a group of friends when he started abusing other patrons. The bar owner asked him to leave, but Skinner refused. Local law officers were called, but when they arrived, Skinner still wouldn't leave. Finally, Marshal Joseph McDaniel was called, and when he entered the bar's side door, he found Skinner and his friends sitting in a booth in the back.

McDaniel walked up to the table, and Skinner and some of his friends laughed. The marshal ignored them and spoke directly to Skinner. "We've got a warrant for your arrest for resisting an officer," he said.

When Skinner refused to stand up, McDaniel reached over, grabbed him by the shirt, and began to drag him out of the booth. Skinner struggled with him, and both men fell to the floor, with Skinner under the lawman. Suddenly, five shots rang out, and McDaniel cried out as Skinner shoved him aside. The marshal had been shot five times with a small-caliber automatic pistol as the two men wrestled on the floor. Three of the bullets struck him in the shoulder, one entered his abdomen, and one bullet went straight to the heart. The marshal was rushed to the local hospital but died shortly after he arrived.

Skinner was immediately arrested and handcuffed by the other officers on the scene.

He was convicted of second-degree murder and deadly assault and sentenced to 35 years in prison.

Ever since that time, the Sultana has been rumored to be haunted. Bartenders working late have seen and heard things they cannot explain. One of the female bartenders recalled an eerie encounter with a ghost one Super Bowl Sunday. She was busy hanging banners and signs on the wall when she felt someone touch her on the shoulder. She spun around, assuming it was one of the bar patrons, but no one was nearby. A short time later, a local man who was shooting pool had almost the exact same experience.

Another young woman who worked at the bar reported someone whispering in her ear while she was locking up for the night. Servers claim to have been lightly pushed by unseen hands in the main dining room. One night, a guest said that she had seen a man in clothing from the 1940s walk past the supply room. Confused, she asked the bartender if someone else was working that evening, but he shrugged his shoulders and told her that he was the only one on duty.

Staff members have reported eerie encounters when, on a dare, exploring the old tunnels under the bar. They claim to have heard footsteps in the darkness, voices that echo off the walls, and the laughter of men who lived and died decades earlier. Those who have experienced these strange events believe those bootleggers still lurk in the mysterious passages as restless spirits.

But what about the innocuous ghost in the 1940s clothing who is believed to haunt the Sultana itself? Could it be the ghost of Marshal

McDaniel, who was shot during the violent incident there in 1947 and bled out on the floor of the bar? Perhaps as his life drained away on the floorboards of the old saloon, his spirit took up residence at the place where he made his final arrest.

THE MURDER OF HAZEL JOHNSON

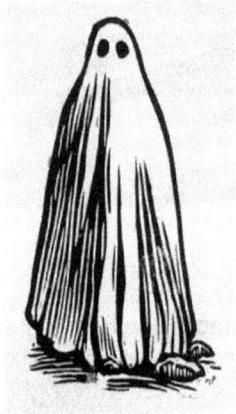

TRAVELERS WHO VENTURED WEST OF WILLIAMS ON ROUTE 66 faced numerous hazards – some of which they didn't expect to find in Arizona. The high elevation of the area meant that snow and ice were common from late Fall to late Spring.

Accidents involving wildlife, including deer and elk, were common. They encountered steep grades that brought traffic to a crawl, and impatient drivers often attempted to pass on the narrow road with its blind curves, which resulted in fatal outcomes. As the road dropped away from the mountains to the high desert, they found a series of sharp twists and turns. Brake failure was not uncommon. Making each hazard worse was a highway with little or no shoulder.

HAUNTED

Death took many forms along this section of the highway, but not all of them occurred behind the wheel.

What started as a cross-country honeymoon trip ended up being a dead-end journey for Hazel Johnson, a young woman who had first faced tragedy two years before her death. Hazel was widowed on March 3, 1924, leaving the pretty 28-year-old with a three-year-old son to raise on her own.

She never expected to find love again but found herself swept off her feet by a charming 32-year-old army veteran named Granville W. Johnson. He wined and dined the pretty widow, and they were married on February 20, 1926. He convinced Hazel to sell her car and purchase a new Hudson automobile for the cross-country trip he proposed as their honeymoon. Granville suggested they take Hazel's son and travel to Missouri to meet his family.

Hazel was thrilled with the idea – but she wouldn't have been if she'd known what her new husband was getting up to behind her back.

Unknown to her, Granville had purchased several life insurance policies on his new wife – naming himself as beneficiary – almost as soon as the ink on their marriage license was dry.

The newlyweds pulled the widow's money out of the bank, packed up their new Hudson, and left California, heading east on the National Old Trails Highway. On May 2, they stopped for the night at the Mountain Springs Ranch motor camp, which was just two miles outside of Williams, Arizona.

The tourist camp offered a small grocery store and a collection of rustic cabins, each with an attached garage. The cabins had the bare necessities – like a table and cots – and while

Hazel Johnson and her three-year-old son

nothing fancy, they were typical of other motor camps of the time. Hazel saw it as an overnight stay that would be both comfortable and safe – or so she thought.

Later that night, the peaceful quiet of Mountain Springs Ranch was shattered by the sounds of a man's screams. Granville Johnson was running frantically through the camp, covered in blood, carrying his three-year-old stepson. He was shouting that his wife had been murdered.

Granville pounded on the door of one of the other cabins just after 1:00 A.M. He was raving that Hazel was dead and begging someone to

Mountain Springs Ranch, west of Williams

The cabin at Mountain Springs Ranch in which Hazel was murdered and her body was discovered

keep an eye on his son. Another guest was also awakened, and the three men returned to the Johnson cabin, where they found Hazel's body. She was bloody and had been brutally slain. She had apparently been sleeping when she was attacked because there were no signs of a struggle, and the bed covers were over her body in a natural way. The pillow that her head was on, though, was soaked with blood.

By now, the owner of the camp, who lived in the building with the store, had been awakened, and he had called the sheriff and the Williams town marshal. Officers soon arrived at the scene, followed by the local coroner. His examination of Hazel's body showed that she'd been struck twice in the head with a sharp-edged instrument. One wound was on the forehead, and the other was on the back of the head.

When questioned, Granville stated that he had left the camp around 11:00 P.M. to drive to Williams so that he could try out the new carburetor that he had replaced earlier in the day. He said he returned just before 1:00 A.M. and found his wife had been murdered.

The police weren't buying his story, and he was placed under arrest while the investigation continued.

According to the owner of the camp, when Johnson and his family had rented the cabin, the man had asked him if anyone slept in the camp store at night and whether the gate was left locked or unlocked overnight. He even asked to be shown how the gate operated in case he wanted to wake his family and leave in the middle of the night.

When officers checked the Johnson cabin, they found fresh tire tracks coming and going from the garage. A guest told them how he had seen Johnson driving back and forth in front of the camp earlier in the day. An investigator suggested he might have been putting extra miles on the Hudson's odometer to make it look like he had driven into town.

When daylight arrived, officers more thoroughly searched the camp for clues. They quickly found a camping hatchet that had evidently been thrown from the door of the cabin where Hazel was killed. There was a mark in the soft dirt where the hatchet had struck. It bounced several more feet and landed in some grass. There was blood all over the blade, making it clear this had been the murder weapon.

But who had used it to kill Hazel?

That question was quickly answered – when officers studied the handle, they found "G.W. Johnson" carved into the wood.

Criminal genius this man was not.

The trial was short, and the jury deliberation lasted less than an hour. Convicted of murder, Johnson was sent to the Arizona State Penitentiary, where he was scheduled to be hanged in May 1928. His sentence was commuted to life in prison on the morning he was supposed to be hanged, however. It was here where he spent the rest of his life, except for a brief time when he escaped and was later recaptured in San Francisco after two months on the lam in 1936.

And his escape is an odd story all its own.

While incarcerated, Granville's behavior had earned him a prison trustee position, and he was allowed to work at a service station across the road from the prison. One day, he stole money from the safe and paid an accomplice to drive him to San Francisco. He lived the high life while he was there, staying in nice hotels, eating at exclusive restaurants, and drinking so much liquor that he was sent to the hospital under an assumed name to dry out.

It was at the hospital where his crimes came back to haunt him, so to speak. Johnson demanded to know who the woman who came into his room at night was and kept waking him up. When he asked her what she wanted, he claimed she had always disappeared. He also asked the nurses each morning, "Did I talk in my sleep?"

Johnson became so unnerved by the strange woman – and by the dreams that caused him to believe he was talking in his sleep – that he placed several calls to the Arizona Penitentiary, trying to disguise his voice, and asking if anyone was looking for Granville Johnson. The calls were promptly traced – as Johnson likely knew they would be – and the police quickly found him at the hotel he'd returned to after checking out of the hospital. He was returned to the penitentiary – his trustee days now behind him – and he died behind bars in 1950.

And once he was returned to prison, he never again spoke of the woman who mysteriously haunted his sleep.

DEATH COMES TO ASH FORK

IN 1882, THE ATLANTIC AND PACIFIC RAILROAD – WHICH later became the Santa Fe Railroad – chose an area known as Ash Fork for a siding stop. The area had been named for the trees that grew at the fork of nearby Ash Creek.

The newly formed Ash Fork Livestock Company drove their cattle to the recently built railhead, and it slowly turned into a town as the cattle business thrived. In 1893, Ash Fork was completely decimated by a fire but was rebuilt and relocated to the other side of the railroad tracks, where it still stands today.

Ash Fork is now a shadow of its former self. Once a hotbed for tourist activity, a lot has changed for the once bustling community. In 1907, the beautiful Fred Harvey Escalante Hotel became the pride and joy of the rough-and-tumble town. When Route 66 arrived in Ash Fork, the town's economy boomed until the road was split into a divided highway through town, resulting in the loss of several businesses.

In 1948, the Escalante Hotel closed. Next, the railroad line was moved further north, skipping past Ash Fork, and then came the "Big Fire" of 1977 that destroyed most of the businesses that were left. Once the interstate opened in 1984, bypassing the heart of the town, Ash Fork was doomed.

While not a ghost town by any means, Ash Fork is much quieter today than it was during its heyday – although some of the legends of Route 66 remain.

At one time, one of the deadliest sections of Route 66 was Ash Fork Hill, located between Williams and Ash Fork. The hill was a six-percent downhill grade for a winding eight miles, descending 6,500 feet. It caused gut-wrenching fear in

Ash Fork Hill .. another of Arizona's deadly stretches of road

many travelers in the early days – and for good reason.

The regional newspapers were filled with stories of motorists who descended the curving eight-mile road, often nursing a broken brake rod and trying to steer their car to the foot of the hill before losing control and running off the road at the edge of the deep canyon. Some drivers were lucky – others weren't. Once, the front wheel of a Studebaker collapsed, and the driver was unable to get his brakes to work. Eventually, a large rock snagged under the rear axle and stopped the car right at the lip of a steep drop off the side of the highway. The rock was all that saved those in the vehicle from serious injury or death.

There were head-on collisions with vehicles slowly climbing the hill while some out-of-control drivers descended the steep road, only to wind up in a ditch or buried in the sand. Steering gears broke, engines overheated, and tires blew, sending cars careening toward the road's narrow shoulder.

Even in the 1950s, when Route 66 travelers were driving much better cars than motorists two decades before, things weren't much better on Ash Fork Hill. A truck driver was on his way down the hill when his flywheel flew apart and burst through the transmission case. Pieces of the transmission ripped through the floorboard of the truck's cab and struck the driver on the leg. Several hitchhikers who were riding white-knuckled in the back of the truck jumped from the vehicle. One of the men ended up with a broken leg, and another died from internal injuries. A mother and her son were not seriously injured.

The truck, by the way, had been loaded with 21 tons of eggs. Somehow, none of them were damaged.

In 1952, blizzards caused whiteouts – and more head-on collisions – on this stretch of the road. Finally, two years later, Route 66 was rebuilt into a wide new road that was well-paved and had fewer curves.

Even this new highway saw death. In 1962, three lanes of Route 66 near Ash Fork Hill vanished after the road collapsed into a mysterious opening beneath the road.

DEATH COMES TO ASH FORK (AGAIN)

IN 1921, BEFORE THE NATIONAL OLD TRAILS ROAD BECAME Route 66, Ash Fork figured prominently in a tri-state crime spree that included a bank robbery and the murder of two police officers in Los Angeles.

The bandits involved had also robbed banks in Utah and Nevada, but on December 6, their luck ran out in L.A., and after an intense running gun battle, all six men were arrested.

L.A.P.D. officers Harry Clester and W. Brett were tasked with taking the men to jail. With three handcuffed prisoners in each car, Clester drove the bandits' getaway car, and Brett drove the patrol car. But things didn't go as planned. Clester was overpowered and then was shot and killed with his own service revolver. Brett stopped to help but was shot in the head, dying instantly. Five of the suspects managed to stay one step ahead of the law for 12 days before they were captured.

TRUE CRIME

The sixth bank robber, Jake Wendell, escaped the manhunt, stole a car, and headed east on the National Old Trails Road. In Victorville, California, hoping to throw the police off his trail, he dumped his auto in the desert and stole another car. But an observant service station attendant in Daggett, California, spotted Wendell and alerted the police. Telegrams filled with details about the bandit and the car he was now driving were sent to sheriff and police departments as far east as Albuquerque, and the hunt was back on.

On the evening of Monday, December 12, Sheriff Mackey in Oatman, Arizona, received a telegram that Wendell had been spotted in Goffs, California. He was driving a Ford coupe, the telegram reported, and he was likely heavily armed. Mackey shared the news with filling station attendants, hotel managers, and café owners. His diligence paid off when a gas station owner contacted the sheriff and told him that Wendell had just filled up the Ford and was on his way out of town. He also told the sheriff that Wendell had a shotgun, a Winchester rifle, and two pistols in the car.

Mackey immediately contacted Mohave County Sheriff W.P. Mahoney in Kingman, who passed on the information to Santa Fe Railroad detectives in Peach Springs, Seligman, and Ash Forks – as well as Sheriff Warren Davis in Prescott and Deputy Elmer Plummer in Seligman.

Soon, another message arrived – Wendell had been spotted in Peach Springs. Sheriff Mahoney and one of his deputies quickly boarded a train to try and beat Wendell to Ash Fork. In Seligman, they were joined on the train by Deputy Plummer and a Santa Fe officer named Frohman.

But the news was traveling faster than the train. They now learned the Ford driven by Wendell had been found abandoned along the highway about seven miles west of Ash Fork. As luck would have it, they spotted two men walking along the highway about

Route 66 west of Ash Fork

a mile and a half away from the Ash Fork station. One of the men was a railroad section foreman named MacNeal – the other was Jake Wendell.

Wendell had asked MacNeal for help, explaining that his car had broken down on the highway. When he saw the lawmen approaching, he sprinted for the station but was quickly surrounded. Sheriff Mahoney called out for him to surrender. Witnesses later said that Wendell stepped to the door and looked out, but when he saw the officers spread out in front of the section house where he'd taken shelter, he ducked back inside. Moments later, three shots were heard – Wendell had shot himself three times in the chest.

Legend has it that the bullets were deflected by a pocket watch Wendell's wife had given him, so the wounds weren't immediately fatal. The officers patched him up as best they could and put him on the train to Kingman, where the closest hospital was located.

Wendell died on the way there, but not before he signed a statement claiming that he was in the back of the car when Officer Clester was overpowered and that he saw two of his fellow bandits kill the two police officers. Both were later executed at San Quentin in California for the murders.

MOTORING TO SELIGMAN

IN THE MID-NINETEENTH CENTURY, THE AREA AROUND WHAT is now Seligman was known as Mint Valley. In 1886, the residents of

Seligman in the 1940s

nearby Prescott were convinced to finance a railroad line called the Prescott and Arizona Central Railroad, which would connect Prescott with the Atlantic and Pacific line via Mint Valley. With that connection, Mint Valley became known as Prescott Junction. Unfortunately, the new rail line soon went out of business, the line from Prescott to Prescott Junction was torn up, and Prescott Junction's name was changed to Seligman in honor of Jesse Seligman, the prominent New York banker who'd financed the now-defunct railroad.

It turned out to be another railroad that managed to breathe life into the community. The Atlantic and Pacific Railroad became the Santa Fe, and in 1897, it moved its western terminus and roundhouse from Williams to Seligman, which gave a considerable boost to the economy. In 1905, the town gained its own Harvey House, which was called El Havasu.

When Route 66 arrived in Seligman, the town reaped the benefits of the highway and became an essential stop for travelers. As auto travel gained popularity, rail travel suffered, which led to the closure of El Havasu in 1954.

But this was just the start of the town's decline. When Seligman was bypassed by the interstate in 1978, the town was deserted seemingly overnight. All the cars that had once stopped in Seligman were now flying past on the new road a couple of miles south of town.

For the next decade, Seligman went into a spiral of decline. Businesses closed, locals moved away, and buildings were abandoned.

But Seligman was only down, not out. In 1985, the town rallied around brothers Angel and Juan Delgadillo, who led the revival in interest in Route 66, which continues today. Promoting the historical significance of the highway to all who would listen, they were instrumental in getting the road designated as "Historic U.S. 66."

Today, Seligman reaps new benefits from those who share the town's love for Route 66. Many of the old commercial buildings in Seligman have been restored. The **Aztec**

The Snow Cap Drive-In

Motel and Gift Shop and the **Snow Cap Drive-In**, which was founded by Juan Delgadillo in 1953, are greeting a new generation of travelers.

Juan had been working for the Santa Fe Railroad at that time but wanted to find a way to cash in on the post-war influx of Route 66 travelers that were coming to town. At first, he tried to become part of the Dairy Queen chain of eateries, but was turned down, so he searched for other companies, eventually settling on the Snow Cap company in Prescott. Show Cap later folded, but Juan kept the name.

And the Snow Cap is still there, offering ice cream and cheeseburgers to hungry travelers all these decades later.

NO HONOR AMONG THIEVES

ON THE EVENING OF OCTOBER 4, 1919, A GRIM DISCOVERY was made along the National Old Trails Road, about 20 miles west of Seligman. A shepherd who was tending his flock stumbled on the smoldering remains of a man.

Investigators from the Yavapai County sheriff's office determined that the dead man had been shot in the back by a .38-caliber handgun, wrapped in a blanket, dragged about 100 feet from where a car had been parked, soaked with gasoline, and set on fire. Though the body was badly charred, officers were able to discover that he was wearing a military uniform, which indicated he'd been a member

TRUE CRIME

SUPPOSED MURDERER CANADIAN SOLDIER ARRESTED AT VISALIA

The police of the town of Yettem, a small town near Visalia, California, have arrested Michan Martin on an order from the sheriff of Yavapai county charging him with murder. Martin is supposed to be the slayer of a soldier, whose badly burned body was found last week near Yampai, about 65 miles east of Kingman. In Martin's car and on his person was found a medal belonging to the dead man and other effects. The name of the dead man is given as Arthur Duesteunder, who served in a Canadian regiment during the war and who won a medal for valor. His wife resides in Chicago.

of the Twentieth Canadian Infantry during World War I. Tracing the serial number on his insignia, they learned from Canadian authorities that the dead man's name was Arthur De Steunder.

In the weeks that followed, investigators learned that De Steunder had been living in Chicago until recently when his wife had filed for divorce. They also discovered that he had left the Windy City under strange circumstances. According to his sister-in-law:

He answered an advertisement about a month ago and met a man who offered him $10 a week and expenses to make a car trip throughout the western United States. The purpose of the journey was kept a mystery. They spent several days getting ready in Chicago and then departed. We didn't like the man's looks. Arthur's sister met this man and warned Arthur against going.

The stranger who had caused so much concern for Arthur's family was Michan Martin, a 25-year-old Armenian immigrant from Turkey who had come to the United States in 1912 and served in the army during the war. Martin had a prominent crimson wine-stain birthmark on his face, which made it easy to identify him.

Soon, desk clerks, filling station attendants, and waitresses along the National Old Trails Road were confirming that the two men had traveled together. It was also learned that on September 25, both men had been arrested and jailed in Holbrook on suspicion of robbery. A few days later, though, they were released for lack of evidence. Only later did investigators learn that the pair had been financing their trip with robberies of stores and gas stations along the highway.

Later on the night of October 4, Martin registered as Harry Dyer at the Commercial Hotel in Kingman, about 60 miles from where the body of De Steunder had been found. That night at a tavern and in the morning over breakfast, he talked to other travelers and described his solo trip from Rhode Island. A night clerk at the hotel later told investigators that most of Martin's conversations were about the possibility of finding a companion for his long automobile ride across the country.

In other words, he was looking for his next victim.

Martin was arrested in California on October 15. De Steunder's luggage was with him when he was picked up, some of which was bloodstained. Inside one suitcase were De Steunder's military discharge papers. Martin also had a .38-caliber pistol in his possession – the same pistol that had killed De Steunder.

Still, Martin claimed that he was innocent and that he and De Steunder had parted ways in Ash Fork. He swore that he never saw him again after that. No one believed him.

Martin was extradited to Arizona to stand trial but attempted to escape near Needles, California, by jumping off the train. He was captured the next morning, and he went on trial in Prescott on March 25, 1920. He was found guilty of first-degree murder four days later and was executed by the state on Friday, September 9, 1921.

"ORPHAN MAKER OF ROUTE 66"

IN JUNE 1961, HORROR RETURNED TO SELIGMAN AND ROUTE 66 when four young boys, traveling with their parents from Oklahoma to California to visit relatives, had their lives changed forever. Their story would receive national attention and would become one of the bloodiest incidents to occur along the famous highway.

James Dolphus Welch – who was known to friends and family as "JD" – and his wife, Utha, were a typical couple in their early thirties in 1961. JD, a burly six-footer, was a truck driver for Trans-Con, while Utha was a housewife and stay-at-home mother for their four sons -- Jimmy, 12; Billy, 9; Tommy, 8 and 5-year-old Johnny. They were a well-liked couple in their hometown of Spencer, Oklahoma, and were involved in many local activities.

Most of JD's family lived in California, so in June 1961, the family set out from Oklahoma to drive to Tulare, California, to see JD's mother

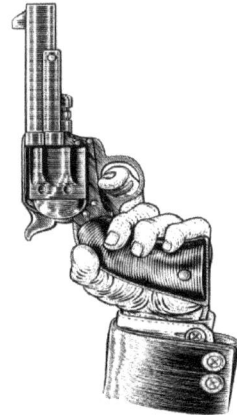

TRUE CRIME

James Dolphus "JD" Welch and his wife, Utha

before she had to have some minor surgery. They planned to return home through Colorado Springs so the boys could see the Rocky Mountains.

The boys were excited about the trip and were keen to do some camping on the road. JD and Utha decided to let them bring along their Boy Scouts pup tent.

On Thursday, June 8, the second day on the road, the family left Amarillo in the morning and drove all day. It was late at night by the time they stopped for gas in Ash Fork and looked for a motel room. Later, the owner told the police that JD thought the room was too expensive and left.

The motel owner never spoke publicly about the incident, despite being the last person to see the Welches alive, which makes me wonder if perhaps he got a look at the family's shiny two-year-old Oldsmobile – JD had only bought it two weeks earlier – and calculating the lateness of the hour and the small boys and quoted a price higher than usual.

We'll never know, and we'll also never know why the family didn't stop in Seligman, where there were more motels. It may have been cost, or it may have been that the boys were nagging their parents about camping. Eventually, around midnight, JD pulled into the side of the road west of Seligman to stop for the night.

It was a bleak and barren spot. The only shelter was from two large piles of rocks, and it was beside one of these that JD pitched his sons' tent. JD and Utha got their sons settled and then went to sleep in the Oldsmobile.

The crime scene as it was discovered the next morning

Johnny was the first one awake the next morning.

He walked over to the car where his parents were sleeping and tried to wake them but got no response. Confused, he ran back to his brothers, saying there was something on mommy's face. Going to check, Jimmy found his mother's face covered with blood. He lifted

Newspaper map showing the location of the crime scene

his father's head and saw that he was also soaked with blood.

JD and Utha had both been shot several times in the head. Even though the tent was just steps away, the four boys had seen and heard nothing.

The weeping and terrified boys desperately tried to flag down help. However, several cars sped past them before salesmen and race drivers Jere Eagle and Dan Cramer from California stopped and realized the horror of the situation.

Highway Patrolman Dan Birdino and Deputy Sheriff Perry Blankenship were the first to arrive on the scene. Blankenship had been notified of the situation by his wife, Bertie, after a driver stopped at Johnson's Café on the east end of Seligman, where she worked as a waitress. Bertie would have a bigger role in this story than she

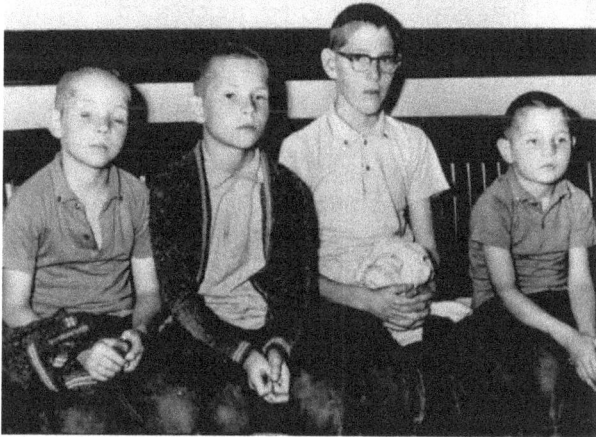

The four Welch boys became known as the "Little Orphans of Route 66" in newspapewrs across the country in 1961

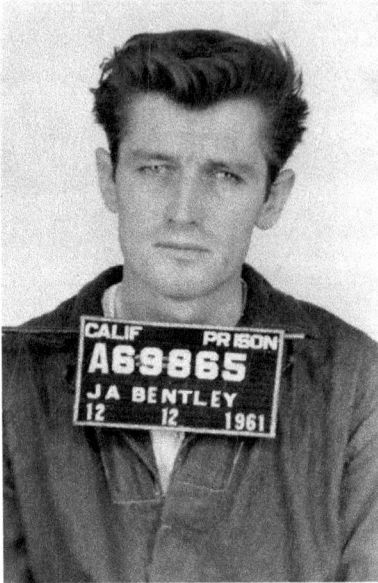

The killer of JD and Utha Welch was James Bentley, who was already on death row at San Quentin by the time he was identified.

could have imagined at the time.

Although around $60 had been taken from JD's wallet, Utha's purse, which contained $147, and her expensive jewelry were untouched.

Despite a few promising leads – a Greyhound bus had stopped at the same place, but this turned out to be some hours after the murders, and clues quickly dried up.

The best lead the local police had was a statement from Bertie Blankenship about a young man she had served late the previous night. He only had a nickel on him, not enough for a cup of coffee, but there was something about him that spooked Bertie, so she gave him the coffee for free, hoping to get rid of him.

Then, a few hours later, the same man returned to the diner and, this time, ordered a full meal, paying for it with a $20 bill. When Bertie asked him why he'd returned, he claimed he'd never been there before and didn't recognize Bertie. She was absolutely certain he was the same man, and she provided investigators with a detailed description.

Law enforcement officials recognized Bertie's description as James Abner Bentley, who lived in Gilbert, Arizona. However, his mother and estranged wife claimed that he had been in Fresno, California, with them on the night of the murders. He hadn't – he'd been in Fresno a month earlier when he'd killed the owner of a liquor store.

When investigators went looking for Bentley, they found him already locked up. He'd been arrested for the robbery and attempted murder of a Phoenix service station attendant in late June.

While the police were convinced Bentley had murdered JD and Utha, for some reason, no one thought of showing his mug shot to Bertie Blankenship so she could identify him. Bertie didn't see a photo of Bentley until a year later after a cellmate of the condemned prisoner had revealed that Bentley alluded to the murders, proudly saying he'd left the children alive. When Bertie was shown an image of Bentley, she immediately identified him as the stranger who had come to the diner – once poor and once with money in his pocket – the night of the murders.

Bentley was charged with the murders of JD and Utha Welch while on death row at San Quentin. He had already been convicted of the murder of the Fresno liquor store owner. Had his death sentence been commuted – and that was a definite possibility at the time as Pat Brown, then Governor of California, was a firm opponent of the death penalty – then Arizona would have proceeded with the prosecution for both the Welch murders and the robbery and attempted murder charge in Phoenix.

But Arizona was able to save itself time and money.

On January 23, 1963, Bentley went to the gas chamber, but this was little consolation for the four boys whose childhood ended so brutally on the side of Route 66.

DINOSAUR CITY AND THE GRAND CANYON CAVERNS

LOCATED 22 MILES NORTHWEST OF SELIGMAN AND A dozen miles east of Peach Springs are the Grand Canyon Caverns. They are situated today along what's been called the longest stretch of old Route 66, which is still in use. For this book, it requires a bit of a side trip away from the path of today's interstate, but it's worth it.

Among the largest dry caves in the United States, the Caverns are still a prime tourist draw along Route 66. They can be found in a slice of beautiful scenery that teems with prairie dogs, mountain lions, bobcats, owls, eagles, hawks, elk, and antelope. A man named Walter Peck (literally) stumbled on the Caverns in 1927 and began charging travelers 25 cents to be lowered underground.

Since the original gravel surface of Route 66 ran just outside the entrance to the cave, he had no problem finding willing customers who were happy to pay to dangle at the end of a rope into darkness.

However, the seeds for his development of the site had been planted years earlier, long before

Route 66 and even automobiles. A preoccupation with all things prehistoric in the Southwest started in the late 1880s and continued to ratchet up into the early twentieth century. Eastern museums unleashed looters into Walnut Canyon, Wapatki, and other southwestern archaeological sites. Diggers crammed picnic baskets full of pottery shards and human remains. Dynamite blasts destroyed ancient walls.

But when paleontologist Roland T. Bird discovered a series of fossilized footprints in Texas that were about 107 million years old, the public's taste for all things prehistoric was secured. The dinosaur has been the king of Route 66 ever since.

Which brings us back to Walter Peck.

Walter was a woodcutter for the Santa Fe Railroad when he found the cave. He was also an avid poker player. One Saturday evening, he was running late for a game of five-card-draw and decided to take a shortcut. He was slogging through some mud left from recent heavy rains and stumbled and fell – finding himself on the edge of a sinkhole that he'd never seen before. He carefully eased up to the rim of the hole and peered into the shadows. In the fading light of the setting sun, he imagined that he saw bones strewn on a ledge far below.

Walter stumbled to the poker game and told his friends what he'd found. The next day, they gathered at the mysterious hole, tied ropes around their waists, and lowered themselves inside. Between the shadows thrown from the kerosene lamps they carried, they discovered that Walter really had seen human bones – there were at least two skeletons in the sinkhole resting near a pair of rotting saddles.

But what startled them most was the size of the caverns below. There were huge rooms hidden away there, carved from the earth. There were passages with formations and walls glistening with yellow that appeared to be veins of gold core.

Walter was so confident that a fortune could be made from the cave that he immediately secured a land lease – then discovered his sack filled with rock samples contained nothing valuable. Disappointed but not willing to give up, he came up with a new idea. On the sinkhole's rim, Walter constructed a winch for a ticket that could be bought with pocket change, and he began lowering adventurous tourists into darkness.

The two skeletons found in the cave managed to generate some publicity for Walter's new attraction. He claimed the bones belonged to two cavemen, showed them to some gullible reporters, and let the story run where it would. The story led to Walter's efforts being quickly condemned by the nearby Hualapai tribe, who insisted the skeletons were two of their own – members of a wood-gathering party who died only a decade before and were consigned to the cave when winter deaths prevented burial in frozen ground. Walter ignored the Hualapai plea to give the bones a proper burial and continued to tell the prehistoric story. However, he had no explanation for how two Neanderthals were found with twentieth-century horse saddles.

Scientific study eventually lent credence to Walter's prehistoric claims – not about the cavemen but about the formation of the cavern. Designated as the largest known dry cavern in the United States, Yampai Caverns – as they were first called – had formed during the limestone development of the Grand Canyon. Fossilized seashells and small sea creatures found in the ceiling date back to the time when the world was only one massive continent.

For all his efforts, though, Walter wasn't having much luck with turning his discovery into a well-paying business. But he soon had some help with improvements. In 1936, the Civilian Conservation Corps built a proper entrance for what was now called Coconino Cavern. The new access had 30 feet of rickety stairs and three 15-foot ladders. Later, a 60-foot swinging bridge was added. It was better than being lowered on a rope – but not much.

By 1940, though, Walter Peck was done. Stan Wakefield leased the property and started giving guided tours. Stan owned Deer Lodge – a gas station and collection of cabins on Route 66 about 20 miles west of Seligman. Aware of tourists' hunger for all things prehistoric, Stan had turned one area of Deer Lodge into a caveman's living room, showing off stalactites, onyx shale, and other oddities.

Later, in the 1940s and the 1950s, Winston Wright, a miner, and a rancher named W.C. Denny vied for control of the caverns. The natural entrance was on a section line – Wright owned half, and Denny owned the other half. When tourists arrived, each tried to get them to take his tour.

In February 1960, Winston Wright published a paper stating that he believed the cave should be taken over as a State or National Park. He outlined improvements that had occurred at the cave since 1940, including trails and wooden walkways and the removal of the original sinkhole entrance.

Soon after the publication of the report, a new elevator was installed to take visitors from the surface to the depth of the cave. Before that, tourists were using a safe entrance with "19 short flights" of a new

When the cave became Dinosaur Caverns, big plans began to be made for an entire city thanks to Route 66

steel stairway. After the elevator was in place, the stairs were kept as an emergency exit.

The new additions brought a new name – Dinosaur Caverns, which capitalized on Walter Peck's original idea. Dinosaur Caverns began widely advertising, promising that travelers would soon be able to stroll the paths of Dinosaur Park – an extensive prehistoric attraction that was slated to include a luxury hotel, service station, riding stables, and a trailer park. The entire "Dinosaur City" would be brought to the public by chief backers J.W. "Bill" Ringsby and his sons, Gary and Don, who ran a trucking line.

The original plans for Dinosaur City were extravagant. Drawings that still exist today show plans for Dinosaur Estates, Fossil Court, Volcano Court, Ledgerock Lane, and Sabretooth Drive. There was even a plan to build a dinosaur across Route 66, with the tail on one side and the head on the other.

The Dinosaur Caverns Visitors Center opened in 1961, and the souvenir shop was stocked with pennants, bumper stickers, plastic caveman clubs, and toys and games featuring *The Flintstones*. This animated series had conveniently started its six-year primetime run in September 1960.

The Dinosaur Caverns' Doll Museum was also opened on the property. It included 50,000 dolls from a private collection in California. There was also "Bob," a mummified bobcat that had been discovered in the cave. The low humidity in the cave, near-constant temperature, and lack of bacteria had left Bob perfectly preserved. Bob became the most photographed curiosity at the cavern, and he soon made his way onto postcards and t-shirts.

The revamped cave held its dedication ceremony on May 12, 1962. Thomas "Cal" Miller – former superintendent of Mammoth Cave National Park – greeted visitors as the site manager. He spent his days squeezing into nooks and crannies, pointing out features of the cave, like Devil's Den, Rainbow Dome, and other marvels.

During the Cold War, Dinosaur Caverns became a fallout shelter where 2,000 people could hide from nuclear fallout for two weeks... although they'd end up a little short of toilet paper after a few days

In the middle of the cave's reopening, the nation was faced with the Cuban Missiles Crisis, leading government officials to turn the cavern into a makeshift bomb shelter. C-rations and water that were placed inside were supposed to sustain 2,000 people for two weeks. They also included 30 sanitation kits, each of which contained three rolls of toilet paper.

Two thousand people.

Two weeks.

90 rolls of toilet paper.

Government bureaucracy at its best.

Despite the success of Dinosaur Caverns, Dinosaur Park was never completed. A chunky stegosaurus could be found looming over the serving counter in the Juniper Room restaurant, and at least two outdoor dinosaurs were sculpted for tourist photos, but future prehistoric plans were abandoned. A motel did open in 1963 called the Caverns Inn, but rumors of the extinction of Route 66 did in all the other amenities.

That blow came in 1978 when the new interstate bypassed the entire Peach Springs area, cutting across the region 20 miles to the south. Soon after, Dinosaur Caverns assumed a new name – Grand Canyon Caverns, in hopes that tourists would connect it to the spectacular park.

It didn't help.

In the 1980s, the number of visitors that came to Grand Canyon Caverns dropped by 80 percent. The restaurant and the dance hall at the Caverns Inn were closed.

But that began to change in the 1990s. New management took over the cave and brought it back from the brink. The resurgence in interest in Route 66 started, and tourists took to the road once again.

And there's one other thing that's managed to keep the place alive – the fascination that we all have with dinosaurs. They are just as popular now as they were in 1927 when Walter Peck stumbled onto the cave, and they've kept travelers coming to the former Dinosaur Caverns nearly a century after they were first opened.

PEACH SPRINGS

A DOZEN OR SO MILES DOWN THE ROAD FROM GRAND Canyon Caverns, Peach Springs is a near ghost town located on the Hualapai reservation. The town dates back to 1883 and owes its existence to the sweet water from a local spring, which was named after a grove of peach trees.

When Route 66 came to town in 1926, it brought a flood of new business and made Peach Springs one of the busiest communities on the highway between Flagstaff and Kingman.

The successful **Peach Tree Trading Post** opened in 1928 and was built from local stone and Ponderosa pine beams. The town also had several cafes, service stations, and motor courts, like the **O.C. Osterman Auto Court.**

In 1925, former Swedish merchant marine John Osterman sold the gas station he'd opened just before World War I to his brother, Oscar. As luck would have it, the bumpy gravel road in front of the station soon became Route 66.

By 1932, highway improvements relocated Route 66 one block north, so Oscar built a new station along the highway, which still exists today. Oscar turned the west end of the building into an office and provided a small bunkroom for employees above the garage. Shortly after the station opened, Oscar added a row of six small cabins. Business was so good that the construction costs for the cabins were paid

OSTERMAN BROS. CAMP GROUND, GARAGE, STORE, AND CABINS, PEACH SPRINGS, ARIZONA

off by the end of the summer. To meet demand, he added another 16 units – with attached garages – at the back of the property.

In 1934, Frank Boyd, who'd grown up on a farm in Kansas, left home to attend college in California. Year after year, during the busy summer months, Frank and his brother returned to Peach Springs and worked at Oscar's station. After he graduated in 1938, Frank decided to settle in Peach Springs. It turned out to be good timing. Around that same time, Oscar decided to get out of the tourism business, and he offered the business to Frank, who jumped at the chance. He made a quick trip back to Kansas to retrieve his new bride, Beatrice, and the couple started their new life together in Peach Springs as the owners of O.C. Osterman Auto Court.

Business boomed, especially after World War II, but in 1946, a fire destroyed a large part of the business. They quickly rebuilt, though, and added a new gas station to complement the auto court.

But the fire wasn't the end of their bad fortune. In 1966, a flood destroyed most of the business, but undaunted, the Boyds rebuilt again. In time, the auto court closed but the gas station and store lived on until 2005. The building still stands today, but a few years ago, it was sitting dark and empty.

While the O.C. Osterman Auto Court no longer exists today, the gas station hung on longer than most businesses in Peach Springs. When the interstate bypassed the town, the community went into a decline that lasted for years. Thankfully, Peach Springs has been at least somewhat revived by the resurgence in interest in Route 66.

VALENTINE

ALONG HIGHWAY "66" VALENTINE, ARIZ. B-212

FROM PEACH SPRINGS, ROUTE 66 PASSES THROUGH Truxton, which is essentially a ghost town, although it wasn't founded until 1951 when it was announced that a dam was going to be built on the Colorado River at nearby Bridge Canyon. Anticipating a heavy flow of trucks and autos on their way to the dam, a service station and garage were built, followed by a café. Although the dam was never built, the businesses thrived thanks to Route 66 traffic. Other businesses, like motels, restaurants, and garages, soon followed.

One of the new businesses was the **Frontier Motel and Café**, which was opened by Alice Wright. It was later sold to a former waitress, Mildred Barker, and her husband, Ray, in the 1970s. Mildred was already beloved in the area for her sweet nature and welcoming attitude, which added to the success of the café and motel.

Mildred was also well-known for sharing her ghost stories. She believed her resident spirits were Native Americans who were killed on Route 66 when traffic was heavy – crossing the highway or walking along the edge of the road. She said that she often looked toward the doorway and saw a Native American man standing there as if he had been injured or run over by a vehicle.

After Truxton, the highway drops into the Crozier Canyon Valley before passing by the forlorn ruins of an old Union 76 station and post office in Valentine – a town once famous for its heart-shaped postmark. Thousands of cards and letters flooded into the tiny post office each year until it was closed in 1990.

On August 15 of that year, post office manager Jacqueline Ann Grigg was murdered by 19-year-old Bryan Buckingham during a senseless robbery that reportedly netted him less than $100 and some postal money orders. The post office was permanently closed after that, and the town's famed heart-shaped postmark was retired.

Valentine itself started in 1883 when the Santa Fe Railroad built a siding that was called "Truxton," which is where the 1951 community of Truxton gained its name.

After a brief period of activity during the Route 66 years, Valentine dwindled to just a handful of homes after the interstate bypassed the community.

Today, only a handful of buildings remain, including a terrible place that, while closed since 1937, retains an atmosphere of menace and tragedy that has never gone away.

TRUXTON CANYON INDIAN SCHOOL

ONE OF THE EARLIEST BUILDINGS TO BE CONSTRUCTED IN Valentine was the Truxton Canyon Training School, which opened in 1903. It was a boarding school for the children of the Hualapai, Apache, Hopi, Mojave, Navajo, and Papago nations. It was designed to "assimilate" these children into white culture and teach them how to leave the "primitive" customs and traditions of their people behind.

The school presented itself as an industrial training institution when it opened, and students spent part of each day in academic classes. During the rest of the day, the boys were taught a trade while the girls learned domestic skills. The students were veritable prisoners at the school, and many of them were taken from their reservations by force. Some of them were so reluctant to leave home and come to the school that they committed suicide instead of submitting to this kind of "education."

The superintendent of the school was Henry P. Ewing, an erratic and well-known man

HAUNTED

who had arrived in the Valentine area in 1883. He served as a county assessor, sheriff, and deputy sheriff until becoming an industrial teacher, then superintendent, after the school opened. He was also an agent for the Hualapai reservation until he lost that job after corruption in his office was uncovered. He was charged with falsifying accounts to defraud the government out of about $1,200.

Students and fellow staff members believed that his legal problems hastened the decay of his mental faculties, which had already been deteriorating for a few years. In 1906, he lost most of his vision but refused to live in town, preferring to remain at a nearby mine that he owned. Over the next several months, he became violently insane, accusing people of poisoning him, and was eventually sent to an asylum in Phoenix. He died there in 1908.

The descent into madness by Henry Ewing was not the only tragedy connected to the Truxton Canyon Indian School. In 1907, Michael Maguire fell behind the wheels of a freight train just a mile west of the school. His right leg was mangled beyond repair. He was immediately brought to the school to be treated but died while being rushed by train to Kingman.

Dr. E.P. Ford was hunting rabbits in some heavy mesquite brush near the school when he somehow accidentally shot himself in the chest with his shotgun. His body was found hours later by his wife and children. It was presumed that he had tripped and fallen, and the gun had discharged when he hit the ground, killing him instantly. Dr. Ford was on staff at the school, and he and his family had only been there about five months when he died at age 35.

On September 13, 1924, a four-year-old student at the school named John Light died after the accidental discharge of a .22-caliber rifle. He had just loaded the gun, and while his seven-year-old brother was trying to take it away from him, the gun discharged, and a bullet passed through John's right shoulder. He died just moments later.

Although, at one time, there were many different buildings on the property that belonged to the Truxton Valley Indian School, only one red brick school building remains. It's a reminder of a different – theoretically less enlightened – time when Native Americans were considered "savages" and unable to cope on their own without guidance and skills given to them by the white man.

Thankfully, it's been closed for many years now, although this doesn't mean the surviving building is truly empty. For decades, rumors have claimed the remains of the school are haunted – perhaps by those who died on the grounds or by the restless spirits of the children who were forced to come here against their will and found pain, loneliness, and confusion waiting for them when they arrived.

For years, stories have been told about eerie lights in the building and on the weed-choked land that surrounds it. Faces have been seen peering out the weathered and darkened windows, and those who tell the stories will say that it's not just the coyotes who cry out in the darkness around the former school.

"GIGANTICUS HEADICUS"

DATING BACK TO 1874, THE ONCE THRIVING MINING community of Hackberry is the oldest town on this stretch of Route 66. When the railroad came through the area in 1882, the town was moved four miles from its original site and became a loading stop for cattle. A nearby silver mine earned almost $3 million before it closed in 1919, turning Hackberry into just another desert ghost town.

Well, almost.

When Route 66 came through in 1926, Hackberry became a tourist town, and various stores and service stations opened to serve the needs of travelers. The best known of these was the Northside General Store, which was connected to a Conoco station. The business – along with all

the others in town – boomed until a few decades later when Hackberry was bypassed by the interstate, leaving the little town stranded 16 miles away from the new highway. The station closed, and just as it had in 1919, the community became a ghost town.

Artist and Route 66 enthusiast Bob Waldmire bought the abandoned store in 1992 and re-opened it as the **Hackberry General Store and Visitors Center**. It's since become a favorite Arizona location for present-day Route 66 travelers. The old store is filled with trinkets and treasures, and the place itself is a museum jammed with memorabilia, souvenirs, vintage cars, old gas pumps, and more.

JUST A MERE SIX MILES WEST OF HACKBERRY IS THE TINY railroad village of Antares, and there, sitting silently along the roadside, is a Tiki-inspired giant that is guaranteed to get the attention of everyone who drives past. This oversized homage to the mysterious statues of Easter Island may not be smiling, but he may be the most welcoming face you'll see in town.

Officially, he's called "Giganticus Headicus," a somewhat sarcastic and pseudo-scientific-sounding moniker that is as deadpan as the sculpture himself. The art piece is the brainchild of former New Jersey artist Gregg Arnold, who got the idea to build this strange, 14-foot head in 2004. He was soon looking for the perfect location to place his creation,

and after paging through a dozen books about roadside America, he decided that somewhere along Route 66 was the ideal spot.

Eventually, he found his way to Antares, a town that was settled when the railroad became stuck on how to get over the nearby mountains and opted to go around them instead. Later, Route 66 followed the same route, and the town flourished for the next few decades.

Interestingly, Antares takes its name from a star, and its name is Greek for "rival of Mars," which refers to the star's red hues. Likewise, the town of Antares was named for its bright, red sands – the same sands from which the giant head now rises.

The structure is set up on what was once the Kozy Korner trailer court, positioned directly in front of an oddly shaped triangular building, and he's become a photo magnet for tourists.

Although Giganticus Headicus is the most popular part of the exhibit, it's not the artist's only creation. A whimsical pineapple seat accompanies the head, and there's also a windmill made from 1950s furniture, some funky robots, and even a "baby rattler" pit. If you're afraid of snakes, don't worry – it's only a pit filled with baby rattles.

A local group started working with Gregg Arnold when he came to town, and they turned the old Kozy Korner building into the Antares Visitors Center, making Giganticus Headicus easy to find when passing through town.

THE ROAD INTO KINGMAN

WEST OF HACKBERRY AND ANTARES, ROUTE 66 LEFT THE mountains and ran straight toward the horizon through the vast Hualapai Valley toward Kingman.

Founded in 1882, Kingman began as a simple railroad siding near Beale's Springs along the Atlantic and Pacific line. Known initially as Middleton, it was renamed for Lewis Kingman, who surveyed the railroad's right-of-way between Needles, California, and Albuquerque, New Mexico.

The first train arrived in town in March 1883, and Kingman, then just a little camp on the side of the tracks, quickly became a central transportation hub for the western states.

HIGHWAY 66 KINGMAN ARIZ

Kingman U.S. Army Airfield

Kingman flourished during the early 1900s and became a boomtown when Route 66 arrived in 1926. It's ironic, though, that the town is such a hub for transportation that most Kingman streets, including Route 66, remained unpaved until about 1940. Stranger still is the fact that, until 1941, Kingman was surrounded by fences to keep livestock from wandering into the streets.

During World War II, an area just east of town became the site of the Kingman U.S. Army Airfield. It became an aerial gunnery training base for 35,000 soldiers and airmen. After the war, the airfield became one of the largest storage depots for obsolete military aircraft in the world.

Accidents were common when the base operated as a training center and when war-damages planes were flown in to be stored or dismantled for salvage.

One accident in January 1944, though, had nothing to do with aircraft. The deadly crash occurred when a freight train slammed into an army bus filled with cadets just outside the main gate of the base on Route 66. The bus was returning with 36 cadets from night gunnery practice when the accident occurred.

According to witnesses, the bus had stopped at a railroad crossing as the Santa Fe freight train approached. After pausing for several seconds, the bus then suddenly jerked forward onto the tracks, directly in the path of the fast-approaching train. It was suspected that the driver's foot slipped off the clutch pedal, causing the bus to move.

The front of the train squarely jackknifed the bus, dragging the crumpled wreckage several hundred yards down the track. The collision killed 27 of the soldiers on the bus and injured eight others.

Soldiers from the base quickly rushed to the scene while medical officers immediately set up a field hospital at the scene. Rescuers climbed over the mass of twisted steel and metal that had once been the bus and were often forced to pry the wreckage apart to bring out the injured and the dead.

The original air traffic control tower still stands at the former airfield today, and below it is a memorial that lists the names of the men who died in this tragic accident. Another memorial there commemorates the deaths of crews that resulted from a midair collision between a B-17 Flying Fortress and a North American T-6 Texan trainer.

A crash occurred on July 6, 1943, and isn't memorialized, but it was just as deadly. Nine airmen were injured, and the co-pilot was killed when a twin-engine training plane crashed on the runway at the airfield.

After the war, Kingman experienced more growth when several major employers moved into the area, including the Ford Motor Company, which opened an auto testing proving ground. Several new neighborhoods were developed in the city to house the skilled workers and professionals employed at the proving ground. Around this same time, the development of the Duval copper mine near Chloride and the construction of the Mohave Generating Station in Laughlin, Nevada, also began contributing to Kingman's growth.

Kingman also has some connections to Hollywood. Clark Gable and Carole Lombard were married at St. John's Methodist Church in 1939 (more about them soon), and actor Andy Devine was raised in Kingman, where his father operated the popular Beale Hotel, located on Route 66. The path of the old highway through town is now named "Andy Devine Avenue," and Kingman celebrates in his honor every September.

Kingman today remains one of the more prominent towns along Route 66 in Arizona, even though it was one of the first to be bypassed by the interstate in 1953.

Clark Gable and Carole Lombard

KILLERS IN KINGMAN

IN 1926, KINGMAN WAS THE SCENE OF A MURDER THAT HAD consequences in at least two different states and made the front pages of newspapers across the country.

TRUE CRIME

At around 8:45 P.M. on October 20, a Crysler with a driver and four passengers – all members of the Bing Kong Tong, a Chinese crime syndicate from Los Angeles – drove slowly down the alley behind the Commercial Hotel, located on East Front Street, or what is now Route 66.

The car stopped at the rear entrance of the American Kitchen restaurant. The owners of the eatery, Don On and Tom King, were Chinese immigrants who had relocated to Kingman from Los Angeles. Both men were in the restaurant that night, cleaning up and preparing to close for the night.

While one man was waiting in the car parked in the alley, the other men entered the back door of the restaurant. One of them addressed King by name. Then, all four assassins opened fire with pistols.

Leaving the owners in pools of blood on the floor of their restaurant, the killers fled back to their car and fled west on the National Old Trails Road back toward California. Mohave County Sheriff W.P. Mahoney and several deputies pursued them at high speed. Gunshots were exchanged as they neared Topock on the Colorado River, where the chase came to an end. The assassins lost control of the Crysler and veered off onto the shoulder of the road, burying it up to its front axle in deep sand.

The killers were placed under arrest, but because of a rise in Tong activity on the West Coast and in Arizona, as well as fear of retaliation, the five men – B.W.L. Sam, Shew Chin, Jew Har, Gee King Long, and Wong Lung – were transferred to the Yavapai County Jail in Prescott rather than the Mohave County Jail in Kingman.

Even though the Chinese residents of Kingman were mostly well-treated, especially the business owners, there was still an underlying prejudice against them. As an example, many property deeds in town contained a clause that prohibited "Negroes, Chinese, Japanese, or Indians" from buying or occupying the residence.

Further evidence of that prejudice can be found in the series of raids that Sheriff Mahoney initiated on the homes of Chinese immigrants in the wake of the murders. He searched their homes, confiscated their guns, and even forced many of them to leave the county.

During the trial of the Tong killers, it was learned that Tom King had been a member of the Hop Sing gang and that he was killed because, during the time he worked as a pit boss at an illegal gambling hall in L.A., he had made a substantial loan to a member of the Bing King Tong. An attempt to collect on the debt had led to a feud between Tongs that resulted in 15 murders before Tom King was killed.

The trial became a national media sensation, one of the first to reveal the inner workings of Chinese organized crime. It was said that the respective gangs spent more than $1 million in legal fees during the 18-month courtroom battle and subsequent appeals, which included recanted testimony and claims of bribery.

In the end, the jury verdict and the sentence handed down by the judge were sustained, and all five men were sent to the Arizona State Penitentiary for execution. Only one of them, Wong Long, was spared the death penalty. He was only 17 at the time of the murders, which led to his sentence being commuted to life behind bars.

A BED FOR THE NIGHT

DURING ITS YEARS AS A TRANSPORTATION HUB ON ROUTE 66, Kingman played host to hundreds of travelers every night of the year, offering motels, hotels, and motor courts for every budget. Some of those spots have become renowned to highway travelers over time, offering stories that have become an essential part of this section of the road.

DURING THE HEYDAY OF ROUTE 66 IN KINGMAN, THE Arcadia Court catered to well-to-do travelers. One of the postcards for the motor court noted, "Quiet and restful. Luxurious furnishings and the finest appointments for the fastidious guest. Healthiest climate (no humidity) and purest water. Special quarters for chauffeurs and maids."

Opened in 1938, the motel offered 15 first-class rooms with attached garages surrounding a hacienda-style courtyard. Eventually, the garages were eliminated to make way for more rooms. In the 1950s, it was remodeled and expanded to 47 rooms – all with air-conditioning, which made it one of the first artificially cooled motels in Arizona at the time. The owners also added a swimming pool, which was the first in Kingman. The name was changed to Arcadia Lodge, befitting an establishment considered the peak of luxury at the time.

After the interstate bypassed the town, many of the auto courts in the community began a slow decline, and the Arcadia Lodge was no exception. As motorists blew past Kingman on the new highway, the motel was left in the dust.

As time passed, the motor court fell into disrepair, and rooms began to be rented on a weekly and monthly basis. The police were frequent visitors, dealing with drug dealers, prostitutes, and sketchy tenants. The fine reputation of the motel was now a distant memory.

After a string of disillusioned owners, the property was sold again in 2001. After a lengthy renovation, the classic motor court was brought back to life to provide a nostalgic overnight stay for Route 66 travelers.

Sadly, though, this period didn't last, and, as of this writing, the Arcadia Lodge was once again for sale, hoping to find that special owner who is willing to breathe life into the old place once again.

ANOTHER KINGMAN MOTOR LODGE WAS THE **WHITE ROCK** Court, which was built by Conrad Minka in 1935. He had purchased property on what was then the west end of town and decided to build an auto court from native stone from a nearby quarry. The unusually bright white stone prompted Conrad to call his new business the White Rock Court.

The guest rooms were built in two sections and laid out in an "L" shape. Each of the "modern cabins" had their own attached garage. The

two-story main building housed the office and the owner's residence, although the second-floor residence would later be converted to additional rooms.

One unusual feature of the White Rock Court was central heating, which was as rare as air conditioning at the time. Conrad accomplished this by building the court over a series of tunnels that connected to a central furnace. In other words, every guest room was set to the same temperature. Take it or leave it.

Sometime after World War II, the garages vanished, and the court grew to 22 units. This wasn't enough to save it, though, and eventually, it fell victim to changing times, so the motel was converted to monthly rental units.

Unlike many motor courts on Route 66, the White Rock Court was built from solid stone and masonry. The construction was so solid that it managed to avoid destruction for many years. Time eventually caught up with it, however, and the once popular auto court has since vanished with time.

IN THE LATE 1930S, JOHN F. MILLER PURCHASED A PIECE OF property on the edge of Kingman, where he planned to open the most glamorous motor lodge in town. Miller was no stranger to the business. He'd built his first hotel in Las Vegas on the corner of Main and Fremont – the Golden Gate Casino – and by December 1939, he'd opened El Trovatore in Kingman.

The first guests to stay in one of the 30 rooms at the new motel paid just $3 a night, but that was no indication of the quality of the place. Miller had vowed to make the place classy – and he did. El Trovatore became so popular that he had to add another 24 rooms to keep up with demand. He also opened a cocktail lounge and dining room that featured unusual walls that were lined with large rocks, giving guests the impression that they were inside a stone structure.

After the interstate bypassed Kingman in 1953, El Trovatore began a series of ownership changes, which led to the appearance and reputation of the place beginning a downhill slide. Year after year, the place became worse and worse, deteriorating into a place known for monthly rentals, parties, drugs, and trouble.

Then, in May 2005, Karen Kreiger bought El Trovatore with plans to revitalize the motel and repair its seedy reputation. Work began on the rooms – new furniture, new carpets, never everything. While the place continued to struggle for years, it's currently open again and greeting travelers who are looking for a place to experience a little bit of Route 66 history.

HOTEL BRUNSWICK

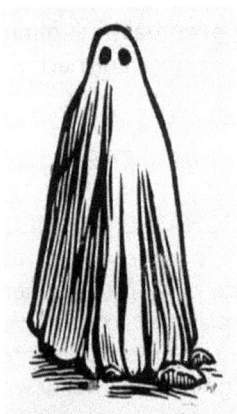

BUILT IN 1909, THE HOTEL BRUNSWICK IN KINGMAN WAS already standing when the gravel road that ran in front of it was designated Route 66.

The three-story stone hotel – once the tallest building in town – has been casting a long shadow over downtown since it opened. It boasts not only a link to Arizona history but a nearly forgotten chapter in Ford family history, connections to Hollywood celebrities – and even a ghost story or two.

John Mulligan arrived in Arizona in the 1870s, around the same time that John W. "Watt" Thompson arrived in the territory from New Brunswick, Canada. Mulligan, who was a stonemason by trade, soon learned that he could make more money using his skills in construction than in mining or prospecting, although he was somewhat successful with both.

In 1881, he built his first house on the southwest corner of what is now Beale and Fourth Street in a rough-and-tumble railroad camp that would soon become known as Kingman. He also later built the Hotel Beale, the Mohave County Jail, and the Elks Lodge, of which he was a charter member.

It was around this same time that he first formed a partnership with Watt Thompson. They worked together on an array of projects that included mining, land speculation, and construction. In 1907, they began work on their most ambitious project, the construction of a stylish, modern hotel on Front Street. Named the Brunswick by Thompson when it was completed in 1909, they planned for this to be one of the finest hotels in the Arizona Territory. They spared no expense when it came to building materials, and Mulligan even traveled to Los Angeles to purchase the fine furnishings they needed.

In 1912, though, the partnership between Mulligan and Thompson unraveled. Speculation about the split continues to this day, but the actual reasons are lost to history. Reportedly, the men never spoke again.

The Hotel Brunswick was divided, literally, with the construction of a wall that separated the building into equal halves. The agreement gave each partner 25 hotel rooms. Mulligan was given the original lobby and the bar. Thompson ended up with the

Hotel Brunswick

restaurant. Oddly, the hotel continued operating under a single name – Hotel Brunswick – and both men were quite successful.

In the summer of 1915, Edsel Ford – the only child of automaker Henry Ford – and a few of his college chums left Dearborn, Michigan, for a grand adventure. Their destination was the Panama Pacific Exposition in San Francisco. However, like an increasing number of tourists, they also wanted to see the exotic cultures of Santa Fe and the pueblos in New Mexico. The natural wonders of sites such as the Grand Canyon and Painted Desert were also attractions, so they followed the National Old Trails Road to Los Angeles before traveling up the Pacific coast to San Francisco.

The adventure was financed by turning it into an unofficial business trip. Along the way, Edsel inspected Ford agencies in many towns – including the one in Kingman – and he often used Ford garages when repairs were needed on the road.

Edsel's travel journal for July 15, 1915, reads:

"Got going from Williams about 11:00. Had lunch at Ash Forks. Loafed along; found it very hot. Bought some gas and oranges at

Seligman. Stutz broke another spring and returned to Seligman. Cadillac and Ford went on to Kingman, arriving at midnight, Brunswick Hotel. "

As evidence of the hotel's prominence in the early days of Route 66, the *Hotel, Garage, Service Station, and AAA Club Directory* published in 1927 listed two recommended lodging options in Kingman – the Hotel Beale and the Hotel Brunswick. However, changes came over time, and by the time AAA published the 1940 Directory of Motor Courts and Cottages, Brunswick was no longer listed.

Mulligan sold his portion of the property in 1925. It was sold again in 1928, and the Brunswick name was dropped. It would be the "Ideal Hotel" for the next two years, but in 1930, it sold again. George LaPlante became the new manager and promised extensive work to modernize the hotel, which was underway. It was during this time that the old front portico with its balcony was removed, and a neon sign was added to appeal to the tourists on Route 66. In the years that followed, several eateries operated from the former restaurant, including Scudder's, Richey's, and Lockwood's Chicken in the Rough.

In 1939, the Hotel Brunswick made its Hollywood connection when Clark Gable and Carole Lombard attended a brief reception in the bar after they were married at St. Johns Methodist Episcopal Church. (Still more Gable and Lombard coming soon)

In 1959, the Thompson side of the hotel was sold to Joe Otero. After another remodel, he opened El Mohave restaurant. It proved to be a popular restaurant for locals and Route 66 travelers. It was also a favorite of Senator Barry Goldwater when he was in Kingman. In 1966, Otero purchased the rest of the property and closed the hotel. He also removed the dividing wall on the first floor and linked the bar and restaurant into one large space.

The restaurant closed in 1980, and the old hotel was left vacant until 1994 when it was acquired by Priscilla and Rennie Davis. They began a new restoration, starting with rebuilding the staircase in its original configuration and replacement of the portico and balcony. For a brief time, the hotel, bar, and restaurant were again open for business. Even the original switchboard, on loan from the Mohave Museum of History and Arts, was returned to its original location. It proved to be a short-lived endeavor, and the hotel was closed again in 1998.

Over the next decade, a series of new owners purchased the property with plans for renovation and the restoration of the hotel. In 2012, it was purchased again, this time by Werner Fleischmann, a Swiss developer. Intermittent restoration work began once more, and the place managed to open again a few years later.

Street Scene looking East   U.S. Highway "66"   Kingman, Arizona

And that's when the owners and staff first heard about the ghost stories that had been plaguing the hotel for nearly a century.

Strange events occurred, which had apparently been going on for years. Mysterious coins appeared out of nowhere in the lobby and hallways. Guests reported apparitions of a man and a little girl. The man was often spotted climbing the steps from the cellar. Ghostly presences were encountered in the rooms and guests told of being tucked in at night or having their head or feet touched by unseen hands.

Some historians have speculated that the hotel's resident ghost may be that of William McRight, a 74-year-old man who was found dead in his room at the Hotel Brunswick on March 7, 1915. He was believed to have died from natural causes, but his body wasn't discovered until he failed to come downstairs for breakfast that morning. A manager went up to his room and found the older man lying dead on the floor, a towel clutched in his hands.

Born in Pennsylvania in 1841, William McRight first came to the Arizona Territory from the California coast in 1874. He initially settled in the town of Signal, where he lived for the next 40 years. He was one of the owners of the profitable McCracken Mines and made a fortune selling off his shares when he decided to retire.

William arrived in Kingman in 1913, and he moved into the Hotel Brunswick. He usually woke each day at 7:00 A.M., ate breakfast, and then spent the day reading, talking, and playing cards with friends. He spun stories about early Arizona for

anyone who wanted to listen – and there were plenty of people who did. He made many friends and was well-liked by travelers who stopped at the hotel for the night.

If William is one of the hotel's resident spirits, he may not haunt the building alone. One of the more recent owners of the Brunswick reported encountering the overpowering smell of lilacs, which she believed was linked to Sarah Mulligan, the wife of one of the original owners, Joseph Mulligan.

Others have – in addition to seeing the ghost of a little girl – heard the scampering of children's footsteps throughout the building, as well as playful laughter and what sounded like a bouncing toy ball.

But if the Hotel Brunswick is truly as haunted as so many believe, then the ghosts currently have no one to interact with. As of this writing, the hotel is closed, but if you're passing through Kingman, keep an eye out for it – you never know when someone might decide to open it again.

COOL SPRINGS CAMP

JUST 20 MILES WEST OF KINGMAN, ROUTE 66 CAME TO THE Black Mountains on the approach to Sitgreaves Pass in 1926. The following year, N.R. Dunton built Cool Springs Camp entirely out of stones that he gathered along the highway. There wasn't much to the place – not at first – but it offered a respite for travelers, especially those driving west from Kingman when 20 miles was a lot farther than it is today.

In 1936, Dunton sold the property to James and Mary Walker from Indiana. The Walkers, along with their four children, moved to Cool Spring that summer and soon remodeled and enlarged the business to include

a restaurant and a bar. When the couple later divorced, Mary ended up with Cool Springs Camp. She remarried a man named Floyd Spidell, who added a full-service garage and eight guest cabins, turning the small camp into a full-fledged travel stop. When Mary and Floyd later divorced, Floyd found himself the sole owner of Cool Springs Camp.

In the years that followed, the camp became a popular destination for travelers and Kingman locals alike. Well known for its famous chicken dinners, people came from as far as 40 miles away for a meal.

The Mobil gas station at Cool Springs even made an appearance in the John Ford movie *The Grapes of Wrath*, starring Henry Fonda as Tom Joad.

In 1952, the highway changed, bypassing this dangerous stretch of road (more about that soon) in favor of a safer and straighter route to Topock, Arizona. After that, business slowed to a crawl, and Cool Springs Camp closed in 1964. Floyd packed up and moved to Kingman.

Cool Springs Camp was abandoned and was mostly forgotten for decades. Vandals slowly destroyed it, and what they didn't destroy simply crumbled and decayed in the unforgiving heat of the desert.

One day in 1991, Cool Springs Camp came back to life and was partially rebuilt as a set for the movie *Universal Soldier*. Unfortunately, the restoration was for one purpose – to blow it up for a scene in the film. The studio moved on afterward, and what they left of Cool Springs was not worth mentioning. It went back to being nothing more than the bare bones of a place that had once been a favorite Route 66 eatery.

In 1997, Ned and Michelle Leuchtner happened to pass through the area, and they noticed the ruins of Cool Springs Camp. They decided to stop and take a look, then decided to do a little research and find out what the abandoned structure had once been. The more they learned, the more fascinated they became, and soon, the reconstruction of the roadside icon became Ned's and Michelle's dream.

They contacted Nancy Waverka, the niece of Floyd Spidell, and made an offer to buy the site. But Nancy refused, citing sentimental reasons, but the couple assured her that they intended to rebuild the camp that her uncle had loved. This finally gave her the peace of mind

she needed, and in 2001, Ned and Michelle became the new owners of Cool Springs Camp.

Three years later, the rebuilding began in earnest, and it has since been fully restored. The camp remains open today, complete with a gift shop and museum, and it's regained its old notoriety as a popular stop on the Mother Road.

"THE COOLEST SPOT IN THE DESERT"

BEGINNING THE RUGGED APPROACH TO SITGREAVES PASS from the east – one of the most feared and dreaded sections of all of Route 66 – travelers would always spot the letters of Ed's Camp spelled out in painted white rocks on the side of a hill.

The camp had been built by Lowell "Ed" Edgerton, who'd come to the desert for the dry air but ended up becoming one of the most mysterious characters of the highway. He opened his business for the sole purpose of cashing in on the ever-increasing flow of tourists through the region – never realizing that he would become as legendary as his business was.

Ed was born in Michigan in 1894 and went west as a young man on the advice of a doctor. Ed suffered from tuberculosis, which was the leading cause of death in the United States at that time. It was often suggested that those with consumption – as it was often known at the time – should seek out the dry air of the Southwest for relief. He initially moved to Southern California but found the climate of Arizona more to his liking, and he spent the next 60 years of his life in Mohave County.

Not much is known about Ed's early years in Arizona, but those who knew him always advised that his stories should be taken with a massive grain of salt.

Later in life, Ed claimed that he studied to be a doctor and had, while working for a mining company in Mexico, amputated a man's leg during the Mexican Revolution. He spun tales about how he had owned a mansion in Los Angeles but had lost it in a property deal that went bad. He also said that, while tracking a mountain lion, he followed the beast into Nevada and became so engrossed in the hunt that he forgot about his wife and five children and figured there was no point in going back. The biggest problem with this story is that there's no record that Ed was ever married, let alone having five children.

When Ed moved to Mohave County, he was able to get a lease on the tailings dump east of Oatman. Tailings were the by-product of the mineral recovery process -- the material left over after the valuable ore was separated from what was left over. Within months, his operation was making more money than the actual mine, and he was then hired by the Tom Reed Mine as foreman of recovery.

Around 1919, Ed bought a parcel of land at Little Meadows in the foothills of the Black Mountains. At first, like so many others who came to the area at this time, Ed planned to make his fortune through a gold strike. With his older brother, Tibor, he worked several mining jobs before realizing he could make a steadier – and much easier – living by providing services to miners and travelers rather than digging into the mountains.

When he opened his trading post, it was nothing more than an open space that was sheltered by a tin roof. He later claimed that when Route 66 came through, he suddenly became so busy that he never had time to add walls.

Whether this was true or not, Ed's business boomed. He soon added an eatery – the Kactus Kafe, which was a proper building -- and a service station, dubbing the whole thing Ed's Camp.

At first, Ed's Camp had no tourist cabins or rooms where travelers could sleep. Instead, they could pitch a tent or sleep in their cars. For those who wanted a little "luxury" and had a little more cash, there was a screened porch where they

might sleep on a cot. Ed charged drivers for water on a per-bucket basis, although that fee was waived if they decided to spend the night. As the place grew, a grocery store and souvenir shop were added, and Ed's Camp became a stop for Pickwick Stage Lines, a coach company that would later become part of the Greyhound bus line. The place began to be advertised as "the coolest place in the desert."

But there was more to Ed than him just being the owner of a store and gas station. Over the years, he studied the rocks of Arizona and became an expert geologist who could identify any Mohave County rock and, say, to within a few miles from where it had come.

He also owned a rare earth mine from which he extracted ore that was shipped to numerous companies, providing at least 30 different minerals that were used in alloy steels, electronic components, ceramics, plastics, atomic devices, and even cosmetics.

He even had – although briefly – a mineral named after him. However, "Edgertonite," which was a mix of iron, yttrium uranium, calcium, columbium, tantalum, zirconium, tin, and other minerals, was quickly renamed Yttrotantalite when it was realized it had already been discovered in Sweden in 1802. However, Ed was likely the first man to find Yttrotantalite in the United States, and he often claimed that he'd provided the material for the first atomic bomb.

Oddly, Ed credited Yttrotantalite with saving his life. According to his story, in April 1957, doctors told him that he had cancer and gave him 30 days to live unless he had major surgery. He refused the operation and returned to Ed's Camp, determined to treat himself. The details of what happened next changed with each retelling, but this is probably his most comprehensive version:

I put on two suits of heavy woolen underclothes and put these swatches [of Yttrotantalite] in between, all around, and then I put three big electric pads around that. I cooked myself for about 72 hours at 130 degrees. I didn't eat anything. I drank warm water. At the end of 72 hours stuff began to loosen inside me ... Rotten goddamn stuff, it couldn't take the heat. I commenced to bleed internally and for up to 90 hours I bled inside – rotten blood first and then fresh blood – and then that quit.

When it was over, Ed nursed himself back to health on a diet of goat's milk, raw eggs, and avocadoes. Two months later, his doctor declared there was no sign of cancer in his body – it was a miracle.

It seems difficult to believe that anyone could survive such extreme temperatures for so long, not to mention experience four days of internal bleeding, but Ed believed that he'd cured his cancer, and instead of having just 30 days to live, he was around for 30 more years. He claimed that he was studied intensively by the Veterans Administration Hospital in Fort Whipple, near Prescott, although there are no records of Ed having been a patient until he died there in 1978. He also told people he had worked with one of the foremost cancer experts in the world – although he declined to name the scientist – as well as claiming that he could predict where in a person's body a cancer might be just by the color of their hair.

It's tempting to dismiss him as just some old desert rat, telling tall tales and living like a hermit, but Ed was so much more than that. While some of his stories may have been embellished – and others, quite frankly, tongue-in-cheek fabrications created to entertain tourists – he was much respected in the fields of geology and mineralogy despite his lack of formal training. He consulted several companies, taught at a local college, and wrote and presented papers on minerals.

Ed was certainly not a hermit, even though many parts of his life have always been a mystery.

Thanks in part to the natural springs on his property and in part because of the improvements that Ed made over the years to the water flow, Ed's Camp truly became an oasis in the desert. Late into his seventies, Ed kept Kingman supplied with pears, as well as apricots, tomatoes, quinces, strawberries, peppers, corn, and grapevines. His pomegranates were so good that they won four ribbons at the Arizona State Fair.

Ed Edgerton died on September 7, 1978, at the age of 83. Although he likely wished that it had been at the place that

he'd called home for most of his life, he passed away at the VA Hospital at Fort Whipple – leaving one last mystery behind.

To this day, no one knows where Ed was buried. Although it has been stated that he was buried in Mountain View Cemetery in Kingman, officials there have no record of his grave. And neither does anyone else. Ed was buried somewhere, of course, but where that might be is unknown, which is probably just how Ed would have wanted it.

Today, Ed's Camp is slowly decaying on private property, but thanks to the enforcement of the NO TRESPASSING signs around the site, it can still be seen off the side of the old highway. The gas pumps are long gone, but the trading post and the café remain, along with the basic tourist cabins that he later built.

If you pass by now, you can even make out a few of the remaining white stones that once spelled out Ed's Camp on the hillside opposite the camp. It's a place that seems like a bleak spot in the desert now, but for many years, it was a paradise for Ed and the thousands of travelers who stopped there during the heyday of Route 66.

SITGREAVES PASS

IN THE EARLY DAYS OF ROUTE 66, DRIVING ACROSS THE country was not a fun and relaxing experience for most travelers. First, there was only a fraction of the amenities that you'd find along today's roadside. There was no one to call if your car broke down and you needed a tow to the closest garage. If you broke down, you usually had to rely on your mechanical skills to get going again.

In the Midwest, motoring from town to town on the highway wasn't

much of a challenge. The road was mostly flat, and the odds were in your favor against breaking down too far from the next town. But the stakes were much higher in Texas, New Mexico, and Arizona, where open expanses of the country meant that you might drive for days to get across state lines.

And the farther west you went, the conditions got tougher. In addition to the long distances,

the heat played a significant role in stranding vehicles. If you were really unlucky, you might wind up with a blown head gasket or a seized engine, neither of which were easily repaired in the middle of nowhere. But if travelers planned ahead – and carried an ample supply of water – even a rookie motorist had a good chance of making it to their final destination.

Of course, all bets were off when it came to crossing the steep mountain grades and other treacherous inclines – especially in Arizona, just outside of the once prosperous gold mining town of Oatman. In that area, the pre-1952 alignment of Route 66 curved and climbed up and over the dramatic terrain of Sitgreaves Pass.

Located in the Black Mountains of Mohave County, Sitgreaves Pass is essentially a gap between the mountains that rises over 3,500 feet in elevation. It was here in 1857 that famed Southwest explorer Edward Fitzgerald Beale completed what was called Beale's Wagon Road, which would later become the path of the Santa Fe Railroad. To honor one of his men, who had died building the trail, he called it John Howell's Pass. The following year, though, Lieutenant Joseph Christmas of the Corps of Topographical Engineers passed through on a survey mission, and he renamed the pass in honor of one of his fellow explorers, Captain Lorenzo Sitgreaves. This name was the one that stuck.

Early Route 66 travelers motoring west to California approached the pass with a fair amount of nervousness. No matter what they were driving, they could rest assured that their vehicle would be put to the test. From above, looking west toward the Colorado River Valley, the two-lane highway looked like a snake following a treacherous path through the broken and rugged terrain. Rising and falling with every hill and gully, the endless switchbacks, hairpin turns, and steep grades were a white-knuckle challenge for even the most experienced drivers.

Oddly, many of the motorists who made the trip in the underpowered vehicles of the day often tackled the sharp hills by going backward because driving in reverse offered power. This trick also solved the possibility of their engine stalling out on a slope because many of the gravity-fed fuel systems of the time were inadequate when it came to steep inclines.

Occasionally, drivers came along who found it impossible to pilot their car up and over the pass. The stories say that locals often staged teams of horses or mules nearby and offered their services to pull vehicles up to the top of the summit – for a price, of course. Several wrecking companies got in on the act, too, cheerfully hooking up cars with their trucks and towing them up and over the pass for a few dollars.

The Summit was a welcome sight to those who made it over the nail-biting curves of Sitgreaves Pass.

For those drivers who did make it to the top, there was a time when they could pull over at the summit and buy themselves an ice cream cone – or better yet, have a cold beer to settle their nerves. The Summit was an ice cream stand and filling station that was located at the highest point of the pass, and it must have been a strange and wonderful sight to anyone who succeeded in taking on the perils of Sitgreaves Pass. It survived until 1967 when a fire reduced it to the ruins that can now be found along the side of the old roadway.

Today, the Oatman Road approach has been replaced by the Yucca bypass that happened in the early 1950s, but it's still an option for the daring drivers who'd like to experience it for themselves. As one of the forgotten and most dangerous sections of Route 66, it offers breathtaking views – and a chance to test your bravery behind the wheel.

GOLDROAD GHOST TOWN

THE ABANDONED TOWN OF GOLDROAD RESTS TODAY IN A canyon just beyond Sitgreaves Pass on westbound Route 66. There isn't much to see in town these days, but looking beyond it, there is a sweeping view of California to the southwest and Laughlin, Nevada, to the west.

Before there was ever a town here, John Moss discovered traces of gold in the area in the early 1860s. However, when silver was found in abundance in the Cerbat Mountains, Moss left his diggings behind and went north to the Chloride area.

Moss may have been the first prospector to prowl around this area, but he wasn't the last. In 1900, a miner named Jose Jerez stumbled onto the find of a lifetime. Jose was searching for a lost burro in the hills when he discovered a rich ledge of gold-bearing quartz. He used his pick to chip off a large sample and took it to an assay office, which thrilled Jose when they told him that it was rich with gold. Immediately, he contacted his partner, a store owner Kingman named Henry Lovin, and the two men wasted no time returning to the site to start digging. Within just a few months, they'd dug a 15-foot shaft that turned them into very wealthy men. Their activity soon attracted the attention of a California syndicate who bought the claim from them for $50,000 in 1901.

The syndicate then turned around and sold their rights to another group of investors for $275,000, and they brought in the necessary equipment to expand their holdings, build a mill, and bring hundreds of thousands of dollars in gold ore out of the ground.

The workers brought in to operate the mine needed food, tools, liquor, and entertainment, so it wasn't long before a makeshift settlement appeared. It wasn't long before there were so many people living near the mine that a post office was established in 1902, and the community was dubbed Goldroad.

Henry Lovin used the money he'd made from the initial gold claim to open a new store in Goldroad, along with a successful freight company and a saloon called the Goldroad Club. Unfortunately, one of his best customers was his former partner, Jose Jerez. He quickly burned through all the money he'd made from the claim and later ended his life by swallowing rat poison.

The Goldroad Mine peaked in the years 1905 and 1906, but the rich veins began to peter out the following year. By the end of 1907, the mine had closed – although it was estimated that over $2 million in gold ore was taken from the mine during its short time in operation.

And while the largest mine in town closed, there were still plenty of smaller claims that continued to pay off over the next 25 years. Goldroad remained profitable until 1931, and it was estimated that another $7 million in gold ore was removed from small mines during this time.

Even after all the mines had played out, the town hung on. The post office closed in 1942, and then a few years later, the entire town was razed to save on taxes. There's nothing left of the original town today.

But Goldroad's story wasn't over yet.

In 1992, Addwest Mineral acquired the defunct mine, and after three years of development, the mine began producing gold again. Miners worked three shifts a day until 1998 when the bottom dropped out of the gold market again.

Idle once again, the mine sat waiting for the day when it would be profitable to operate again. In the meantime, the company operated gold mine tours. In 2007, that profitable point returned as gold prices once again soared. The tours were closed as mining operations resumed and have continued for years.

Though the town of Goldroad vanished in 1942, and travelers can't enter the area around the mine, there are visible remnants of the town's former prosperity. Often blending in with the surrounding landscape, slowing down past the site can reveal rock retaining walls, concrete stairs, old water tanks, and roofless buildings.

Those forgotten reminders remain as a community that once was.

NEXT STOP: OATMAN

LOCATED IN THE BLACK MOUNTAINS OF MOHAVE COUNTY is the community of Oatman. Started as a mining camp after prospectors found gold in the area, the town went through many changes during its history, including a time when it boomed during the first 25 years of Route 66.

Often described today as a "ghost town," it doesn't quite fit the category, but it's close enough, considering that it once boasted a population of 10,000 and now supports just a little over 100 souls year-round.

It's sometimes said that the burros in Oatman outnumber the human residents. A legion of these semi-tame animals – descended from the pack burros turned loose by early gold miners -- roam the town today, growing fat from the carrots and sugar cubes sold to tourists by local shopkeepers.

Early days in Oatman

But it wasn't always this way. During its heyday, Oatman was one of the largest gold producers in Arizona – and it has the rugged history to prove it.

The first prospector to look for gold near the future site of Oatman was a man named Johnny Moss, who came here in the 1860s. He staked claims to two mines, one named Moss and the other Oatman, after Olive Oatman, who was kidnapped by the Apache, sold to the Mojave, and released after five years near the current townsite in 1855.

Mining for gold in the Black Mountains was sporadic until the early 1900s. In 1904, a tent city began to form – complete with a post office – when the Vivian Mining Company began operations. Originally dubbed "Vivian," the mining camp began to grow as miners rushed to the area. Over the next several years, just two of the mines in town produced over

Oatman, Ariz.

$20 million in gold ore. Finally, in 1909, the town changed its name to Oatman to honor the young woman who had been kidnapped by Native Americans years before.

As gold continued to be found in the surrounding area, the settlement continued to boom. By 1915, the town had a newspaper, schools, churches, hotels, saloons, and dozens of other businesses.

In 1921, a fire destroyed much of the town, but it was quickly rebuilt. Three years later, the leading mining company, United Eastern Mines, closed its operations for good. But thanks to the smaller mines – and the rumored arrival of Route 66 – Oatman hung on and continued to be a thriving community.

When Route 66 was in the planning stages in the mid-1920s, several supporters of the new highway wanted to have it run alongside the railroad tracks to Yucca, skipping past the rugged terrain around Oatman. They'd get their wish in 1952, but initially, that plan was rejected. Oatman was still widely regarded as a prosperous mining community at the time, and it had more clout. Even though the drive was more difficult, thanks to that hazardous journey over Sitgreaves Pass, Oatman was soon catering to the many travelers on the new highway.

By 1930, when the estimated amount of money from local mines topped out at $36 million, Oatman had grown to include two banks, seven hotels, 20 saloons, and two dozen stores. The population had grown to over 10,000, and there seemed to be no end in sight when it came to the success of the community.

GENERAL VIEW OF OATMAN, ARIZ.

But it was all about to come crashing down.

During World War II, the government needed other types of metal for the war effort, so miners were taken to other areas, and the Oatman mines were closed, leaving the search for gold to wait for better times. Even so, Route 66 kept the community alive for a bit longer.

In 1952, the alignment of Route 66 was changed to bypass treacherous Sitgreaves Pass and to follow the route that had been initially proposed for the highway back in the 1920s. Oatman was no longer the town it had been in 1926, and there was nothing they could do to stop it.

An article in the *Oatman Daily Miner* described what happened next:

One afternoon in 1952, traffic was coming steadily over Sitgreaves Pass, then it was silent. Someone rushed to Oatman with the news that they had cut the ribbon on the new section of U.S. Highway 66 between Kingman and Topock. Six of the seven service station families started to leave town the following day, and the owners of other businesses followed.

Oatman became a ghost town virtually overnight.

By the 1960s, the town was all but abandoned, although it did win a short reprieve in 1962 when the movie *How The West Was Won* was filmed in town.

In the 1970s, nearby Laughlin, Nevada, started building up as a popular gambling spot, and in the early 1990s, Route 66 again became a popular destination for tourists

worldwide. Oatman started becoming lively again.

Then, in 1995, gold operations in Goldroad reopened, closed, and then reopened again, which had a beneficial effect on Oatman, helping it to turn into the small tourist town that it is today.

Though Oatman is a shadow of its former self, it's certainly worth a visit for Route 66 travelers who want a taste of its former glory. Today, the main street is lined with shops and restaurants, and visitors can enjoy not only dodging the burros that wander the streets but also the gunfighter reenactors who offer daily shoot-outs in the middle of town.

GHOSTS OF THE OATMAN HOTEL

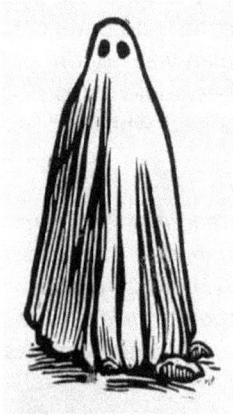

DURING ITS HEYDAY, OATMAN SUFFERED THREE devastating fires, including one in 1921, which wiped out much of the town's business district. Smaller, wood-framed structures went up in flames, but the fire spared the now-famous Oatman Hotel.

Originally called the Durlin Hotel, the popular establishment was built in 1902 by John Durlin, and it continued to play host to scores of travelers after the fire – until the town nearly disappeared after mining operations stumbled in 1924 with the closing of one of Oatman's largest mines. Thankfully, though, the advent of Route 66 allowed the town and the hotel to hang on, catering to the many travelers on the new highway.

HAUNTED

One of the hotel's greatest claims to fame is that Clark Gable and Carole Lombard spent their honeymoon night there on March 29, 1939, after getting married in Kingman. In the years that followed, the couple often returned to the hotel for the peace and quiet it offered them. Clark was known to spend many nights playing poker with local miners. Sadly, Carole was killed in a plane crash in January 1942. Though devastated, Clark continued his life and career and married again.

Since that time, the old hotel has been known by several names, but it was changed to the Oatman Hotel in the 1960s when the local population had dwindled to only about 100 people.

Although the hotel no longer accepts overnight reservations, it has become a history museum that's dedicated to Oatman and some of the famous hotel guests who enjoyed staying there during its heyday. But that's not the reason that the Oatman Hotel has become the biggest attraction in town – that's because of its ghosts.

The most famous resident spirits are, of course, Clark Gable and Carole Lombard, who evidently had so many fine memories of the old hotel that they now refuse to leave. Continuing to celebrate, visitors and staff often hear the pair whispering and laughing from the room when it is empty. According to one report, when a professional photographer took a picture of the empty room, the ghostly figure of a man who resembled the famous actor appeared on the developed print.

But Clark and Carole are not alone. Other ghosts reportedly haunt the hotel, too. The second floor shows how the hotel rooms looked during the glory days of the business, and one room is notorious for the distinct outline of a sleeping body that's found in the dust on the bed. Upon closer inspection, nothing else in the room appears to be disturbed. The staff suspects the sleeping spirit is a former chambermaid often spotted in that room.

Another guest room is said to be haunted by an Irish miner who once lived there. Distraught because his family died when on their way to America, he became a heavy drinker. One night, he had a little too much and passed out behind the hotel. He never woke up. It is said that he has haunted his old room in the hotel ever since. The staff refers to this spirit as "Oatie," who is often spotted around the hotel. He's also blamed for the hotel's spectral pranks, like opening the window in his former room

and pulling the covers off the bed. There have also been reports of the room being very cold – even on a hot Arizona day.

Downstairs in the hotel's saloon, there are believed to be several playful spirits at work. They've been said to lift money off the bar and raise glasses into the air. Lights turn on and off, eerie voices are heard, toilets flush in the empty bathroom, and footprints have been known to mysteriously appear on recently cleaned floors.

Lucky for the Oatman Hotel, their bevy of unusual guests seems playful and friendly, and they aren't in the habit of scaring away the paying customers.

MAKING A RUN FOR THE BORDER

TRAVELERS ON ROUTE 66 WEST OF OATMAN DESCENDS ON an incline for about 25 miles of some of the most beautiful and rugged landscapes on all of the Mother Road. At that point, motorists reached Topock, which marked the end of Arizona's stretch of Route 66.

However, just a mere six miles outside Oatman was an outpost called **Riverview Court.** Built in 1930, it was the simplest of tourist facilities, with just six small, one-room cabins with parking spaces along one side of the property. There was also a gas station that supplied the bare necessities for crossing the desert and a garage that offered small repairs.

One thing you can say about the spot, though, was that the owner must have had a vivid imagination when he came up with the name Riverview Court – the Colorado River was about 17 miles away from its front door.

The cabins and service station are long gone now. A few ruins and a small clearing are the only clues that the roadside business ever existed there.

END OF THE LINE IN ARIZONA

SITUATED ON THE EASTERN EDGE OF THE COLORADO RIVER, Topock started when the Atlantic and Pacific Railroad built a wooden bridge across the river in 1883. The settlement that sprang up on the Arizona side of the waterway was mainly just a railroad station and a steamboat landing at first. The original name was "Mellen" in honor of Captain John Alexander "Jack" Mellon, a Colorado River steamboat captain and owner of an important shipping company. However, the name was misspelled.

A few years later, in May 1890, the wooden bridge was replaced by the Red Rock Bridge at the cost of almost half a million dollars. This bridge, built by the Atchison, Topeka & Santa Fe Railroad, was a cantilevered truss bridge.

At about this time, the settlement's name was changed to Topock, a term thought to have come from the Mohave Indian word for "water crossing" or "bridge."

The National Old Trail Highway's route was laid from California to Kansas, crossing the Colorado River at Topock. At that time, road travelers crossed the river on the Needles Ferry. However, in 1914, when a flood took the ferry out of commission, planks were put on the Red Rock Bridge so that automobiles and wagons could cross the bridge between trains.

Two years later, the Trails Arch Bridge was completed in February 1916 to accommodate road travelers. At the time of its construction, it was the longest-arched bridge in America. Though it was a big improvement over sharing a bridge with a train, the arch bridge could only accommodate one-way traffic. That wasn't a huge problem at the time since there wasn't a lot of automobile traffic

The Trails Arch Bridge was completed in 1916 and was still being used when the National Old Trail Highway was laid out across it.

Colorado River Bridge   Highway 66

The Red Rock Bridge for Route 66 in 1947

on the roads, but that would change when Route 66 barreled through, bringing more cars to the area than the builders of the bridge could have imagined.

Things became even more complicated during World War II when military trucks and vehicles used Route 66 to get from one side of the country to the other. Not only was traffic jammed by the one-way bridge, but it also had a weight limit of only 11 tons, which was an issue for trucks carrying equipment and supplies.

Soon, engineers began to look for a new way for Route 66 travelers to cross the Colorado River. When the Santa Fe Railroad opened a new bridge for their trains in 1945, the rails were removed from the old Red Rock Bridge, reinforcements were made, and the bridge was opened for automobile traffic in 1947.

It served its purpose for the next 20 years, but when Route 66 was replaced by Interstate 40, a new four-lane steel girder bridge was built, and the old Red Rock Bridge was abandoned. After 22 additional years of sitting and rusting in the sun, it was finally dismantled in 1988.

And what about the Trails Arch Bridge that was abandoned in 1947? It's still there, but it's now supporting gas and utility lines that cross the river. It also lives on in the minds of movie fans, who recognize it from the film *The Grapes of Wrath* and the opening credits of *Easy Rider.*

FAREWELL ARIZONA...

And with that, we bring our journey through the American Southwest to an end. With Texas, New Mexico, and Arizona in the rearview mirror, we motor on toward California and our final stop on Route 66 at the Santa Monica pier.

BiBLiOGRAPHY

There are a few special acknowledgments that I'd like to make as we come to the end of his journey.

First, thanks to **Mark Moran** and **Mark Sceurman** of **Weird N.J.** and **Weird U.S.** fame! I was lucky enough to get to be part of their "weird empire" starting back in 2004 and lucky enough to get to do **Weird Illinois**, as well as help with books about a few other states. I've learned a lot from them about what makes road-tripping so much fun and how to find the truly "weird," whether at home or out on the open road.

I'd also like to thank **Kathy Weiser** for her hard work and dedication with **Legends of America** over the years. She's a true aficionado of Route 66 and the American West, and I have been inspired by her for at least a decade and a half now. We'd hoped to get to pull off some sort of project like this together one day but could never work it out to make it happen. But thanks for everything, Kathy!

And thanks to radio legend **Steve Dahl** (and sons **Patrick, Matt**, and **Mike**) for their live broadcasts from Route 66 in the 1990s. The daily shows were hilarious and fun, and while they never made me want to pack up kids in an RV and travel from California to Chicago, they certainly inspired me to take the trip again!

Antonson, Rick – *Route 66 Still Kicks*, New York, NY, Skyhorse Publishing, 2012

Baker, T. Lindsay – *Eating Up Route 66*, Norman, OK, University of Oklahoma Press, 2022

Birchell, Donna Blake – *Haunted Hotels and Ghostly Getaways of New Mexico*, Charleston, SC, History Press, 2018

Branning, Debe – *Arizona's Haunted Route 66*, Charleston, SC, History Press, 2021

---------------------- - Grand Canyon Ghost Stories, Helena, MT, Riverbend Publishing, 2012

Clark, Marian – *Route 66 Cookbook*, San Francisco, Ca, Council Oak Books, 2000 edition

Dregni, Eric – *The Impossible Road Trip*, Beverly, MA, Quarto Publishing Group USA, 2021
--------------- - (Editor) *Greetings from Route 66*, Minneapolis, MN, Voyageur Press, 2010

Hinckley, Jim – Ghost Towns of Route 66, Minneapolis, MN, Voyageur Press, 2011
----------------- - *Illustrated Route 6 Historical Atlas*, Minneapolis, MN, Voyageur Press, 2014
----------------- - *Murder and Mayhem on the Main Street of America*, Tucson, AZ, Rio Nuevo Publishers, 2019
----------------- - *Route 66: America's Longest Small Town*, Minneapolis, MN, Voyageur Press, 2017
------------------ - *Route 66 Encyclopedia*, Minneapolis, MN, Voyageur Press, 2012
----------------- - *Travel Route 66*, Minneapolis, MN, Voyageur Press, 2014

Krim, Arthur – *Route 66: Iconography of the American Highway*, Staunton, VA, George F. Thompson Publishing, 2014

Lee, Ken – *Route 66 Abandoned: Under a Western Moon*, Charleston, SC, Arcadia Publishing, 2023

Miller, Blue – *Abandoned Route 66*, Charleston, SC, Arcadia Publishing, 2021

Morrow, Jason Lucky – *Famous Crimes the World Forgot*, Tulsa, OK, Historical Crime Detective Books, 2014

Never Quite Lost – "The Final Mystery of Ed's Camp," published June 2, 2022

Olsen, Russell A. – *Route 66 Lost and Found*, Minneapolis, MN, Voyageur Press, 2011

Phoenix, Charles – *Addicted to Americana*, Altadena, CA, Prospect Park Books, 2017

Polston, Cody – *Ghosts of Old Town Albuquerque*, Charleston, SC, History Press, 2012
----------------- - *Haunted Albuquerque*, Charleston, SC, History Press, 2021
----------------- - *Wicked Albuquerque*, Charleston, SC, History Press, 2017

Repp, Thomas Arthur – *Route 66: Romance of the West*, Lynwood, WA, 2002

Ross, Jim and Shelee Graham – *Secret Route 66*, St. Louis, MO, Reedy Press, 2017

Scott, Quinta – *Along Route 66*, Norman, OK, University of Oklahoma Press, 2000

Sonderman, Joe – *Route 66 Roadside Signs and Advertisements*, Minneapolis, MN, Voyageur Press, 2016

Wallis, Michael – *Route 66: The Mother Road*, New York, NY, St. Martin's Press, 1990

Wexler, Bruce – *Route 66 Ghost Towns and Roadside Relics*, New York, NY, Chartwell Books, 2016

Witzel, Michael Karl – *Route 6 Remembered*, St. Paul, MN, Motorbooks International, 1996
--------------------------- and Gyrel Young-Witzel, *Legendary Route 66*, Minneapolis, MN, Voyageur Press, 2007
--------------------------- - *Strange Route 66*, Beverly, MA, Quarto Publishing Group USA, 2018

Wood, Andrew F. and Jenny L. Wood – *Motel America*, Portland, OR, Collectors Press, Inc., 2004

SPECIAL THANKS TO

April Slaughter: Cover Design
Becky Ray: Editing
Samantha Smith
Athena & the "Aunts" - Sue, Carmen & Rocky
Orrin and Rachel Taylor
Rene Kruse
Rachael Horath
Bethany Horath
Elyse and Thomas Reihner
John Winterbauer
Cody Beck
Trey Schrader
Tom and Michelle Bonadurer
Lydia Rhoades
Cheryl Stamp and Sheryel Williams-Staab
Joelle Leitschuh and Tonya Leitschuh
Scott and Hannah Rob
Victoria & Reese Welch
And the entire crew of American Hauntings

ABOUT THE AUTHOR

Troy Taylor is the author of books on ghosts, hauntings, true crime, the unexplained, and the supernatural in America. He is the founder of American Hauntings Ink, which offers books, ghost tours, events, and the Haunted America Conference, as well as the creator of the American Oddities Museum in Alton, Illinois.

He was born and raised in the Midwest and divides his time between Alton, Illinois and wherever the wind decides to take him. See Troy's other titles at: www.americanhauntingsink.

www.ingramcontent.com/pod-product-compliance
Lightning Source LLC
Chambersburg PA
CBHW062045080426
42734CB00012B/2564